Planning Your Qualitative Research Project

Even conscientious students can approach a qualitative research project for the first time by embarking on an unsystematic march through a welter of material. Also, because of the emphasis on the interdisciplinary nature of qualitative research, students can often think that their task is to reconcile it as being suitable to support their chosen research questions. The enormity of this task is often not appreciated by new researchers.

This book demonstrates a proven way forward by means of a very structured approach. It shows that when planning a qualitative research proposal, researchers should adopt an approach where they ask themselves the following four questions:

- What research paradigm informs my approach to my research area?
- What theoretical perspective do I choose within the paradigm?
- What methodology do I choose?
- What methods are most appropriate?

The book begins by offering a scaffolding for new qualitative researchers for the development of proposals based on the four central questions identified. This is followed by examples of the write-up of two central types of research projects: studies on participants' 'perspectives' on phenomena and studies on how participants manage or 'cope with' phenomena. Five research proposals are then outlined in separate chapters in order to illustrate ways in which these two central 'types' can be varied and applied when engaging in five other types of studies, namely, Policy Studies, Life History Studies, Retrospective Interactionist Longitudinal Studies, Interactionist Historical Studies and 'Problem-focused' Studies.

Planning Your Qualitative Research Project is a key text for any student embarking on a qualitative research project. It provides worked examples and valuable models which can be used as guides for plans and proposals, answering key questions and providing a comprehensive guide to your project.

Tom O'Donoghue is at The University of Western Australia, Australia.

Planning Your Qualitative Research Project

An introduction to interpretivist research in education

Tom O'Donoghue

Routledge
Taylor & Francis Group

LONDON AND NEW YORK

First published 2007
by Routledge
2 Park Square, Milton Park, Abingdon, Oxon OX14 4RN

Simultaneously published in the USA and Canada
by Routledge
270 Madison Ave, New York, NY 10016

Routledge is an imprint of the Taylor & Francis Group, an informa business

© 2007 Tom O'Donoghue

Typeset in Galliard by
HWA Text and Data Management, Tunbridge Wells
Printed and bound in Great Britain by
The Cromwell Press, Trowbridge, Wiltshire

British Library Cataloguing in Publication Data
A catalogue record for this book is available from the British Library

Library of Congress Cataloging-in-Publication Data
A catalog record for this book has been requested

ISBN 10: 0-415-41484-9 (hbk)
ISBN 10: 0-415-41485-7 (pbk)
ISBN 10: 0-203-96772-0 (ebk)

ISBN 13: 978-0-415-41484-5 (hbk)
ISBN 13: 978-0-415-41485-2 (pbk)
ISBN 13: 978-0-203-96772-0 (ebk)

To Ian Melville
For friendship, generosity and keeping me young

Contents

Tables

Preface

Over the last 30 years qualitative research has emerged to rival quantitative research as a serious approach to inquiry in a variety of social science areas, including education. This has been a welcome development, as has been the acceptance over the last decade that, far from being oppositional, the two broad approaches are complementary. At the same time, however, there is still a lot of scope for providing a series of guides for beginning researchers on how to go about planning qualitative research projects. This is not to argue that there is a shortage of works on various aspects of qualitative research; on the contrary, a great number of texts exist. A particular group of such texts consists of works laying out the epistemological foundations of the approach. Another group consists of texts which elaborate on the great number of theoretical positions derived from such epistemological foundations in response to the desire to pursue particular research avenues. And then there is the large body of work detailing approaches to the gathering and analysis of qualitative data. Nevertheless, there are very few books which attempt to tie all of these orientations together in the form of primers or guides to assist beginning researchers in planning their qualitative research projects. This book is a contribution to filling the lacuna.

One of the difficulties faced by new researchers due to a lack of books like this one is that many of the texts within the various groups outlined above stress that qualitative research is interdisciplinary, drawing from academic disciplines as wide-ranging as psychology, sociology, anthropology and linguistics. The position adopted here is that while some approaches to qualitative research can be interdisciplinary, qualitative research does not always have to be so. Also, to seek to plan research projects within an interdisciplinary framework necessitates an academic training of both great depth and breadth since to achieve competence in the central concepts of any one of the academic disciplines mentioned above takes years of sustained and concentrated study. Yet, many conscientious students approaching a qualitative research project for the first time, particularly in order to produce a thesis as part of the requirements of a university degree, often do not have this position made clear to them. Consequently, they regularly embark on an unsystematic dredge through a wealth of material, driven by a belief that they have, somehow, to master not only the central concepts and methods of investigation of a number of disciplines, but also those of the sub-schools within them, some of which are diametrically opposed to one another. Also, because of the emphasis on the interdisciplinary nature of qualitative research, students often seem to think that their task is to reconcile competing positions, develop their own eclectic stance and then defend it as being suitable to undergird their chosen research questions.

This is not to argue that it is a waste of time to engage in the latter exercise; indeed, cognitive dissonance has long been considered to be a valuable learning experience. On the other hand, the enormity of the task of constructing an eclectic theoretical framework for one's qualitative research project is often not appreciated by new students. Consequently, they dig deeper and deeper, often only to find that they have simply wandered into a swamp from which, without expert guidance, they find it extremely difficult to extricate themselves. I regularly have students come to me after engaging in various introductory programmes desperately trying to disentangle, compartmentalise and connect together such strange bedfellows as discourse analysis, positivism, case study research, telephone interviewing techniques, dilemma analysis, post-structuralism, autoethnography, and non-participant observation.

I find with many students that one way forward is to take a particular structured approach. I also ask students to keep in mind that I do not dismiss the possibility that after they have worked through this approach a number of times they may eventually, and quite legitimately, reject it and embark, this time with confidence, on developing once again their own eclectic conceptual frameworks. Nevertheless, I hold that without a structured approach as initial scaffolding when they embark on planning their initial research projects, many are unlikely to ever come out of the swamp of confusion. The structured approach I promote requires students to consider that their chosen area of research needs to be considered in terms of how it connects to:

a. an underlying research paradigm;
b. a specific theoretical position within the paradigm;
c. a specific methodology consistent with the paradigm and the theoretical position; and
d. set of methods for data gathering and analysis consistent with the specific methodology.

This book follows the logic of the above approach. It is specifically concerned with planning qualitative research projects where the research paradigm is interpretivism, the specific theoretical position is symbolic interactionism, the specific methodology is grounded theory and the research methods are semi-structured interviewing, participant and non-participant observation, and document analysis.

Finally, it needs to be re-emphasised that this is a book about planning research projects. It is not another book dealing specifically with any one of the four parts of the structured approach outlined above, although reference will be made throughout to significant positions and to various specialised texts to help students in their planning. The early chapters provide, in expository form, the scaffolding referred to already. This is followed by examples of the write-up of two research projects of the central types addressed by this book. Five research proposals are then outlined in separate chapters. The purpose of including these proposals is to illustrate some products of working through the planning process being advocated, with some extension on the basic ideas which are central to the book's focus. Finally, most of the examples used throughout the book relate to projects in which the author and his students have been engaged at The University of Western Australia over the past decade. These, however, are also projects which could just as easily have been undertaken, with minor variations, in most of the English-speaking world.

Acknowledgements

Ideas presented in this book have evolved from reflections on my experiences in teaching postgraduate programmes in qualitative approaches to educational inquiry and conducting seminars in the United Kingdom, Ireland, Australia, Singapore, Hong Kong, Malaysia, The Philippines and Papua New Guinea. The many research students I have worked with on these programmes, along with those I have supervised at thesis level, have played a major part in stimulating my thinking. I am also deeply indebted to many colleagues for encouraging me to write this book. Two, however, must come in for special mention in this regard, namely, Professor Keith Punch at The University of Western Australia and Professor Clive Dimmock at the University of Leicester. My thanks also go to the following students for permission to include aspects of their postgraduate research work: Michael Brennan, Ron Chalmers, Simon Clarke, Tony Curry, James Kent, Lucy Riley and Angela Yiannakis. The constant support of Anne Chapman, Sally Male, Gary McCulloch, Denis McLaughlin, Marnie O'Neill, Tony Potts, David Pyvis, and Alan Walker is also greatly appreciated

Part I

An overview of the research process

Chapter 1

Introduction

For many years it has been common to place the process of engaging in research alongside experiencing and reasoning as the principal ways in which people attempt to understand their environments (Cohen and Manion 1985). While many of us have been socialized into assuming that such engagement is the most sophisticated of the three activities, Candy (1989: 1) has argued that it 'seems to be as much a natural human function as breathing'. On this he quoted Emery (1986: 1) as follows:

> Research ... is an ancient and ubiquitous activity. Curiosity about others and the worlds in which they live has always been displayed through conversation, asking questions, working together to see what happens after different kinds of actions are performed, talking or gossiping about others to tease out intentions and other reasons for behaviour, clarifying and understanding circumstances; all are fundamental research functions.

Candy (1989: 1) concluded his consideration of this point by arguing that it is upon such slender foundations that 'the whole massive superstructure of "research" is based'.

Notwithstanding the basic foundations of the research process, however, an important challenge for anyone contemplating engaging in it is to try to find a pathway from one's 'natural' research inclination into this 'massive superstructure' which Candy talks about. One way of proceeding is to view the initial stage in the research process as consisting of two major steps. The first step has its origins in an observation one makes. This observation may arise from viewing something on TV, reading something in the newspaper, hearing something on the radio, becoming cognisant of a particular policy issue, or being faced with some difficult decision to make. What may quickly follow is some curiosity, perplexity, confusion or doubt on one's part. This curiosity, perplexity, confusion or doubt, in turn, prompts one to want to know something. The result is that one begins to engage in research.

The second major step in the initial stage of the research process often follows quite rapidly. Here the practice, as Bouma (2000: 25) has put it, involves 'moving from an ordinary everyday question to a researchable question by focusing on one aspect of the issue arousing your interest'. Bouma further argues that the goal in this step is to produce a clear statement of the problem to be studied. Such a statement of a problem must explicitly identify the issues on which the researcher has chosen to focus. This, as he sees it, requires one to 'clarify the issues' and narrow the 'focus of concern' (Bouma 2000: 36).

Harry Wolcott, the famous educational anthropologist, suggested a way of thinking to help one engage in these related processes of clarifying the issue and narrowing the focus. His position is that as inquiry proceeds, the idea that prompted it should become both better formed and better informed (Wolcott 1992: 7). To this end he suggested three categories which 'form a modest typology' of the ideas that guide inquiry: reform-driven ideas, concept-driven ideas, and 'big' theory-driven ideas. This can be represented diagrammatically as shown in Table 1.1.

It is arguable that most educational research has its origin in reform-driven ideas. On this, it is important to keep in mind that Wolcott uses 'reform' as a blanket term to include 'problem-oriented' and 'decision-oriented' research. What underlies all research questions articulated within the category, however, is an 'assumption on the part of the researcher that things are not right as they are or, most certainly, are not as good as they might be' (Wolcott 1992: 15). Examples of research questions which could be posed in this vein include the following:

* What is the most effective leadership style to adopt in schools?
* Does smoking affect academic performance?
* What is the extent of truancy in inner-city high schools?
* Does a concurrent programme of teacher education where students engage in teaching practice throughout their years of undergraduate study produce better-skilled teachers than a consecutive programme where students first of all study for a degree in a substantive subject-area and then undertake a one-year teacher preparation programme?

The researcher who poses questions such as these usually feels that all is not well with current practice and is prompted to bring about change directed at trying to improve the situation.

Table 1.1 A typology of ideas that guide inquiry

Inquiry based on reform-driven ideas	Inquiry based on concept-driven ideas	Inquiry based on 'big' theory-driven ideas

Wolcott's second category of ideas that guide inquiry are those identified as 'concepts'. These come in all shapes and sizes: 'Concepts point in an orienting consciousness-raising, but saucily independent manner' (Wolcott 1992: 11). He went on to state that working at this level with, for example, a concept like 'culture', 'can provide a focus without allowing the seeming absence of theoretical structure to become overbearing' (Wolcott 1992: 11). The main concern of those adopting such an approach is with attempting to describe aspects of culture, an activity often referred to as ethnography. Goetz and LeCompte (1984: 17) described the activity thus:

> The purpose of educational ethnography is to provide rich, descriptive data about the contexts, activities, and beliefs of participants in educational settings. Typically, such data represent educational processes as they occur. The result of these processes are examined within the whole phenomenon; isolation of outcomes is rarely considered.

Researchers who are informed by a cultural perspective in their investigations are said to succeed if their research reports enable readers to behave appropriately in the particular cultural settings they purport to describe (Bogdan and Biklen 1984: 38).

LeCompte and Preissle (1993: 137–8) have provided a number of other examples to illustrate how research can be concept-guided. They pointed out that Sindell (1974) developed research questions in his study of the socialization of Mistassini Cree children from factors identified as important in Bandura's social learning theory. They also pointed out that Spindler's (1974) examination of the impact of the school on attitudes towards urbanization among inhabitants of a rural German village drew explicitly from assimilation theory. Another trend they highlighted is the tendency in much contemporary research on adolescent alienation from school to draw heavily on the concepts of hegemony, symbolic violence and the political context of knowledge and meaning (LeCompte and Preissle 1993: 138).

Wolcott's third category of ideas that guide inquiry encompass those ideas that relate to an overall 'grand' or 'big theory'. He quoted the sociologist Robert Merton in this regard, where Merton spoke of 'the all inclusive systematic effort' to develop a unified theory that explains 'all the observed uniformities of social behaviour, social organization and social change' (Merton 1968: 39). Wolcott argued that those who 'think theory' in this 'grand' sense are attempting to 'link up in someone's – perhaps even their own – Big Theory, everything that matters to everyone' (Wolcott 1992: 7).

This book is about undertaking a particular type of research from the point of view of Wolcott's third category of ideas that guide inquiry, namely, that of 'big theory'. The argument running throughout is that educational research can, in fact, be underpinned by one of four major 'big' theories, namely, positivism, interpretivism, critical theory, and postmodernism. Also, it is held that each of these 'big theories' can, in turn, be broken down into a number of related theoretical perspectives. For example, the interpretivist 'big theory' embraces such theoretical positions as hermeneutics, ethnomethodology, symbolic interactionism and phenomenology. This categorization of 'big' theory can be represented as shown in Table 1.2.

The specific aim of this book is to provide new researchers with a guide to planning qualitative research projects based upon interpretivism as the 'big theory' and upon symbolic interactionism within it. At the same time, as readers progress through the work they should come to recognise that all research, including that guided by concept-driven ideas and problem-focused ideas, can ultimately be mapped back to show that it has 'grand theory' or 'big theory' foundations. Yet, it is not a book which explicitly seeks to engage readers in such a backward-mapping exercise. Instead, in setting out to demonstrate how research projects can be planned by adopting interpretivism as one's 'big theory' – and adopting within it the theoretical position of 'symbolic interactionism' – it is recognised that one can also plan research projects based upon one of the other 'big theories'.

Before moving directly to such planning issues, however, it is necessary to clarify a number of central ideas so that the theoretical foundations of the remainder of this book are clearly established. The rest of this chapter provides such clarification. First, consideration is given to the position that the idea of research as being guided by 'big theory' is more usually talked and written about as being research which is 'paradigm guided'. To this end, the notion of a research paradigm is explained and the four major 'big theories' already outlined are considered in terms of how each constitutes a research paradigm. Consideration is also given to the matter of how research questions are posed differently depending upon the research paradigm one adopts.

The chapter then moves on to argue that a paradigm's approach to research requires us to adopt a view of the process as involving much more than simply rushing headlong into selecting appropriate methods for the investigation of a problem. Certainly, examining any problem or hypothesis does require the use of methods in the form of techniques to gather and analyse data. However, once we have grasped the notion of what is involved in a paradigm-guided approach to research we quickly come to recognise the need for a strategy, plan of action, process, or design to link our paradigm-guided questions with particular methods. This is what is referred to when we argue for the need for an appropriate methodology. A wide variety of such methodologies exist, ranging from survey research to ethnography, from experimental research to grounded theory, and from discourse analysis to heuristic inquiry.

Overall, then, the intention of the remainder of this chapter is to provide an overview of:

- the idea of paradigms
- the basic ideas of the four major paradigms
- the distinction between methodology and research methods.

Table 1.2 Interpretivist paradigm and related theoretical perspectives

'Big' theories	*Four major theoretical perspectives within the interpretivist 'big' theory*
Positivism	
Interpretivism	• Hermeneutics • Ethnomethodology • Phenomenology • Symbolic interactionism
Critical theory Postmodernism	

Such an overview should provide appropriate scaffolding for an understanding of *why* one particular type of qualitative research project can be planned where:

- the paradigm is interpretivism
- the specific theoretical position adopted within the paradigm is symbolic interactionism
- the methodology is grounded theory
- the research methods are semi-structured interviewing, participant and non-participant observation, and document study.

This understanding should, in turn, place one in a better position to understand the remaining chapters of the book, where the emphasis is very much on *how* research projects based on such a framework can be planned.

Research paradigms

At this point it is important to once again recall Wolcott's (1992) third type of research, namely, that of 'grand theory' or 'big theory'. As has already been pointed out, the more sophisticated term used when referring to such research is to talk about it as being 'paradigm guided'. In considering what is meant by this it is important to recognise from the outset the point made by Punch (1998: 28) that paradigm is a complex term. He elaborates as follows:

> As used in social science it [paradigm] means a set of assumptions about the social world, and about what constitutes proper techniques and topics for inquiry. In short, it means a view of how science should be done. It is a very broad term, encompassing elements of epistemology, theory and philosophy, along with methods. Paradigms have been the subject of vigorous debate.
>
> (Punch, 1998: 28)

Usher (1996) is helpful in developing this point. He proceeds by high-lighting some aspects of the thinking of Thomas Kuhn whose major work, *The Structure of Scientific Revolutions* (1970), played a significant part in 'changing our understanding of science, research and scientific method' (Usher 1996: 14).

In Kuhn's work the concept of the paradigm is defined both as 'the entire constellation of beliefs, values, techniques, shared by members of a given scientific community' (Kuhn 1970: 75) and 'as an exemplar or exemplary way of working that functions as a model for what and how to do research, what problems to focus on and work on' (Usher 1996: 15). On this, Usher states:

> Paradigms are frameworks that function as maps or guides for scientific communities, determining important problems or issues for its members to address and defining acceptable theories or explanations, methods and techniques to solve defined problems. When a paradigm becomes settled and dominant within a scientific community, Kuhn calls the research carried out 'normal science'. This way of doing research is largely characterised by routine, problem-solving discontinuities (which Kuhn calls 'scientific revolutions'). Here a paradigm shift occurs, dominant paradigms are overthrown and new paradigms take their place.
>
> (Usher 1996: 15)

He concludes by saying that a paradigm shift involves a new way of looking at the world and hence new ways of working, or new ways of doing 'normal' science.

Over the last 30 years or so there has been much talk and debate about the various major paradigms which exist and which influence the production of research in education. Some researchers and theorists have produced 'typological charts listing the principal schools of contemporary research methodology along with some definitive statements for each' (Carspecken 1996: 1). These include charts where paradigms are compared according to their ontological and epistemological assumptions. Such charts, of which that of Guba and Lincoln (1994: 109) is probably the most best known, are valuable in that they illustrate a range of frameworks which are of help in locating and clarifying the paradigm within which we might wish to locate our research. Also, they help to remind us that all educational research is either implicitly or explicitly conducted within a framework of theoretical assumptions.

One could engage in a review of the various charts which exist. To do so, however, would be to confuse many readers from the outset. In order to make sense of them one would need quite a background in philosophy in general, and philosophy of science in particular. The contention is that a more practical way to proceed is to commence by outlining a simple typology of paradigms. The particular typology chosen here to such an end is that developed by Connole *et al.* (1993: 38–9), with its four paradigms – positivist, interpretivist, critical, and postmodernist. This is much simpler than the typologies of Guba and Lincoln and much more valuable as an initial heuristic device or scaffolding. Overall, it lays the foundation for the main body of the text, which considers in detail how to engage in research based on the second of the major paradigms identified, namely, the interpretivist paradigm, with the theoretical position being that of symbolic interactionism – about which much more will be said in Chapter Two; the methodology being grounded theory – about which much more will be said in Chapter Four; and the research methods being semi-structured interviewing, participant and non-participant observation, and document study.

Four major paradigms

Connole *et al.* (1993: 38–9), as stated above, argue that research methodologies can be grouped according to four main paradigms: positivism, interpretivism, critical, and postmodernism. Each paradigm is based upon sharply different assumptions about epistemology – the study of how knowledge is generated and accepted as valid – and about the purposes of research. A useful starting point in elaborating on this is to consider the position of the philosopher Jurgen Habermas (1972), who contended that those who adopt the research approach associated with the positivist research paradigm are pursuing one of three human 'cognitive interests', namely, the interest in technical control. It is this interest which leads us to want to know all the facts and figures associated with the area of interest, and the answers are provided by empirical-analytic knowledge. The basis of such knowledge, it is claimed, involves careful and controlled observation, where the observer takes a dispassionate position independent of the object of observation.

Smith and Lovatt (1991: 57), in elaborating on what is involved in pursuing technical knowledge, focus on the practices associated with both the behaviourist form of psychology and the functionalist form of sociology. These disciplines, they argue, which are based on fairly specific ideas about human behaviour and human society respectively, have developed precise research approaches with positivist foundations. The typical initial strategy is that of formulating hypotheses, setting up a clinical observation, and recording observations. The latter are regarded as objective devices and, hence, reliable. The next step is to quantify the data and present the findings by means of statistics. The final set of statistics is seen as providing knowledge which is both objective and generalizable, and which, it is held, can be used to predict and control events.

The second major research approach is that based upon the interpretivist paradigm. This approach emphasizes social interaction as the basis for knowledge. The researcher uses his or her skills as a social being to try to understand how others understand their world. Knowledge, in this view, is constructed by mutual negotiation and it is specific to the situation being investigated.

Habermas contends that those engaged in research within the interpretivist paradigm are pursuing the second human cognitive interest, namely, the interest in understanding the meaning behind something. This contrasts sharply with the positivist's interest in prediction and control. Also, a very different notion of how one knows something is emphasised. Again, the nature of what is involved is addressed by Smith and Lovatt. They argue that this second way in which one knows something, can be seen in the method used in attempting to convey understanding through textbooks like the present one. In such situations the writer uses words to convey ideas and meanings to the reader. Smith and Lovatt (1991: 75) clarify this point:

> The only way that you can prove to us (or we can know) that you have understood my ideas with the meaning that we intended, is for you to paraphrase in your own words, the meaning that you have gained from my words. In other words, a very important way that we come to know something is through a negotiation of meaning through communication.

They conclude by saying that the way one proves one knows these things is through either a verbal or written account, although often the meanings of such accounts still need to be negotiated between the speaker and the listener, or the writer and the reader.

Habermas holds that those who engage in research within the third paradigm, namely, the critical paradigm, operate on the assumption that knowledge is problematic and capable of systematic distortion. The contention is that it can never be value free, but always represents the interests of some group within society. Consequently, it is argued, knowledge has the potential to be either oppressive or emancipatory. The purpose of the researcher working within the critical paradigm is to unmask the ideologies which maintain the status quo 'by restricting the access of groups to the means of gaining knowledge' and by raising their 'consciousness or awareness about the material conditions that oppress or restrict them' (Usher 1996: 22). The emphasis is placed on understanding the causes of 'powerlessness, recognising systemic oppressive forces and acting individually and collectively to change the conditions of life' (Usher 1996: 22). Equally stressed alongside the emphasis on social critique is, however, the importance of being guided by this critique in taking social action to improve the quality of human life.

The fourth research paradigm is that of postmodernism. A particular position underpinning this fourth paradigm is that 'knowledge claims are governed by privileged sets of rules and social relations' (Connole *et al.* 1993:

12). Overall, as Usher puts it, what the fourth paradigm does is challenge 'the powerful view that there is a determinate world which can be definitively known and explained' (Usher 1996: 23). Also, the various theoretical approaches associated with it do not relate to Habermas' three cognitive interests. Rather, collectively they represent an epistemological break with other research paradigms. Thus, they seek to challenge our understandings of knowledge as being based on truth.

Research paradigms and the posing of research questions

From considerations so far it should be clear that what differentiates one paradigm from another is that each offers a rationale for its choice, for the kinds of research questions it can address, for the varieties of research design it uses and for an introduction to its methods. Husén (1988: 18) elaborates on this as follows:

> The paradigm determines how a problem is formulated and methodologically tackled. According to the traditional positivist conception, problems that relate, for example, to classroom behaviour should be investigated primarily in terms of the individual actor, wither the pupils, who might be neurotic, or the teacher, who might be ill-prepared for his or her job.

LeCompte and Preissle (1993: 139) illustrated this notion by focusing in particular on how research questions are posed differently depending upon the paradigm which one is adopting. The problem they chose in order to illustrate this is that of the 'at-risk' student, or potential dropout. They demonstrated that if one adopts the positivist position known as 'functionalism' then the research questions which can be asked are as follows:

1 What are the characteristics of the dropout population?
2 What role do dropouts, as a group, play in the social system of the school?
3 To what extent does dropping out serve to remove from schools those students for whom formal schooling is inappropriate or wasteful of public resources?

To pose these questions is to approach students as conscious 'dropouts' who choose to leave school prematurely. This is to view the issue as a person-centred one, with an emphasis on the self-esteem, family background, motivation and intelligence of the student. However, if one favours the 'critical' approach one poses questions like the following:

1 What patterns of resistance do students – and teachers – employ to resist the hegemony of the dominant order in schools?

2 What processes operate within the school to push students out?

Such questions arise when one shifts one's focus to viewing students as 'push outs' who are actively encouraged in their departure by school practices which require investigation focusing on such issues as 'the bureaucratic organization of schools and the time schedule, the behaviour of students and staff, the structure of the curriculum, and the general relationship between schools and the structure of opportunity in the larger society' (LeCompte and Preissle 1993: 140).

LeCompte and Preissle (1993: 139) go on to illustrate how different sets of questions can be raised yet again within other paradigms and, indeed, within sub-positions within these paradigms. For example, still staying with the same issue, they state that if one favours the 'postructuralist' approach one can pose questions like the following:

1 Which students' or other school participants' experiences are ignored by contemporary researchers?

2 How do such students define and structure the school experience?

To summarise, then, on this matter of different 'types' of research questions, the argument is that the adoption of a different paradigm can predispose a researcher to approach a research problem differently in terms of the questions asked. This situation will, in turn, lead the researcher to choose different research methodologies and research methods.

Methodology and research methods

To argue along lines like those above is to argue that research needs to be thought of as being about much more than simply choosing a *method*, or 'a program or set of procedures for designing, conducting and reporting research' (Lancy 1993: 8). As Crotty (1998: 3) puts it, methods are 'the techniques or processes used to gather and analyse data related to some research question or hypothesis', while the notion of 'methodology' constitutes the link between the paradigm-related questions and the methods. The latter is so in the sense that methodology is 'the strategy, plan of action, process or design lying behind the choice and use of particular methods and linking the choice and use of methods to the desired outcomes' (Crotty 1998: 3). Crotty elaborates on this where he argues that 'in developing a research proposal, while we need to put considerable effort into answering what methodologies and methods will be employed in the research we propose to do, we also need to ask how we justify this choice and use of methodologies and methods' (Crotty 1998: 2). He argues that the answer to the second of these questions lies with the purposes of our research – in other words, with the research question that our piece of inquiry is seeking to answer. However, he also holds that there is more to it than that: 'Justification of our choice and particular use of methodology and methods is something that reaches into the assumptions about reality that we bring to our work (Crotty 1998: 2). This is to once again highlight the importance of how one positions oneself from a paradigm's perspective.

I find it helpful to bring all of this together by rearranging and paraphrasing Crotty's (1998: 2) outline where he argues that when we view research through this lens we ask ourselves four questions. My rearrangement and paraphrasing of these questions is as follows:

1   What research paradigm informs our approach to our research area of interest?
2   What theoretical perspective do we choose within this paradigm regarding our research area of interest?
3   What methodology do we choose as a result of our location of the research area of interest within a particular theoretical perspective derived from a particular paradigm?
4   What methods are most appropriate to use in light of our chosen methodology?

The remaining chapters of this book are concerned with outlining an approach to developing research proposals where the paradigm is interpretivism, the specific theoretical position is symbolic interactionism, the methodology is grounded theory, and the research methods are semi-structured interviewing, participant and non-participant observation, and document study.

The chapters which go to make up the book were outlined in the Preface. It is now important to note that they are organised into two parts. Part One consists of this chapter and five others. Chapter Two details some basic principles of interpretivism and outlines how the theoretical position of 'symbolic interactionism' is located within it as one of a number of related theoretical positions. Chapter Three is based on the contention that there are two basic types of studies which can be developed from the symbolic interactionist view of the individual, namely, studies aimed at generating theory regarding the perspectives which participants hold with regard to something and studies aimed at generating theory regarding how participants 'manage', 'deal with', 'or 'cope with' situations. The focus is on considering how to develop appropriate research questions for engaging in these two basic types of theory-generation studies.

Chapter Four goes on to provide an exposition on what is meant by 'theory' in the sense in which the term is used with regard to the types of studies being promoted in this book. It also considers the types of populations with which it is 'normal' to work when generating such theory. Furthermore, it provides an overview on the range of arguments which are used as a justification for the value of engaging in studies aimed at theory generation. Finally, Part One of the book is brought to completion with Chapters Five and Six, where the aim is to provide exemplars of the two main types of theory-generation studies considered so far.

Part Two of the book is based upon the notion that, along with the two main types of symbolic interactionist studies which are the basis of considerations in Part One, it is also possible to engage in related types of studies. The first four of these types are 'policy studies', 'life history studies', 'retrospective interactionist longitudinal studies' and 'interactionist historical studies', while the fifth type is of the 'problem-focused' variety. Chapters Seven, Eight, Nine, Ten and Eleven consider each of these separately. The point not to lose sight of, however, is that while studies with terms such as 'policy', 'life history', and 'problem-focused' in their titles can be underpinned by a variety of foundations other than those of interpretivism and symbolic interactionism, the concern in Part Two of the book is with studies where interpretivism and symbolic interactionism are chosen as the central foundations. Each chapter makes this very clear, illustrating what is involved through the outline of a series of research proposals.

It is in these proposals that one is also brought face-to-face for the first time with details on research methods, or techniques for the gathering of qualitative data. The emphasis throughout is on three main types of data-gathering approaches, namely, semi-structured interviewing, participant and non-participant observation, and document study. Furthermore, the approaches recommended are those which have been standard since qualitative research approaches gained popularity within education studies over the last 25 to 30 years. There are some excellent texts which provide overviews on these approaches, including the recent works of Punch (2005), Silverman (2005) and Woods (2005). There has also been an increase in the last number of years in works which illustrate the potential of computers for speeding up access to documentary material (McCulloch 2004) and for using widely available internet technology in conducting interviews with participants at a distance when we are unable to meet with them in person (Mann and Stewart 2002).

Finally, it should not be assumed that this book champions the interpretivist paradigm over other paradigms, or symbolic interactionism over other interpretivist theoretical positions. Instead, it is strongly influenced by the adage, 'be guided by the question'. In adopting this position it is also held that it is not helpful for the new researcher to spend too much time attempting to reconcile a number of paradigms in order to develop an eclectic position to guide a research project. At this stage of one's career, where one is faced with a complex research area which seems to have affinities with various paradigms, one would be better employed breaking it up into a number of sub-projects, each grounded in the appropriate paradigm. After completing this process the new researcher, if interested in pursuing the research approach outlined in this book, can select an interpretivist sub-project for investigation. This is a view which sees that the sub-projects could then be collated, perhaps by an overall project director, in a work which would present them as a series of discrete, but complementary studies leading to some overall conclusions for theory, practice and future research. This allows for a variety of possibilities, not least that of engaging in what we might call a 'second level of analysis' of the theory generated. For example, those attracted by the critical theory paradigm might usefully interrogate their newly-generated theory with symbolic interactionist underpinnings by drawing upon some of the central political concepts utilized by critical theorists. This, however, it should be stressed, is not the same as developing an empirical study from the outset based upon the central assumptions of the critical theory paradigm. For some excellent primers on the latter approach one has to look elsewhere (e.g. Carspecken 1996).

The thinking behind this book also does not favour the view that symbolic interactionism, phenomenology and other theoretical positions within the interpretivist paradigm can be combined loosely to underpin an eclectic research approach. This is not to argue against eclectic research approaches in principle; rather, it is to maintain that they need to be supported by rigorous logical arguments which make crystal clear what is involved. And here I return again to the ideas of Wolcott. In a consideration of the wide variety of research approaches available, he has stated that 'in the real world of science, the most seasoned veterans probably are conversant with no more than one or two different approaches' (Wolcott 1992: 18). My understanding of the point he was making here is that it is better, particularly when starting out on one's early research projects, to base them upon an in-depth command of one research approach rather than a superficial grasp of many. It is in such a spirit that this book has been conceptualised and written.

Chapter 2

The general background

Introduction

This chapter is an exposition on issues which need to be considered by way of general background to understanding the interpretivist paradigm and the place of the symbolic interactionist theoretical position within it. The chapter opens by detailing some basic foundation principles of interpretivism. A brief historical account of interpretivism as it unfolded in the form of symbolic interactionism is then outlined. Thirdly, the chapter provides an exposition on the concept of 'perspectives', a central concept within symbolic interactionism. Finally, three important distinctions which many tend to blur in developing eclectic approaches to interpretivist research of the sort discouraged in the previous chapter are clarified: the distinction between behaviour and action; the distinction between 'perspectives' and 'perceptions', and the distinction between 'perspectives' and 'attitudes'.

Foundation principles

For the interpretivist, the individual and society are inseparable units. From this, it follows that a complete understanding of one is not possible without a complete understanding of the other. Also, society is to be understood in terms of the individuals making it up, and the individuals are to be understood in terms of the societies of which they are members. In other words, the individual and society are inseparable; the relationship is a mutually interdependent one rather than a one-sided deterministic one. At the same time, it is possible to separate the two units for the sake of analysis. This book does so by concentrating on the individual or, more correctly, on individuals and groups of individuals, while never overlooking the societal dimension.

One of the most basic ideas of interpretivism regarding the individual is that all human action is meaningful and hence 'has to be interpreted and understood within the context of social practices' (Usher 1996: 18). It follows from this that an understanding of the meanings that create, and are created by, interaction between human beings is essential to an understanding of the social world and the myriad phenomena which it contains. Consistent with this view, interpretivists examine the meanings that phenomena have for people in their everyday settings. The concern is with the study of 'how people define events or reality' and 'how they act in relation to their beliefs' (Chenitz and Swanson, 1986: 4).

A number of assumptions underpin the interpretivist approach to research. In particular, these assumptions involve everyday activity, freedom, meaning, interaction and negotiation. Blackledge and Hunt (1985: 234) are very helpful in developing this position through an elaboration on four of the major assumptions. Firstly, they state that everyday activity is the building block of society. As they see it, every aspect of society can be traced back to the way people act in everyday life. They illustrate this by pointing out that what keeps the educational system together is the day-to-day activity of teachers, learners, administrators, inspectors and other educational professionals. Furthermore, any changes in education or society are brought about by changes in such activity. Thus, the argument goes, if we want to understand education we must begin by looking at everyday activity in the different education sectors.

The second assumption highlighted by Blackledge and Hunt reiterates that of Blumer (1969: 2) when he stated that everyday activity is never totally imposed; there is always some autonomy and freedom (Blumer 1969: 2). This, as it is put, 'is not to say that there are no constraints on the way people act; nor does it imply that people are uninfluenced by their background' (Blackledge and Hunt 1985: 236). Rather, as Blackledge and Hunt (1985: 235) conclude, 'what is insisted upon is that people can and do create their own activity to some extent; everyday life is produced by people employed within the system acting together and producing their own roles and patterns of action'.

The third assumption highlighted by Blackledge and Hunt is that everyday activity nearly always involves a person interacting with other people rather than acting in isolation. As a result, individuals not only give meaning to their own actions, they also give meaning to the actions of others. Put differently, it is contended that 'people mutually interpret the behaviour of other people with whom we interact. It follows from this that subsequent action depends on our interpretation' (Blackledge and Hunt 1985: 236). Also, the argument is that our interpretation of other people's activity is influenced by what we currently consider we know about them, including our knowledge of their age, race, intelligence, and motivation.

A fourth assumption highlighted by Blackledge and Hunt is that everyday activity involves a process of 'negotiation' of meaning and, through this, we come to modify our understandings and views. They go on as follows:

> It is important to note that the analysis of action must include a study of the participants' meanings and interpretations. However, it would be

incorrect to think that meanings and interpretations remain static and unchanging. It is clear, for example, that people do modify their views. Also, over time, participants in various circumstances tend to come to have shared understandings and interpretations. The sharing is brought about through a process of 'negotiation' of meaning. Negotiation is seen as a continuous process, not something that happens once and is finished. It occurs in subtle ways, with modification to the participants' understanding of what is going on. Shared assumptions develop.

(Blackledge and Hunt 1985: 236)

They conclude by stressing that the term negotiation does not imply that all parties have the same power at their disposal.

Each of the four assumptions of interpretivism outlined so far also apply specifically in the case of symbolic interactionism which, as has been stated repeatedly, is a major theoretical position within the interpretivist paradigm. This position, as the historical exposition in the next part of the chapter points out, derives from the Chicago School of Sociology of the 1920s and 30s, particularly the ideas of its chief exponent, George Herbert Mead, whose work was popularised by Herbert Blumer. Indeed, it is Blumer who is attributed with having first coined the term 'symbolic interactionism'. Key concepts which have been developed to articulate this particular theoretical approach within interpretivism are 'self', 'interaction', 'self-interaction', 'voluntarism' and 'common symbolic language'. Of these, the concept of 'self' is of primary importance to the understanding of the symbolic interactionist approach to research.

Mead (1934) postulated that the individual develops a sense of self through interaction with others. As such, the self is created in childhood when a person begins to make judgements about the way he or she is perceived by others. The process continues through life and involves individuals taking the role of others as a means of looking back at themselves from the perspectives of the people with whom they interact. In this regard, one constructs an image of how one believes one is seen by others. Furthermore, this image changes throughout life because of social interaction.

The significance of the concept of 'self' lies in its potential for facilitating each individual in the engagement of self-interaction. The self becomes an object for the individual to consider, assess, communicate with, and act towards. This ongoing interplay between an individual – subject – and self – object – enables individuals to anticipate the reaction they may receive if deciding to act in a particular way. On this, Schwartz and Jacobs (1979: 23) observe that self-interaction allows the person to 'really "see" others' reactions to his [*sic*] own actions before these reactions occur'. For Mead (1934), and for his successors who operate within the symbolic interactionist theoretical approach, the concept of self relates directly to the way people attach meaning to, and act towards, particular objects and phenomena.

In an elaboration on Mead's ideas, Blumer (1969: 2) formulated three principles. First, he stated that 'human beings act towards things on the basis of the meanings they have for them'. On this, Woods (1992) has argued that, unlike approaches which hold that human behaviour is determined by structural societal forces, or is the product of internal psychological drives, the view of the symbolic interactionist is that individuals attach their own meanings to 'things', e.g. material objects, people, institutions, concepts, in their environment and then act towards them on the basis of these meanings. In other words, people are volitional rather than organisms which merely respond. They are organisms who have to manage by constructing and directing their line of action. Here we are back to the notion that meanings influence actions.

Blumer's second principle is that social interaction is the source from which meanings are derived. Thus, the meanings that a person has for a thing in his or her world are created by the actions of other people. This principle asserts that 'the meaning of a thing for a person grows out of the ways in which other persons act towards the person with regard to the thing' (Taylor and Bogdan 1984: 9). In other words, people learn how to see the world from other people. What is also implied is that the meaning each person has for a thing may be constantly adjusted by the actions of other people. This new meaning also has its effect on human actions. Another way of putting it is that meaning is acquired from one's experience of the world and because one is constantly interacting with the world that meaning may be confirmed, modified, reinforced, or changed.

Blumer's third principle is that meanings are 'handled in, and modified through, an interpretive process used by the person in dealing with the things he [*sic*] encounters' (Blumer 1969: 2). He goes on to say that there are two steps in this process. Firstly, one points out to oneself the things that have meaning. One then selects, checks, suspends, regroups and transforms the meaning in the light of the situation in which one is placed and the direction of one's action. This process, which is an essential component of social life, is the means by which individuals align their actions with others and with groups. It is through this interpretive process that shared meanings are attributed to the full range of objects that comprise the human experience. This is to reject a view of human action as deriving from such internal forces as instincts, drives and needs, and also to reject the concept of 'attitude' as an internal tendency – a matter taken up in some detail in the fourth part of this chapter. It is also to reject those theories which view the actions of an individual as determined by such large scale external forces as '"social system", "social structure", "culture", "status position", "social role", "custom", "institution", "collective representation", "social situation", "social norm" and "values"' (Ritzer 1994: 301). Rather, human action, as Meltzer, Petras and Reynolds (1975: 2) have put it, is seen as arising out of 'a reflective and socially derived interpretation of the internal and external stimuli that are present'.

By now astute readers may be a little unsettled by the way in which the terms 'understandings', 'meanings' 'beliefs' and 'perspectives' have been used so far. They have good reason to be, as the exposition to this point has been allowed to proceed in a manner which mirrors the practice in much of the literature, namely, to use these terms interchangeably. What is important to note here is that to engage in this practice is not technically incorrect and the terms largely mean the same thing. Rather, the contention is that it is a confusing practice. To deal with this situation, the term which has been selected for use consistently from this point onwards is that of 'perspectives'. An elaboration on what is meant by the term is presented in the third part of this chapter. For the moment, however, it is sufficient to keep in mind Woods' (1983: 7) definition of perspectives as 'frameworks through which people make sense of the world'. Charon (2001: 4) puts it similarly when he states that perspectives are made up of words which are used by the observer to make sense out of situations. He goes on to state that 'the best definition of perspectives is a *conceptual framework*, which emphasizes that perspectives are really interrelated sets of words used to order physical reality'.

To recap then in light of the position taken above, it is held that the value of adopting an interpretivist approach to research, and of the symbolic interactionist theoretical approach within it, is that it can uncover people's perspectives on a phenomenon. The important reality, it is argued, is what people perceive it to be. This reflects a tradition in social science that fundamentally depends on observations taken in people's natural settings and interacting with them in their own language and on their terms (Kirk and Miller 1986: 9). This is the point Matza (1969) was making when he argued that research methods should respect the nature of the empirical world. The emphasis, as Woods (1992) puts it, should be on 'naturalism' and on 'unobtrusive methods'. In this way, the issues which are focused upon for study are those which are issues for the participants being investigated, rather than those which might exist from the outset as problems in the mind of the researcher which he or she deems worthy of investigation

In summary, a researcher adopting a symbolic interactionist theoretical approach when conducting research within the interpretivist paradigm is concerned with revealing the perspectives behind empirical observations, the actions people take in the light of their perspectives, and the patterns which develop through the interaction of perspectives and actions over particular periods of time. In such an approach, the researcher is the primary data-gathering instrument, using guiding questions aimed at understanding a phenomenon through semi-structured or open-ended interviews with the people involved and in their own surroundings. Other important means of gathering data are through an examination of documents and other records, and on-site observations. These methods rely on the interactional, adaptive, and judgemental abilities of the human inquirer. Also, they can lead to the production of a vast amount of data about a small number of people. In later chapters, examples of how data can be gathered and analysed are outlined and expositions are presented on what the product of analyses could look like and the value of such products to the academic, the professional and the general community. At this point, however, it is considered appropriate to give the reader a greater understanding of the historical background to the interpretivist paradigm, with particular reference to the symbolic interactionist theoretical approach within it as espoused by the Chicago School of Sociology

The historical background

Interpretivism, as should be clear from discussions so far, is not a homogenous position, although the various theoretical positions within it do tend to share the four major assumptions identified by Blackledge and Hunt (1985) which were outlined in the previous section. Also, some of these theoretical positions are very prominent. In tracing the origins of a number of them, Husén (1988: 17) opened by focusing on that tradition within educational research where the concern is with modelling the activity of those working in the natural sciences, with the emphasis on 'empirical quantifiable observations which lend themselves to analyses by means of mathematical tools'. The task within this tradition is to establish causal relationships in order to provide an explanation. Also, it is a tradition deemed valuable because of the contention that it allows for the prediction of future behaviour on the basis of present action.

The interpretivist paradigm is based on different assumptions. On this, Husén highlights the distinction made by Wilhelm Dilthey (1833–1911) in the 1890s between 'erklaren' and 'verstehen'. The former refers to 'explanation' and is associated with positivism, while the latter refers to 'understanding' and is associated with interpretivism. Furthermore, in making this distinction, Dilthey maintained that the humanities have their own logic of research, pointing out that the difference between natural sciences and humanities is that the former tries to explain, while the latter tries to understand. He also maintained that there are two kinds of psychology, 'the one which by means of experimental methods attempts to generalise and predict, and the one that tries to understand the unique individual in its entire, concrete setting' (Husén 1988: 18). Husén draws our attention to the emergence of similar positions in the same period, such as that espoused by Henri Bergson (1859–1941) in France, 'who maintained that the intellect was unable to grasp the living reality which could only be approached by means of intuition' and that of John Landquist in Sweden who 'advanced the epistemology of human knowledge about human affairs' (Husén 1988: 18).

Various other interpretivist positions also emerged around the same time. Amongst the most well known of these within the discipline of philosophy was the phenomenological philosophy of the German, Edmund Husserl

(1859–1938). Again, Husén (1988: 18) offers a good summary of the basic assumptions of this position:

> It [Husserl's phenomenology] emphasised the importance of taking a widened perspective and of trying to 'get to the roots' of human activity. The phenomenological and later the hermeneutic approach is holistic. It tries by means of empathy ('Einfuhlung') to understand the motive behind human reactions. By widening the perspective and to understand human beings as individuals in their entirety and in their proper context, it tries also to avoid the fragmentation caused by the positivistic and experimental approach that takes out a small slice which it subjects to closer scrutiny.

Symbolic interactionism constitutes another theoretical position yet again within the interpretivist paradigm. Also, it is an approach which can be sub-divided into a number of schools. The notion of a school, as used here, is that offered by Ritzer (1994: 66) who defines it as 'a group of academics who share a common time and place, have a high degree of interaction with one another, and have a common way of doing their subject'. The most well-known of the symbolic interactionist schools is that of the Chicago School of Sociology which was established in 1892, which went into decline around 1935, and which has re-emerged with various degrees of force at different periods in time up to the present day.

   Ritzer (1994) has provided us with a very scholarly overview of the development of the Chicago School, and it is this overview which provides the basis of the account throughout the remainder of this section of the chapter. He starts off by noting that the city of Chicago grew dramatically between the 1840s and 1892, the year of the establishment of the school of sociology at the University, while also reminding us it constituted an 'open-air laboratory' with 'its neighbourhoods; its racial and ethnic diversity; its problems, such as stockyards; and its occupations, even deviant occupations such as prostitution' (Ritzer 1994: 69). He concludes that 'the youth and dynamism of both the city and the University made them conducive to new and important developments in many domains, including academic fields' (Ritzer 1994: 69). The University responded by encouraging its departments and faculty members to do original thinking and research regarding the city, to publish their results and to become involved in public service. The hope was that all this activity would be of assistance in coping with the city's social problems.

   A significant lead was given in pursuit of the University's mission by the philosophy department under the direction of the world-famous thinker, John Dewey, himself a key figure in the new school of philosophy which came to be termed 'pragmatism' and which was primarily an American response to the modern world. When Dewey came to Chicago in 1894, he brought George Herbert Mead (1863–1931) with him. While Mead was a professor in the philosophy department, he attracted a lot of students from the sociology department to his courses, and particularly to a course entitled 'advanced social psychology'. Through this and other activities, Mead played a very major role both in the development of sociology at the University and also in its development as a distinctive academic discipline. While he wrote very little during his academic life, his lecture notes were copiously documented by his students who published them posthumously in a book entitled *Mind, Self and Society* (Mead 1934). The concern in the book is with Mead's central ideas, namely, the emergence of mind and self in the process of social interaction.

The key figures located within the Chicago sociology department in those early years were Albion Small, who became head of the department in 1892, and W.I. Thomas. Of these two individuals, Thomas made by far the greatest contribution to academic scholarship. In terms of contributing to social theory, he was responsible for promoting the notion of 'subjects' definition of the situation' as a central idea within the Chicago School. Ritzer (1994: 82) has summarised this notion as follows:

> This means that what matters most is the way in which people, not sociologists, define their social lives. Additionally, it means that people's definitions matter as much as or more than the actual situation. If people define a given situation in a particular way, then that is what matters. This kind of subjective orientation leads the sociological researcher in the direction of ethnography and away from the kinds of studies that are easily analysed statistically.

Thomas is also well-known for pioneering two research approaches, namely, the 'self-reported life history' and what we now term 'document study'. The use of these two approaches in the collection of empirical data was a major departure from the armchair theorizing and library-study approaches dominant up until then. The product of Thomas' labour along these lines is best exemplified in the five-volume work published between 1918 and 1920, *The Polish Peasant in Europe and America* (Thomas and Znaniecki 1918–1920) which he co-authored with a Polish peasant, Florian Znaniecki. This is a work based partly on letters, newspaper accounts, records of court trials, sermons, pamphlets, and other documentary sources, and partly on the self-reported life history of Wiszniewski. Interestingly also, Ritzer notes that Thomas did not use the specific methods that were to come to dominate later Chicago research, namely, face-to-face observation and interviewing.

The other important member of the Chicago school of sociology at the time, Robert Park (1864–1944), favoured the use of participant observation – participating directly in the lives of the people being studied – in his research aimed at writing about 'city life in vivid detail' (Ritzer 1994: 77). He would, as Ritzer (1994: 77) puts it, 'go into the field, observe and analyze, and finally wrap up his observations'. On the other hand, he was opposed to the statistical analysis of data, dismissing the approach cynically as 'parlor magic' because, as he saw it, its use 'prevented sociologists from analysing not only subjectivity, but also the idiosyncratic and the peculiar'. For Park, all these things 'tended to be washed away when the researcher was dealing only with a sea of numbers' (Ritzer 1994: 77). The dominance of this view resulted, for a while, in the marginalisation of the important work in quantitative methods that was being undertaken at the time by William Fielding Ogburn and others within the sociology department at the University of Chicago. On the other hand, it did not hinder the emergence of an alternative school of symbolic interactionism at the University of Iowa. While not of concern within this book, it is instructive to realise that the Iowa School was also centred on such concepts as the 'nature of self' and 'interaction', yet was associated with positivism in working from the assumption that 'it is possible to obtain knowledge of the social world through detached study and the application of quantitative techniques' (Layder 1995: 63).

During its heyday researchers associated with the Chicago School produced a major corpus of work, most of which consisted of participant observation studies of urban life. These included *The Hobo* (Anderson 1923), *The Taxi Dance Hall* (Cressey 1932), *The Gang* (Thrasher 1927), *The Ghetto* (Wirth 1928) and *The Gold Coast and the Slum* (Zorbaugh 1929). A related set of studies was conducted on the life histories of juvenile delinquents and criminals. Included in this set were *The Natural History of a Delinquent Career* (Shaw 1931), *The Professional Thief* (Sutherland, 1937) and *The Jack-Roller* (Shaw 1966).

The Chicago School went into decline in the 1930s. Thomas and Small had, by now, left the University, Park had retired and Mead had died. Also, there was a major move to positivist science in sociology within the University of Chicago sociology department and to the accompanying use of advanced modes of statistical analyses. Two major scholars, Herbert Blumer and Everett Hughes, however, continued to work within the department and laid the basis for a renewal of the interpretivist thrust in the late 1940s and early 1950s. Among the best-known members of the resultant Second Chicago School were Erving Goffman, Howard Becker and Eliot Friedson. Since then also, symbolic interactionism within the tradition of the Chicago School has continued to be promoted in various textbooks, including those of Rose (1962) in the 1960s, Meltzer *et al.* (1975) in the 1970s, Ritzer (1983) in the 1980s, and Ritzer (1994) and Layder (1995) in the 1990s. More recently, Prus (1996) produced a text aimed at highlighting once again the importance of symbolic interactionism of the Chicago School type in investigating what he sees as central in social life, namely, intersubjective experience and meaning. It is also arguable that this position permeates such very influential texts as Hage and Powers' (1992) *Post-industrial Lives* and Castells' (2000)

The Rise of the Network Society. In addition, Atkinson and Housley (2003: xiv), speaking as sociologists, hold that 'we are all interactionists now…in the sense that many of the key *ideas* of interactionism have become part of the contemporary mainstream of sociological thought'.

The engagement in symbolic interactionist research within the field of education took off in earnest in the USA in the 1970s, at a time when a host of other research approaches involving the use of qualitative research methods were also gaining in popularity. As would be expected, the symbolic interactionists 'held to the basic and optimistic assumption' (Bogdan and Biklen 1992: 24) that participants would grant access to a research site if they could. They also had an 'empathic' perspective; that is, 'they called for sympathy and understanding towards those whom they studied' (Bogdan and Biklen 1992: 24). Such assumptions and approaches led to quite a degree of conflict between themselves and other researchers, and not just those committed to the use of quantitative research methods. Nevertheless, a significant number of books and papers emerged on various aspects of life in educational settings which were underpinned by the symbolic interactionist theoretical approach and which were the product of the use of in-depth interviewing, participant and non-participant observation, and the study of primary-source documents.

Woods (1992: 339) notes that there was a similar development in the United Kingdom. Catalysts, he argues, were provided by Young's (1971) edited collection, *Knowledge and Control*, and the Open University's (1972) course, *School and Society*. Works from such key symbolic interactionists in the Chicago School tradition as Blumer, Becker and Hughes, were reproduced, although other theoretical approaches, and not only from the interpretivist paradigm, were also represented. Out of this, Woods has observed, emerged two scholarly movements, namely, one adopting a more deterministic Marxist-oriented line and the other a more interactionist one. The main thrust of the latter has been summarised in the following words:

> British interactionists (more or less) used the school as a social laboratory, opening up the 'black box' that hitherto had been impervious to the 'input-output' studies that had prevailed hitherto. Here was a fascinating new world, where action did not simply take place as a product of external structural and cultural forces but, rather, was constructed within classrooms. How this occurred and with what consequences seemed a crucial question, not only for sociology but also for education. Sociology of education in Britain had only really begun in the 1950s, and while important work was done on background factors and their relationship to achievement, the standard survey approaches gave no assistance with understanding the processes of what actually went on in schools, how it was experienced by teachers and pupils, what different perspectives

they brought to bear, how they related together, and how conflict was resolved if that was a consequence.

(Woods 1992: 340)

Out of this movement emerged a large number of symbolic interactionist studies on various aspects of education and focusing on the various participants in the educational process (Blackledge and Hunt 1985: 231–89; Woods 1983). A number of methodological commentaries also emerged in order to provide guidance for other researchers (Burgess 1984; Finch 1986; Hammersley and Atkinson 1983; Woods 1986).

The remainder of this chapter clarifies some of the central concepts within symbolic interactionism not considered so far; concepts which have the potential to cause confusion. Such clarification is necessary before proceeding in the remaining chapters to outline an approach aimed at providing beginning researchers with a systematic approach for engaging in some basic symbolic interactionist-type research on educational topics. It is also important to realise at this point that the approach which will be outlined does not attempt to relate symbolic interactionism to the other interpretivist positions already mentioned, or to such other well-known positions as phenomenological psychology and ethnomethodology. This is to eschew the temptation to argue that a beginning researcher should spend a significant amount of time trying to construct some grand synthesis of interpretivist positions to underpin a research project. Such a stance is taken on the grounds that while the different interpretivist positions are underpinned by the same general foundation principles, they nevertheless developed out of an interest in addressing different, even if related, research questions. In other words, the stance is that one should 'be guided by the research question' *within* paradigms as well as *between* paradigms. Thus, one needs to look elsewhere to get an understanding of what is involved in undertaking research using phenomenological psychology approaches, ethnomedology approaches and other interpretivist approaches as distinct research approaches in their own right, rather than trying to combine some or all of them under some general umbrella term like 'qualitative research'.

The concept of 'perspectives'

It has already been pointed out that there is a tendency in the literature on interpretivism to use the terms 'understandings', 'meanings', 'beliefs' and 'perspectives' interchangeably and that while this practice is not technically incorrect since the terms largely mean the same thing, it is confusing. The position taken in this book is one which addresses the problem by using the term 'perspectives' consistently. Woods (1983: 7) gets to the heart of what perspectives are when he defines them as 'frameworks through which people make sense of the world'. Charon (2001: 4) arrives at a similar definition, but starts from a very basic position in stating that perspectives are made up of words. It is these words, he argues, that are used by the observer to make sense out of situations. He goes on to state that, as a result, 'the best definition of perspectives is a *conceptual framework*, which emphasizes that perspectives are really interrelated sets of words used to order physical reality' and that the words we use cause us to make assumptions and value judgements about what we are seeing and not seeing. He also puts it another way (Charon 2001: 3) when he states that 'point of view' is 'the very best definition of what a perspective is'.

Becker *et al.* (1961: 34) adopt a similar position when they define perspectives as:

> A coordinated set of ideas and actions a person uses in dealing with some problematic situation, [they] refer to a person's ordinary way of thinking and feeling about and acting in such a situation. These thoughts and actions are coordinated in the sense that the actions flow reasonably, from the actor's perspective, from the ideas contained in the perspective. Similarly, the ideas can be seen by an observer to be one of the possible sets of ideas that might form the underlying rationale for the person's actions and are seen by the actor as providing a justification for acting as he does.

Charon (2001: 3) puts it another way yet again when he states:

> A perspective is an angle on reality, a place where the individual stands as he or she looks at it and tries to understand reality....a perspective is an absolute basic part of everyone's existence, and it acts as a filter through which everything around us is perceived and interpreted. There is no possible way that the individual can encounter reality 'in the raw', directly, as it really is, for whatever is seen can only be part of the real situation.

This means that while human beings are limited by their perspectives in that they cannot see outside of them, these perspectives are also vital in that they make it possible for us to make sense of the world.

To make the latter point is not to argue that there is no truth at all, or that all opinions about reality are equally correct. The unfortunate situation is, as Charon puts it, that many people do believe that there is no truth at all. Reality, he argues, does in fact exist; 'there is something actually happening out there in the world – but we cannot know it completely or in any perfectly accurate way because we always see it through filters we are here calling perspectives' (2001: 6). Crotty (1998: 44) makes the same point in a different way when he states that 'we do not create meaning. We construct meaning. We have something to work with. What we work with is the world and objects in the world'.

Another basic idea associated with perspectives is that they develop when people must choose between alternatives (Potts 1997: 19). Nevertheless, if certain sorts of situations occur repeatedly, the perspective may become a fixed part of an individual's way of coping with reality (Becker *et al.* 1961: 35). Also, there may be a need to distinguish between immediate and long-range perspectives. Furthermore, any situation may not be interpreted in the same manner by everyone. At the same time, however, group perspectives, as has already been pointed out in the first part of this chapter, tend to develop. These are taken-for-granted ways of thinking and acting evolved by a group which has to confront similar problematic situations (Becker *et al.*1961: 36). As Becker *et al.* (1961: 36) put it, they occur 'when people see themselves as being in the same boat and when they have the opportunity to interact with reference to their problems'. Such group perspectives apply to specific situations. They are ways of thinking and acting which have occurred as a result of certain institutional constraints, and serve as an answer to the problems these constraints cause (Potts 1997: 20).

It also needs to be recognised that not only can our perspectives change many times throughout our lives, but they can also change from situation to situation, and can do so many times during the same day. In other words, few of us have one perspective that we can apply to every situation we come across. In this regard, symbolic interactionists speak of perspectives as being 'situational'. Charon (2001: 7) elaborates on this as follows: 'In the classroom my perspective is that of teacher-sociologist; in my home it becomes father or husband; on a fishing trip it changes to "seasoned fisherman"'. Each situation, he concludes, calls forth a different role, which means a different perspective.

Clarifying other key concepts

This final part of the chapter, as flagged in the introduction, clarifies three important distinctions which many tend to blur in developing eclectic approaches to interpretivist research: the distinction between 'behaviour' and 'action'; the distinction between 'perspectives' and 'perceptions', and the distinction between 'perspectives' and 'attitudes'.

Behaviour and action

One of the most basic ideas already mentioned regarding how the individual is viewed within the interpretivist paradigm is that all human action is meaningful and hence 'has to be interpreted and understood within the context of social practices' (Usher 1996: 18). In considering this, it is necessary to take on board immediately the importance of the term 'action'. Interpretivists speak of 'human action' rather than 'human behaviour' (Connole *et al.* 1993: 34). The significance of this is that while positivist scientists speak of events having 'causes' and 'human behaviour' is seen as the outcome of external influences, interpretivists speak of 'human actions' as having 'reasons'. In other words, actions are preceded by intentions which arise out of the perspectives which individuals hold; a position also consistent with the notion promoted at the end of the previous section of this chapter that one of the components of perspectives is that of 'reasons'. Furthermore, the position is that these perspectives create interaction between humans and are, in turn, created by this interaction.

Connole *et al.* (1993: 118–9) take up the distinction outlined above between 'behaviour' and 'action'. They point out that interpretivists deny that explanations of human activity can be elicited and measured by empiricist methods alone. On this, they draw attention to the view of Popkewitz (1984: 40–2) that we need to shift the focus of attention behind people's visible behaviour to the processes of negotiation of *appropriate* behaviours and, in so doing, investigate the social rules being used by those interacting. Connole *et al.* (1993: 119) elaborate on this view:

> Among several points he made was a reference to the classic distinction between two kinds of causation. The first is an event or action being brought about because of a prior event. The second is something done in order to cause a predicted consequence. In one the direction of cause–effect influence is forward in time as something occurs due to something happening before it. In the other the direction is backwards, with something being done at one time due to an intended future event. It is clear that all human behaviours cannot be adequately understood without bringing in the possibility of the second, conscious, intentional, in-order-to, cause–effect relationship.

This is the kind of thinking which has resulted in interpretivists favouring the use of the term 'action' over the term 'behaviour'.

Perspectives and perceptions

One regularly finds the concept of 'perceptions' utilised in interpretivist studies where there is no clear outline of the underpinnings in terms of epistemology, research paradigm and theoretical approach. This is not very helpful because of the centrality of 'perspectives' in symbolic interactionism. Another complicating factor is that the concept of 'perception' is, in fact, a central concept itself within other theoretical approaches. Charon develops this point in a very helpful manner by first of all labelling symbolic interactionism as a distinct theoretical approach within one of two types of social psychology (Charon 2001: 21), namely, 'psychological social psychology' and 'sociological social psychology'. The notion of 'perception' is central to the former, which has its roots, to a large extent, in Gestalt psychology which developed in the late nineteenth and early twentieth centuries:

> Gestalt psychology emphasizes the central importance of 'perception' in human behaviour: The human being acts according to how the situation is perceived. Gestalt psychologists have attempted to isolate various principles of perception in order to better understand how the individual organizes the stimuli he or she confronts. Gestalt psychology as such is entirely psychological in its orientation, but because of the work of some Gestaltists a social dimension was added to the framework, which greatly influenced the direction of social psychology.
>
> (Charon 2001: 21)

Sociology, on the other hand, spawned sociological social psychology, which 'is distinct from much of psychology by de-emphasising the person as cause; it is distinct from much of sociology by de-emphasising the power of social patterns and society at large' (Charon 2001: 21). The main focus is on 'social interaction', which can be defined as the on-going, back-and-forth action that participants take towards one another. Also, while psychological social psychologists tend, by and large, to use surveys and laboratory experiments, sociological social psychologists focus on researching real-life events, such as interaction in a meeting or in the waiting room of a doctor's surgery.

A most important stream within sociological social psychology is symbolic interactionism. Here, as has been laboured repeatedly in this book so far, the concept of 'perspectives' is central. This is not to say that symbolic interactionists do not have a view on 'perceptions'. They do, but it has much lesser status within this theoretical approach than does 'perspectives'. Charon (2001: 8) sums up this lesser status when he states that 'perspectives are not perceptions but are guides to our perceptions; they influence what we see and how we interpret what we see.' He takes up the same point in a different context when he states that language guides the individual through what his or her senses experience: 'It constitutes the individual's *perspectives*, and thus serves the function of alerting the individual to some parts of the environment and not to others' (Charon 2001: 65).

Perspectives and attitudes

In considering the symbolic interactionist's preference for the concept of 'perspectives' over that of 'attitudes' it is useful to consider once again the distinction made above between psychological social psychology and sociological social psychology. The basic question to be answered by those who espouse the former school is how other people around us influence our thoughts, feelings and behaviours. By far the most important topic investigated by this branch of social psychology has been attitudes and attitude change. An attitude within this scholarly approach is usually defined as a person's set of beliefs and feelings towards an object, or class of objects, that predisposes the person to act in a certain manner when confronted by that object, or class of objects.

Symbolic interactionists, who are sociological rather than psychological social psychologists, conceptualize the individual very differently from those who are comfortable with the concept of 'attitude'. The latter, as already stated, is usually defined as being a fairly fixed and stable quality of an individual over time; and the image of the individual which is associated with it is that 'of a consistent, whole organism, responding to stimuli in situations according to this attitude brought to the situation' (Charon 2001: 38). In other words, an attitude is carried around from situation to situation. The external environment acts as a stimulus. The person first responds internally to an object, or to a class of objects. Then the person responds externally after having that internal response.

Symbolic interactionists reject this view as it promotes a notion of the individual as not being in control of his or her own action. As they see it, it is a view which is premised on a notion that the individual is passive and thus does not use the attitude; instead, the attitude directs the individual. By contrast, their concept of the individual is of an active being and they stress the importance of active definition of the situation. This is why they prefer the concept of perspectives. This concept captures the notion of a human being who interacts, defines situations, and acts according to what is going on in the present situation. Furthermore, because perspectives are conceptualized as dynamic and changing guides to interpretation and then to action, such action can never be totally predictable. The next chapter now seeks to outline a systematic way for engaging in research where one of the central concerns is trying to grasp participants' perspectives and how they act in the light of their perspectives.

Chapter 3

Posing the questions

A central position expounded throughout this book is that the interpretivist view of the individual, and particularly that based upon the symbolic interactionist theoretical position, is of one who is a manager of his or her environment. Elaborating on this position can lead to the development of different types of studies, as later chapters demonstrate in the form of research proposals. Nevertheless, it seems to me that before we can launch into pursuing any of these types of studies, we must first of all come to grips with more fundamental matters. In this regard, my contention is that there are two basic types of studies which can be developed from the symbolic interactionist view of the individual, particularly when it is considered in light of Blumer's three principles as outlined in the previous chapter. Furthermore, I contend that these form the foundation framework for engaging in all other kinds of related studies.

The two basic types of studies which can be developed from the symbolic interactionist view of the individual are as follows:

1 Studies aimed at generating theory on the perspectives which participants hold with regard to something;
2 Studies aimed at generating theory on how participants 'manage', 'deal with', 'or 'cope with' a phenomenon.

Part Two of this chapter considers how to develop appropriate research questions for engaging in each of these two basic types of studies. Before moving to this, however, a number of points need to be clarified in order to get a clearer view of what each type involves.

The two basic types of studies

Studies of the first type can be viewed as 'frozen in time' studies. The concern is with generating theory about the perspectives which a group or groups have with regard to some particular phenomenon at a particular point in time. Thus, I have had students engage in studies on such areas as primary school principals' perspectives on what are 'good' schools, teacher educators' perspectives on what is a professional teacher educator, key stakeholders' perspectives within Fundamental Christian schools on their schools' programmemes for the pastoral care of staff, high school principals' perspectives on the role of schooling in the promotion of the academic development of students, and NESB university academics' perspectives on the role which English-language proficiency played in their appointments to their positions. Such studies are valuable for reasons which will be discussed in some detail in the next chapter. At the same time, however, it is important to highlight here their lack of a longitudinal dimension. In other words, they tend not to be concerned with investigating the processes involved in the participants' construction of their perspectives, nor do they set out to track the perspectives from the initial point of investigation onwards to see how, if at all, they change.

Studies of the second type outlined at the commencement of this chapter, namely, those studies aimed at developing theory regarding how participants 'manage', 'deal with', 'or 'cope with' a phenomenon, do have a longitudinal dimension to them. One way of grasping what is involved here is to consider the notion that when we ask how do participants 'manage', 'deal with', 'or 'cope with' situations, we are asking a particular type of question in 'shorthand' form. Phrasing the same question in its more extended form is really to ask a number of interrelated questions. To put it simply, as symbolic interactionists what we are really doing when we pose the question: 'how do participants 'manage', 'deal with', 'or 'cope with' situations?' is asking what are the patterns that can be detected over a particular period of time from an investigation of:

i.   the perspectives which the participants have on a phenomenon at the outset;
ii. how the participants act in the light of their perspectives;
iii. the changes, if any, which take place in the participants' perspectives as a result of their actions;

and so on, as the cycle repeats itself time and again. In other words, there is a major focus on trying to generate theory about process.

It is necessary to elaborate a little on point iii above regarding a focus on 'changes, if any, which take place in participants' perspectives as a result of the responses to their actions'. What is being referred to here has already been taken up in some detail in the previous chapter in the exposition on the nature of 'perspectives' in noting that participants' perspectives may remain the same, may be reinforced, may be modified, or may change as a result of how they respond to how others respond to their actions. This, in turn, it will be recalled, may influence participants to act the same as they did initially, to modify their actions, to reinforce their actions or to change their actions.

The challenge to the researcher is to try to detect patterns arising out of this constant interaction through in-depth studies carried out over definite periods of time.

It is also necessary to highlight the centrality of the term 'theory', or more specifically, that of 'generating theory', in each of the two types of central research questions which are the focus of attention in this chapter. Such a situation is different from that adopted by researchers who take a positivistic stance and are primarily interested in verifying or testing hypotheses about the nature of social life. To make this observation is not in any way to find fault with the work of positivist researchers. Rather, it is helpful in so far as it puts in context the publication of Glaser and Strauss' highly influential book, *The Discovery of Grounded Theory* (1967) – which will be considered in the next chapter within the context of its emergence historically – and the consequent great interest which it sparked in developing, or generating, social theory and concepts. A useful summary of how theory is defined in this and various other works of Glaser and Strauss is that it is an integrated framework of well-developed concepts and the relationships between them that can be used to explain or predict phenomena.

Another point in need of elaboration regarding what is involved in each of the two types of studies which are the focus of this chapter centres on the practice of attributing the same meaning to the terms 'deal with', 'manage' and 'cope with' in symbolic interactionist studies and, indeed, sometimes even to the terms 'handle', 'respond to' and 'exercise control over'. I hold that while it is important for those commencing work in the field to recognise this practice, it is also important to recognise how two of these terms, namely, 'manage' and 'cope with' can be particularly confusing. Confusion centred on the use of 'manage' arises because readers unfamiliar with the interpretivist way of thinking are almost programmememed to think of, and use the term only in terms of, scientific management. Thus, when one poses a question regarding how a group of participants manage some phenomenon or other, they automatically think that what is being asked is how are they managing in relation to how scientific management theorists state they *should* be managing. To take an example, imagine that a research project is being conducted in a factory setting. The data on one senior executive who reports that he suffers from stress indicates that he is regularly absent from work, comes in late in the mornings, and drinks alcohol to excess. The scientific managerialist would be likely to speak of this participant as not managing in the work place. The symbolic interactionist, on the other hand, in taking a non-judgemental approach, would be likely to speak in terms of the participant's regular absence from work, coming in late in the mornings, and drinking alcohol to excess as his way of managing his situation.

A similar confusion centres on an alternative way of using the term 'cope' to the way in which it is used by symbolic interactionists. What is being referred to here is the practice in a particular body of scholarship within psychology which has grown up around a psychological model of coping. Those working according to this model tend to evaluate responses according to either implicit or explicit criteria as to what *should* be involved in coping. In other words, they utilize pre-established standards to investigate the degree to which a person's responses can be judged to represent the level to which he or she is coping. Again, to use the example of the senior executive noted above, those working within the parameters of the psychologist's model of coping would view his actions as indicative of him not coping very well with his situation, while the symbolic interactionist would view them as the strategies he uses in order to cope.

To conclude on the latter point, then, the argument which has been made is that while symbolic interactionist studies of the second type noted at the beginning of this chapter are generally stated in terms of how participants 'deal with', 'manage', or 'cope with' particular phenomena, these terms mean the same thing within the interpretivist paradigm. Nevertheless, they can be confusing because the terms 'manage' and 'cope with' are also well-known terms associated with other paradigms and other theoretical positions, and in these situations they have a different meaning to what they have for interpretivists. Accordingly, the term used consistently throughout the remainder of this text is that of 'deal with'. This is because it is the most neutral of the various terms used by interpretivists and has the least potential to create misunderstanding.

Formulating studies in relation to questions on perspectives

Overall, the contention so far is that two main types of studies can be developed from a consideration of the central ideas of the symbolic interactionist theoretical approach located within the interpretivist paradigm. In order to progress from here in the development of a research plan, a number of steps need to be taken. Clearly, the first step that needs to be taken is to decide which of the two types of studies is appropriate for one's research area of interest. Once this has been settled upon, one needs to formulate one's focus of research into an appropriate statement of the aim of what is to be pursued. For example, if one decides on the first type of study one would formulate an aim along the lines of the following adopted by various postgraduate students of mine over the last number of years:

> The aim of the study is to generate theory on teachers' perspectives on parental involvement in school decision-making in the state school system in Western Australia.
>
> The aim of the study is to generate theory on the perspectives of Japanese teachers in Australia on what is effective teaching.

The aim of the study is to generate theory on the perspectives of teachers in a state school system on the school development planning process in the schools.

The aim of the study is to generate theory on the perspectives of key stakeholders on the quality assurance policy which is implemented in one private school sector

The aim of the study is to generate theory on the perspectives of teachers in Catholic schools on how to develop sustainable learning communities.

The aim of the study is to generate theory on the perspectives of teachers in Fundamental Christian schools on the nature and purpose of schooling.

Similarly, if one decides on the second type of study one would formulate an aim along the lines of the following studies also undertaken by various postgraduate students of mine over the last number of years:

The aim of the study is to generate theory on how those university lecturers responsible for preparing distance education materials deal with the process.

The aim of the study is to generate theory on how teachers in Fundamental Christian schools deal with the teaching of 'Human Origins'.

The aim of the study is to generate theory on how Western Australian parents deal with the home schooling of their children with disabilities.

The aim of the study is to generate theory on how school administration teams deal with their work in a restructured educational system.

The aim of the study is to generate theory on how parents of children in the School of Isolated and Distance Education in Western Australia deal with their work as home tutors.

The aim of the study is to generate theory on how parents of children diagnosed with Attention-Deficit/Hyperactivity Disorder deal with the schooling of their children with the disorder.

Each of the questions in these two groups is straightforward and unambiguous in light of the parameters established so far. Nevertheless, before the students settled upon these questions it was vital for them to establish that the issue of focus was a real issue for the participants and not just of academic interest to themselves as outsiders. If this had not been established, the likelihood is that the researcher would have designed a theoretically sound and neat research plan which could not have been implemented as she or he would have come up against a brick wall of non-responses. To put it another way, there is no point in designing a study about participants' perspectives on something unless we are convinced before we commence the study that it is something about which they have fairly well formed views and that they feel sufficiently free to discuss these views.

Returning now to the matter of making progress in the development of a research plan, the second step which needs to be taken is that of taking one's stated aim and rephrasing it as a general question. In the case of the first example given above for studies of type one, this means that it would be restated as follows: What are teachers' perspectives on parental involvement in school decision-making in the State school system in Western Australia? Similarly, the first example given above for studies of type two would be restated as follows: How do those who prepare distance education materials deal with the process?

At this point it is not so obvious how to proceed further. Certainly, our general research question, whether it relates to a type one or a type two study, is not very helpful on its own, particularly given the position expounded in the previous chapter that semi-structured interviews should constitute a central data-gathering method in both types of studies. What is being alluded to here is that it would be unlikely to be very productive to commence one's interviews by approaching participants and simply asking them to elaborate on their perspectives on the phenomenon under investigation. For one thing, they are likely to respond immediately, and quite understandably, with the question: 'What do you mean by perspectives?'. Secondly, semi-structured interviewing necessitates that we engage in conversations with participants through more down-to-earth questions.

The issue, then, is how to arrive at appropriate down-to-earth questions such that they will yield a quantity and quality of data which, when subjected to analysis, will allow us to generate theory regarding the participants' perspectives. Over the years of engaging in studies with aims along the lines of the two types of studies outlined at the commencement of this chapter, I have found it very helpful to focus my thinking along the following lines:

1 The general research question which is generated from the overall aim is always too broad to be answered directly.
2 What we need is a very specific set of data collection questions. A data collection question is, as Punch (2000: 27) puts it, 'a question which is asked in order to collect data in order to help answer the research question'. Punch elaborates on this by saying that sometimes many data collection questions will be involved in assembling the data necessary to answer one research question.
3 Some researchers term their list of data collection questions an 'aide memoire', or a semi-structured interview guide. For symbolic interactionist studies of the types under consideration in this book, such a guide consists of those lists of questions deemed most appropriate at the beginning of the research in terms of having the potential to engage the participants in conversations across as wide a range of areas

as possible. The objective is to yield data such that it is possible to grasp as fully as possible their perspectives on the phenomenon under investigation.

4 Notwithstanding the value of the position outlined in each of the preceding four points, we are still no wiser regarding how to develop a suitable list of data collection questions. One possible way of doing it which suggests itself would be to brainstorm colleagues and friends, have some informal conversations with individuals similarly located to those in mind for the study, and see what would come out of this activity. However, such an approach would not be very systematic and to pursue it would not involve following any particular chain of logic.

5 Much more productive is to take seriously the question stated above which participants would be likely to give us by way of reply if we were to bluntly ask them what were their perspectives on something, namely 'What do you mean by perspectives?'. The remaining part of this section of the chapter seeks to demonstrate that the exercise of unravelling into a number of component parts what we do in fact mean by the concept of perspectives gives us a very useful framework for logically arriving at a comprehensive list of data collection questions.

Much of the previous chapter focused on distinguishing the concept of perspectives from a variety of other concepts, particularly that of 'perceptions' and 'attitudes'. A number of useful definitions of perspectives was also offered, particularly Woods' (1983: 7) 'frameworks through which people make sense of the world' and Charon's (2001: 4) 'conceptual frameworks'. These definitions have operated very well in this book so far by way of scaffolding the exposition and keeping considerations focused. Nevertheless, the astute reader must once again be having some uneasiness, this time in relation to the meaning of the term 'framework'. In particular, it is unlikely to have escaped many that the use of 'framework' in any definition implies a number of interrelated parts. In this case, what is being referred to are the interrelated parts of a perspective. This, then, begs the question: 'What are the parts that do in fact interrelate in any perspective?'.

Becker *et al.* (1968: 28–30) progress towards answering the latter question when they contend that perspectives have several components, namely, a definition of the situation – a collection of ideas outlining the sort of situation in which action must be taken; an outline of the types of activities one may rightly be involved in; and finally, criteria of judgement. These components certainly correspond with the various aspects of the concept of perspectives as considered in the previous chapter. They pose problems, however, when considering how they might be used to develop guiding questions to facilitate the conducting of a research project with symbolic interactionist foundations.

Before developing this point further it is important to clarify what is meant when referring to guiding questions. In particular, it is important to note that they are not logical subsets of the general research question such that if they were each dealt with, we would somehow have addressed the central research question. If we fail to take this point seriously we could find ourselves forgetting that, ultimately, our purpose is not even to answer a general research question, but rather to fulfil an aim, namely, to generate theory. Instead, what we are seeking in developing guiding questions is a set of questions which are deduced from our understanding of the central research question. Furthermore, this set of questions should be sufficiently comprehensive to facilitate the development at the commencement of our research project that which was already pointed out as being desirous, namely, an extensive list of data collection questions which at that point would seem to have the potential to engage the participants in conversations across a very wide range of areas in order to yield data regarding their perspectives.

It is certainly possible to pose guiding questions by utilizing the component parts of perspectives identified by Becker *et al.* and noted above. In other words, we can pose questions about 'one's definition of the situation', questions about 'the sort of situation in which action must be taken', questions about 'the types of activities one may rightly be involved in', and questions about 'criteria of judgment'. However, my experience is that it is very difficult to then translate these sorts of questions into data collection questions. Much more helpful in this regard is the position of Blackledge and Hunt (1991: 234); a position which is much clearer with regard to what is being referred to, while also being consistent with the views of Becker *et al.*. Blackledge and Hunt hold that the interrelated parts of the framework which goes to make up a 'perspective' consist of the participants' aims or intentions, their strategies, what they see as being significant for them, the reasons they give for their activity, and what they see as the expected outcomes of their activity. This 'unpacking' exercise allows us to construct the following structure for the development of guiding questions in relation to the general research question regarding a study where the aim is to generate theory about participants' perspectives on a particular phenomenon:

1 What are the aims or intentions of the participants with regard to the phenomenon under investigation and what reasons do they give for their aims or intentions?
2 What strategies do the participants say they have for realising their aims and intentions and what reasons do they give for utilising those strategies?
3 What do the participants see as the significance of their aims or intentions, and their strategies and what reasons can they give for this?
4 What outcomes do the participants expect from pursuing their aims or intentions and what reasons can they give for this?

The following is an example of how one student worked through each of the steps outlined in this chapter and used the above framework to arrive at a set of guiding questions for his study.

Aim of the study

The aim of the proposed research is to generate theory regarding mathematics teachers' perspectives on how they engage their students in learning mathematics in the context of the State's Curriculum Framework for guiding the work of secondary school teachers in Western Australia.

General research question

What are the perspectives of mathematics teachers on how they engage lower secondary state school students in ways commensurate with the mathematics learning outcomes of the Curriculum Framework?

Guiding questions

1   What are Western Australian lower secondary mathematics teachers' intentions with regard to engaging students with mathematics under the Curriculum Framework? What reasons do they give for these intentions?
2   What strategies do the teachers say they use to achieve these intentions? What reasons do they give for selecting these strategies?
3   What is the significance of these intentions and strategies for the teachers? What reasons do they give for the significance which they attribute to these intentions and strategies?
4   What are the outcomes that Western Australian lower secondary mathematics teachers expect from implementing their chosen strategies aimed at engaging students with mathematics under the Curriculum Framework? What reasons do they give for these expected outcomes?

The student then proceeded to take each guiding question to help him develop a series of data collection questions so that the research could get underway. For example, he developed the following list of data collection questions from the first guiding question:

1   'Engagement with mathematics' is a key term in the Curriculum Framework. What do you think the 'official' meaning of the term is? Why?
2   What do you think about this use of the term? Do you agree with it? Why?

3 Are there any ways in which you disagree with the intended meaning? If so, what are they? Why?
4 Is it important to you in your teaching that your students are engaged with mathematics? Why?
5 How can you tell if your students are engaged with mathematics?
6 How can you tell when your students are not engaged with mathematics?
7 What are you trying to achieve when engaging your students with mathematics? Why?
8 How realistic is all of this?
9 What would the implications for teaching and learning be if the students in your mathematics classes were not engaged with mathematics?

By developing a similar set of questions from each of the other three guiding questions, the student had every reason to feel confident that he could begin his research armed with a body of data collection questions with sufficient potential to engage the participants in conversations across as wide a range of areas as possible to yield data that would facilitate the development of theory regarding their perspectives. At the same time, however, he was open to the possibility that some of the data collection questions would be unproductive and would have to be dropped, while other more productive ones might suggest themselves during the interviews and would be pursued enthusiastically.

In my own research I have also experimented with trying to come up with guides to indicate how guiding questions themselves can also be broken down further in order to make it easier to develop data collection questions. One effort in this regard is exemplified in the following extract from a short research proposal developed in conjunction with my colleagues, Associate Professor Anne Chapman and Dr David Pyvis.

Project title

Teachers and the curriculum delivered to international students in university offshore programmes: An interpretivist study.

The issue that the project will address and its justification

The overall aim of the study is to generate theory about the perspectives of teachers regarding the curriculum which they deliver to international students in offshore programmes. The study is justified on the grounds that students' learning experiences are shaped largely by their teachers mediating the 'written' curriculum and the notion that the nature of the mediation is influenced largely by the teacher's perspectives on that curriculum. To date, very few studies based upon such a position have been undertaken in relation to offshore university education. Because studies of 'perspectives' are inductivist they need to proceed through small-scale in-depth qualitative projects. Accordingly, this project will open up the area through a preliminary study of four offshore programmes involving staff from a number of Australian universities.

Background

There has been an expansion in the provision of university programmes for overseas students throughout much of the Western world, including the United States, Canada, the United Kingdom, and Australia. Specifically regarding the situation in Australia, statistics show that in Semester 2, 2003, 21.5 percent or 174,732 of the nation's university student population were international students (IDP 2003). A significant number of these were enrolled in 'offshore education programmes' of all 38 public universities. The major market is Southeast Asia, with more than 70 percent of all Australian university offshore programmes being in China – including Hong Kong – Singapore and Malaysia (AVCC 2003).

Currently, the following typology of models of offshore delivery can be identified:

- *Twinning programmes*. Programmes of Australian universities offered offshore with the involvement of an overseas partner. Students generally have the same material, lectures and examinations as those at the offshore campus.
- *Franchised programmes*. A local offshore institution delivers an Australian university programme.
- *Moderated programmes*. A local offshore institution teaches its own programmes with quality assurance provided by an Australian university. The Australian university then offers 'advanced standing' to graduates of the local programme.
- *Offshore campuses*. An Australian university establishes a campus offshore where local and Australian staff are hired to deliver programmes, and onshore staff also may teach for periods of time.
- *Online programmes*. Programmes are delivered through the internet, with support from Australian onshore staff.

The development of the various programmes adds a new dimension to university study. There is, for example, a concern to understand the particularities of the educational experiences of tertiary students enrolled in such programmes. Equally, there is a need to develop an understanding of the various aspects of the experiences of the teachers involved in the delivery of these programmes, including an understanding of their perspectives on the curriculum they deliver.

General research question

What are the perspectives of teachers from Australian universities who teach international students in offshore programmes on the curriculum which they deliver?

Research design and conceptual framework

The central aim of the study seeks to generate theory about the perspectives of teachers from Australian universities teaching international students in offshore programmes on the curriculum which they deliver. To pose such an aim is to adopt a 'theory laden' research agenda where symbolic interactionism is the underlying theoretical position. The central tenet of this paradigm is that in order to understand social reality, one has to study how individuals interpret the world around them; the particular view that an individual has of the social reality is constructed and negotiated by individuals acting according to the perspectives they confer on the phenomena in their environment (Woods 1992).

Definition of terms

An 'offshore programme' is where international students are located in a different country to that of the institution providing their education services (Davis *et al.* 2000).

'Theory' is 'a set of well-developed concepts related through statements of relationship, which together constitute an integrated framework that can be used to explain or predict phenomena' (Strauss and Corbin 1990: 15).

'Perspectives' are frameworks through which people make sense of the world (Woods 1992). Such frameworks have the following interrelated components:

1 participants' intentions and the reasons they give for having these intentions;
2 participants' strategies for realizing their intentions and the reasons they give for utilising these strategies;
3 the significance which participants attach to their intentions and strategies and the reasons they give for this;
4 the outcomes which participants expect to result from their actions and the reasons they give for this.

'Curriculum' consists of:

1 the range of curriculum objectives sought and how these objectives are characterized;
2 the underlying values and beliefs which underlie the objectives;
3 how teachers and students are grouped in relation to this pattern;
4 the content prescribed for the realization of the objectives;
5 the methods recommended for dealing with the content
6 the approaches used to assess the students' work.

Guiding questions

The principal research question will be addressed through the sub-questions in the following matrix developed from the intersection of the component parts of the terms 'perspectives' and 'curriculum' (see Table 3.1)

These questions will be broken down further into an *aide-memoire* of data-gathering questions (Punch 2000: 27), i.e. questions suggesting themselves as the most productive line of inquiry at the commencement of the study. As the study unfolds, some of the guiding questions may prove themselves to be redundant, while others may arise.

A postgraduate student I was supervising was taken by this approach and articulated it in a slightly different way, again with the intention of making easier her task of formulating an extensive list of appropriate data collection questions. Her effort in this regard is exemplified in the following extract from her research proposal.

The aim of the study

The aim of the study is to develop theory regarding the perspectives of the key stakeholders on the curriculum for 'Teaching Greek as a Second Language' in Western Australia (WA) under the 'Seconded Teachers from Greece' (STG) programme.

The background

Since 1915, the Greek community of Western Australia has set out to maintain the Greek language and culture by providing instruction through after-hours classes held during the week and on Saturday mornings. Over the years, as the Greek population grew, so did the demand for extra classes and different locations for tuition. In time, the original Hellenic Community after-hours Greek School had other competitors in the field, offering Greek language and cultural tuition to the growing clientele. Simultaneously, adult classes began at Perth Technical School (TAFE) in the early 1970s.

Table 3.1 A matrix for curriculum research

	... the range of objectives sought?	... the underlying values and beliefs?	... how teachers and students are grouped?	... the content prescribed?	... the methods prescribed?	... the approaches to assessment?
What are their intentions and reasons regarding ...						
What are their strategies (with reasons) for realizing intentions regarding ...						
What significance (with reasons) do they attach to ...						
What outcomes (with reasons) do they expect from ...						

In the early 1980s, The University of Western Australia became the first tertiary institution to offer Modern Greek as a tertiary level subject to adult learners. Soon, various secondary schools began to offer Modern Greek on the curriculum with varying levels of success and longevity. In 1991, St. Andrew's Greek Orthodox Grammar School became operational as the first Greek Orthodox Day School in Western Australia. It was built solely for the purpose of maintaining and promoting the Greek language and culture for Greek and non-Greek background students.

The need for locally trained teachers in the Greek language grew, but the supply was inadequate. To assist with the shortage of teacher availability and to add an authentic dimension to the teaching of the Greek language in Australia, the Greek government invested funds in sending seconded teachers to Australia. Western Australia acquired its first seconded teachers in 1983. Seconded teachers were assigned to an Australian city for a period of three to five years and their brief was to provide professional development for the existing teachers of Greek language in Australia, to teach the Greek language and culture and to promote Hellenism. The number of seconded teachers sent to Australia has grown considerably since 1977 when the first three teachers were sent to Melbourne, Victoria. Unfortunately, the common perception over the years has been that the level of performance of the seconded teachers has been inadequate and ill suited to the needs of its recipients.

This study arises out of a desire to assist seconded teachers from Greece to become better acclimatised and better equipped to handle the demands of the Australian education system and to adjust to the differences in teaching methodologies, particularly in the field of teaching Greek as a second language. It is accepted that a first step towards realising this desire involves the development of an understanding of the perspectives of the major stakeholders regarding various aspects of the curriculum offered by the seconded teachers. This is based on the premise that any actions taken to address perceived problems in teachers' professional lives are unlikely to succeed unless they take cognisance of the perspectives of major stakeholders. The key stakeholders are seconded teachers, staff in host schools, parents of children in host schools, and the wider Greek community.

The general research question is as follows

What are the perspectives of the key stakeholders on the curriculum for 'Teaching Greek as a Second Language' in Western Australia (WA) under the 'Seconded Teachers from Greece' programme?

Data collection questions

With regard to each of the stakeholder groups, the following guiding questions will be explored to investigate the central aspects of their perspectives:

1   What are their intentions with regard to 'Teaching Greek as a Second Language' in WA under the 'Seconded Teachers from Greece' programme and what reasons do they give for their intentions?
2   What strategies do they say they will use with regard to 'Teaching Greek as a Second Language' in WA under the 'Seconded Teachers from Greece' programme and what reasons do they give for using these strategies?
3   What significance do they attach to their intentions and strategies, and what reasons do they give for this?
4   What outcomes do they expect will eventuate from the pursuit of their intentions and strategies, and what reasons do they give for this?

Each question will be explored in relation to each of the four main components of curriculum, namely, objectives, content, teaching methods, and modes of evaluation. The primary sources of data collection will include semi-structured interviews, document analysis, participant observation and field notes. This approach can be represented diagrammatically as shown in Table 3.2.

It is recognised that different stakeholders are likely to have stronger views on certain components of the data collection questions than they have on others. Nevertheless, the full complement of components is outlined in order to safeguard against assuming that some stakeholders may not have strong views on some of them. Each of these components will be fleshed out into a series of data collection questions.

The same careful planning needs to be undertaken regarding the second type of studies, namely, those aimed at generating theory regarding how participants deal with a particular phenomenon. Such studies, it will be recalled, necessitate trying to discover patterns over a period of time from an investigation of:

  i.   the perspectives which participants have regarding a phenomenon at the outset;
 ii.   how the participants act in the light of their perspectives;
iii.   the changes, if any, which take place in the participants' perspectives as a result of their actions.

The approach to initial data gathering regarding participants' perspectives is exactly the same as for the first type of studies. Subsequent data-gathering sessions aimed at uncovering changes, if any, in perspectives over time, however, while likely to be guided at the beginning by the same schemes as those developed for use in the initial session, may take new and unexpected turns as participants relate their positions. Researchers have to be prepared to pursue any new line of thought on the part of the participants even if they

Table 3.2 Another matrix for curriculum research

Research questions	Seconded teachers	Staff in host schools	Parents	Wider Greek community
Intentions for programme and reasons for intentions	*Re: Objectives *Re: Content *Re: Methods *Re: Evaluation	*Re: Objectives *Re: Content *Re: Methods *Re: Evaluation	*Re: Objectives *Re: Content *Re: Methods *Re: Evaluation	*Re: Objectives *Re: Content *Re: Methods *Re: Evaluation
Strategies for achieving intentions and reasons given	*Re: Objectives *Re: Content *Re: Methods *Re: Evaluation	*Re: Objectives *Re: Content *Re: Methods *Re: Evaluation	*Re: Objectives *Re: Content *Re: Methods *Re: Evaluation	*Re: Objectives *Re: Content *Re: Methods *Re: Evaluation
Significance of reasons and strategies for participants and reasons given	*Re: Objectives *Re: Content *Re: Methods *Re: Evaluation	*Re: Objectives *Re: Content *Re: Methods *Re: Evaluation	*Re: Objectives *Re: Content *Re: Methods *Re: Evaluation	*Re: Objectives *Re: Content *Re: Methods *Re: Evaluation
Expected outcomes for participants and reasons given	*Re: Objectives *Re: Content *Re: Methods *Re: Evaluation	*Re: Objectives *Re: Content *Re: Methods *Re: Evaluation	*Re: Objectives *Re: Content *Re: Methods *Re: Evaluation	*Re: Objectives *Re: Content *Re: Methods *Re: Evaluation

have been unanticipated. This is because, as has already been argued, it is that which is important to the participant which is paramount, not what might be important to the researcher. At the same time, however, researchers should still be guided when developing their data collection questions – even those which suggest themselves 'on the spot' – by a desire to canvass across the five areas of participants' aims or intentions, their strategies, what they see as being significant for them, the reasons they give for their activity, and what they see as the expected outcomes of their activity.

It is also important when engaged in studies of the second type to investigate how participants act in the light of their perspectives. Ideally, this should be done by adopting the approach of Wolcott (1973) when he shadowed a school principal for an extensive period of time, after which he went on to write *The Man in the Principal's Office*. Over this period he was not only in a position to make copious notes regarding the principal's actions, but also to regularly seek clarification in order to make sure that what he thought he was observing was in fact what was happening. The importance of engaging in such clarification is what some interpretivists are referring to when they caution us to make sure that 'a blink is not a wink'.

Most researchers, and particularly new researchers, do not have either the time or the resources required for adopting the approach of Wolcott. Consequently, they have to do the best they can. Normally, this involves planning a set of interview questions regarding participants' actions to be asked as recall questions during the same session when one is interviewing them about their current perspectives on the phenomenon in question. It is also possible, however, to develop a picture of participants' actions by communicating with them at regular times between interviews through phone and email contact, as well as by encouraging them to keep a diary. Some of the details of what is involved are outlined in Chapter Six.

Given the extent to which there has been mention in this chapter so far of interviewing, observations and document study, it would be reasonable to expect that one should now be offered a detailed exposition on such data gathering and data analysis approaches. I hold, however, that such an exposition makes more sense when outlined within exemplars of research proposals and of actual studies undertaken and also if one first of all has a fairly clear idea as to what the outcome of such data gathering and analysis would be. So far all that has been indicated regarding the latter is that it should result in the development of theory. But what might that mean? And, equally important, what might be the value in such theory? The following chapter now turns to these matters.

Chapter 4

What is theory and what is its value?

The last chapter was concerned with the two basic types of interpretivist studies which can be pursued based on symbolic interactionist foundations. The aim of such studies, it will be recalled, is to generate theory regarding the perspectives which participants hold with regard to a particular phenomenon, and regarding how participants 'deal with' that phenomenon. This chapter now considers what is meant by theory within these types of studies. It then goes on to consider the sorts of populations with which it is normal to work when generating such theory. Finally, it provides an overview on the range of arguments which are used as justifications for the value of engaging in studies aimed at theory generation.

What is theory?

Lewins (1992: vii) provides us with a very good starting point in considering what is theory. He characterises social science research as being mainly theory testing or theory generation. He clarifies the distinction as follows:

> Compare, for instance, two common statements from medical practitioners: 'I think the patient has hepatitis but I will need to do some tests to confirm it'; and 'I think we will need to do some tests to see if we can establish why the patient is ill'.

In the first example, the starting point is a theory about why the patient is ill. This guides the choice of evidence needed to confirm it. The approach is different in the second example. Here the doctor hopes to arrive at 'a theory or a diagnosis' (Lewins 1992: vii) after the evidence has been gathered. Lewins goes on to illustrate his point further by asking us to compare the following examples from a statement in a courtroom:

Example 1: The prosecution argues that the accused committed the crime and we will produce evidence to support the claim.

Example 2: At an earlier stage in the case the police asked: 'Who committed
            this crime?'

Again, theory testing is implied in the statement by the prosecution and
theory generation is implied in the question by the police.

Put briefly, the steps in theory testing are as follows. First, hypotheses
are developed. These are propositions which accord with 'the simple
propositional logic; that is, if this theory is true, then I should be able to
observe the following (if A then B)' (Lewins 1992: 47). This is followed
by 'operationalisation'. What is involved here is the making of decisions
as to what will count as evidence for the sub-concepts in the hypotheses.
We then test the hypotheses by carrying out the research and analysing the
results.

Theory generation research, by contrast, involves ending with a theory
rather than starting with it. Here it is useful to recall the definition of theory
presented in the previous chapter, namely, that it is an integrated framework
of well-developed concepts and the relationships between them that can
be used to explain or predict phenomena. This is a definition which gets
one away from any notion that theory has to be so involved that it is really
too complex to concern the great majority of us. Rather, it emphasizes that
theories are statements about how things are connected. To put it another
way, theory consists of two parts, namely, the things to be connected and the
connection itself. LeCompte and Preissle (1993: 120) elaborate on this by
stating that the things to be connected are the concepts, and the connections
or relationships 'show how concepts, categories, or constructs can be linked
together once they have been identified'.

Another value in the definition offered above is that it makes clear
that while theory can function as a predictor of phenomena, it does not
necessarily have to do so. LeCompte and Preissle (1993: 119) approach this
matter in a slightly different way. They speak of certain theories centring 'on
understanding and interpretation of the meaning of constructs rather than
explanation of phenomena'. On this, they elaborate as follows:

> Theories which explain general phenomena may be predictive ('every
> actions causes an equal and opposite reaction'). They also may be
> retrodirective or descriptive. Retrodirective and descriptive theories are
> similar in that both are explanations of phenomena tied to particular
> situations, but they differ in their time referent. Retrodirective theories
> address things which happened in the more or less distant past, such as
> historical explanations of the causes of specific revolutions; descriptive
> theories are more oriented to things close in time, such as an explanation
> of how a given university faculty responded to the policies of a dean.
>
> (LeCompte and Preissle, 1993: 118)

Again, this distinction is very helpful for present considerations. To speak in LeCompte and Preissle's terms, this book is not concerned with theories which are predictive. Rather, the concern is primarily with theories which are descriptive, although some consideration is also given in the chapters in Part Two to the generation of retrodirective theories. Such theories are worthy of generation even if their qualities do not include prediction. While the final part of this chapter, as already indicated, will consider in detail what these qualities are, it is useful to start thinking about the matter at this point. In this regard, one could not do much better than to ponder LeCompte and Preissle's (1993: 119) point that while theories which explain individual cases cannot be used to predict the cause of a different kind of case, 'they can be used in a comparative fashion to alert researchers to themes or events which might be common to similar phenomena under different conditions'.

Another way of looking at this is to highlight the distinction which is often made between 'nomothetic theories' and 'ideographic theories'. The former are developed as general laws of human behaviour which have predictive qualities, while the latter are designed to explain particular events or human actions within specific cultural contexts. Again, this book is concerned with the development of ideographic theory rather than nomothetic theory. Ideographic theory corresponds somewhat with the well-known notion of substantive theory, while nomothetic theory has a correspondence with formal theory. Strauss and Corbin (1990: 174) make the distinction between substantive and formal theory as follows: '... any substantive theory evolves from the study of a phenomenon situated within one particular context. A formal theory, on the other hand, emerges from a study of a phenomenon examined under many different types of situations'. By way of example, they state that if one is interested in 'status' one could study the status of executives within an organisation. Because the theory which would be generated would be the product of a study of the phenomenon within one particular situational context, it would be substantive theory. On the other hand, one might, as they put it:

> ... study status in several types of situations, say: the status of politicians at the national level, the status of persons within families, the status of socialites within a given city, and the status of various professional ranks within academic institutions.
>
> (Strauss and Corbin 1990: 174)

This level of study is what is required in order to generate formal theory. They summarise by saying that it is not the level of conditions that makes the difference between substantive and formal theories, but the variety of situations studied.

To recap then, the focus in this book is on the generation of ideographic or substantive theory, with the orientation being more on things close in time than on how things happened in the more or less distant past. In considering what might be involved in this regard it is now useful to progress to considering that ideographic or substantive theory is not some homogenous entity. Rather, different varieties of theory can be developed through analysis of data produced in studies of the types considered in the previous chapter. The remainder of this section of the chapter is concerned with outlining the most common of these varieties.

The first variety of theory which can be considered is 'description'. On this, Taylor and Bogdan (1998: 135) state:

> ... any good qualitative study, no matter how theoretical, contains rich descriptive data; people's own written or spoken words, their artefacts, and their observable activities. ... researchers try to convey a sense of being there and experiencing settings firsthand ... researchers attempt to give readers a feeling of 'walking in the informants' shoes' – and seeing things from their point of view. Thus qualitative research should provide 'thick description' of social life.

Lewins (1992: 26) also makes the point that description in research reports is never just 'mere' description. He states that when we describe anything, whether it is for everyday purposes or for scientific research, 'we describe it with the categories and concepts of our major preoccupation in mind'.

A second variety of theory which can be considered is that of concepts which can be generated from the data gathered in the research. Strauss and Corbin (1990: 61) define concepts as 'labels placed on discrete happenings, events and other instances of phenomena'. They go on as follows:

> Science could not exist without *concepts*. Why are they so essential? Because by the very act of naming, we fix continuing attention on them. Once our attention is fixed, we can begin to examine and ask questions about these phenomena (now, of course, labelled as concepts).
>
> (Strauss and Corbin 1990: 62)

To put it another way, concepts are vital because they give us a language by which we can speak about a phenomenon. This is particularly important when investigating an unexplored topic. Once a set of concepts has been developed, whole new areas can be identified for research because we now have a language for articulating the issues involved.

Bogdan and Biklen (1982: 156) provide a list of what they call 'families of codes' which can be used to analyse data and lead to the generation of a variety of concepts, including the following:

1   Concepts that describe the setting under investigation.
2   Concepts that refer to 'sequences of events, changes over time, passages from one type or kind of status to another' (Bogdan and Biklen 1982: 156). They are generated by collecting data on a person, group, organization or activity over time and perceiving 'change occurring in a sequence of at least two parts' (Bogdan and Biklen 1982: 156).
3   Concepts that refer to regularly occurring kinds of behaviour.
4   Concepts that refer to 'particular happenings that occur infrequently, or only once' (Bogdan and Biklen 1982: 156).
5   Concepts that refer to 'the tactics, methods, ways, techniques, plays and other conscious ways people accomplish various things' (Bogdan and Biklen 1982: 156).
6   Concepts that refer to 'regular patterns of action among people not officially defined by the organizational chart' (Bogdan and Biklen 1982: 156).

These by no means constitute the total sum of concepts which can be developed. Nevertheless, it is possible to classify the total variety of concepts into two types, namely, those derived from an 'emic' – from phonemic – perspective and those derived from an 'etic' – from phonetic – perspective; emic represents an insider's perspective and etic represents the outsider's. In other words, concepts can be organised in terms of (a) those which represent participants' 'definitions of the situation', participants' perspectives, and participants' ways of thinking about people and objects; and (b) those generated by the researcher where it is considered that several pieces of data seem to have certain structural properties in common, yet are not identified as such by the participants.

A third variety of theory which can be considered is that of categorising. Strauss and Corbin (1990: 61) define a category as a classification of concepts. This classification, they state, is discovered 'when concepts are compared against one another and appear to pertain to a similar phenomenon'. The concept then which is developed is a higher order, more abstract concept, called a category. A category can, in turn, be developed into its 'properties' and its 'dimensions'. The properties of a category are its characteristics or attributes. Strauss and Corbin (1990: 71) offer the example of 'watching' as a category. Amongst its properties are 'frequency', 'extent', 'intensity' and 'duration'. Each of these properties can be 'dimensionalized' or broken down into its dimensions. Thus, the dimensions of 'frequency' extend from 'often' to 'never', the dimensions of 'extent' extend from 'more' to 'less', the dimensions of 'intensity' extend from 'high' to 'low', and the dimensions of 'duration' extend from 'long' to 'short'. Again, with such categories at one's disposal one is armed with a framework by which one can speak about phenomena in ways hitherto not possible and one can locate specific instances of a phenomenon somewhere within the framework. On this also, Woods offers some useful advice relating to tests of adequacy which can be brought to bear in the generation of categories, along with indicators as to when initial attempts may need to be revised (Woods 2006: 26).

A fourth variety of theory which can be considered is that of propositions. A proposition is defined by Taylor and Bogdan (1984: 134) as 'a general statement of fact grounded in the data'. They go on to offer the following example of a proposition: 'Attendants use evasion strategies to avoid getting caught violating institutional rules'. They explain that, like concepts, propositions are generated by poring over the data. 'By studying themes … and relating different pieces of data to each other' they say, 'the researcher gradually comes up with generalizations' (Taylor and Bogdan 1984: 134). Woods views the process in similar light. As he sees it, 'categories can be put together in separate groups around a common theme'. The researcher might then try to 'conceptualise the material and raise it to a higher level of understanding, so that it might inform our general understanding of such issues' (Woods 2006: 32). It is through this process that propositions can be arrived at.

A fifth variety of theory is that of models. Lewins (1992: 21) describes a model as a simplified representation of something existing in the world. Its function is to provide a fairly clear picture of something which in reality is somewhat more complicated. Lewins (1992: 21) gives, as an example, a street directory, stating:

> It is obvious that particular streets and places do not exist as parallel lines and dots, but such a scale representation of the real world is explanatory to the extent that it becomes possible to answer questions such as 'where am I?' when one is lost.

In summary, a model is constructed in order to try to denote in a relatively simple manner the crucial parts of a very intricate situation.

The sixth variety of theory which can be considered is that of typologies. These, to put it simply, are classification schemes. Again, they can be both classification schemes used by the participants and those generated by the researcher. Furthermore, they point to relationships and interconnections, thus providing a foundation for comparison. A particular form of typology is Weber's (Aran 1967) 'ideal type'. It provides a basic method for comparative study because it is founded on the 'earned distinctions' of individuals. As such, it is seen as providing a 'rationalizing reconstruction of a particular kind of behaviour' (Aran 1967: 204). Shils and Finch (1949: 90) have explained that:

> An 'ideal type' is formed by … the synthesis of a great many diffuse, discrete, more or less present and occasionally absent concrete individual phenomena which are arranged … into a unified analytical construct.

It should not be inferred, however, that being classified as belonging to a 'type' indicates that a predetermined or inflexible set of actions will always be enacted by particular individuals when they are faced with a specific set of conditions. Rather, an 'ideal type' is a device which allows us to establish similarities as well as variation in a concrete phenomenon. Therefore, the basis of a typology which is comprised of 'ideal types' is that under specific conditions, individuals who are considered to belong to a particular 'type' will tend to engage in actions and interactions which are similar to others of this 'type'. When, on occasions, individuals engage in actions which are atypical of the 'type' to which they have been assigned in relation to the way they deal with a particular phenomenon, it should not be adjudged that the overall typology has failed, or that it has some inadequacies. The efficacy of a 'grounded typology' lies not only in its capacity to describe regular and predictable patters of actions and interactions, but also in its capacity to focus attention to 'intervening conditions' (Strauss and Corbin 1990) which can lead to atypical actions.

While the six varieties of theory mentioned above are by no means the only way in which one can characterise what is possible through analysis, it is important also to note that theory development of the type considered in this book does not include the development of 'laws' or of 'causal theories'. These levels of theory relate to nomothetic rather than ideographic studies. Laws 'posit the recurring nature of particular relationships' (Lewins 1992: 21) and causal theories posit 'the conditions under which the event being explained happens'. Silverman (2005: 349) summarises the point being made here in very simple terms when he states that 'why' questions are usually best answered by quantitative methods.

Selecting participants

In order to obtain data for the generation of theory of the sort considered in the previous section of this chapter one usually, though not always, needs to select participants for interview and observation. Stating this immediately poses for many the following question: 'How many participants do we need to have?'. From considerations so far it is clear that since the studies in which we are interested are ideographic one is, by definition, restricted to understanding particular events or human actions within specific cultural contexts. This immediately places a limit on the number of participants required. Equally, one is not obliged to work with a large number of participants located within such limits since the aim is to generate theory rather than test hypotheses. To put it simply, a much smaller number of participants is required to generate heuristic devices or 'tools' by which we can speak intelligently about the phenomenon under investigation than is required if we are trying to discover 'findings' which are generalizable from the results of a study of a sample of a population to the total population.

Knowing, however, that one is not expected to work with a large number of participants still does not indicate how many is enough. The challenge in this regard is a methodological one, where methodology, as will be recalled from Chapter One, is viewed as a strategy, plan of action, process, or design to link our paradigm-guided questions with particular methods. At this point it is necessary to backtrack a little and call to mind that the methodology, which it was indicated in Chapter One would be explicated in this book because of its relationship to the interpretivist paradigm and the symbolic interactionist position within it, is that of 'grounded theory'.

Punch and Wildy (1995: 2) state that grounded theory is best defined as a research strategy whose purpose is to generate theory from data. This strategy, as Charmaz (2002: 675) puts it, consists of guidelines that aid the researcher in the following ways:

> ... (a) to study social and social psychological processes; (b) to direct data collection, (c) to manage data analysis, and (d) to develop and abstract theoretical frameworks that explain the studied process.

Charmaz goes on to explain that grounded theory researchers collect data and analyze it simultaneously from the initial phases of research. Furthermore, as they proceed they take the view that some of the data collection questions developed in the initial stages of a study could become redundant as a study progresses, while other unanticipated ones could emerge.

The manner in which data gathering and data analysis proceeds where the methodology is that of grounded theory will be considered in some detail in the exemplar in Chapter Six. Here, however, it is instructive by way of further background to recall Punch and Wildy's (1995: 2) observation that the history of grounded theory is, in fact, quite short. A useful overview on this history is provided by Creswell (2005: 396–7). Here, as in most other accounts, the origins of grounded theory are traced back to the 1960s when Glaser and Strauss published two major works in medical sociology concerned with dying in hospitals (Glaser and Strauss 1965, 1968). In 1967 they also published a companion 'how we did it' book, entitled *The Discovery of Grounded Theory* (Glaser and Strauss 1967). According to Strauss and Corbin (1994: 275), this work had three purposes: to offer a rationale for theory that was grounded, to suggest the logic for and specifics of grounded theories, and to legitimate qualitative research undertaken in a rigorous manner.

Over its short history grounded theory has split into two different, yet largely related, positions. Charmaz (2000) refers to these as objectivist and constructivist. The objectivist position, she states, emphasises the viewing of data 'as real in and of themselves' (Charmaz 2002: 677). This position, she goes on, 'assumes that data represent objective facts about a knowable world. The data already exist in the world, and the researcher finds them' (Charmaz

2002: 677). Thus, it is a position very much in harmony with the positivist paradigm. Strauss and Corbin (1990), on the other hand, with Chicago school of sociology influences, brought grounded theory in the direction of the interpretivist paradigm by developing an approach which 'places priority on the phenomena of study and sees both data and analysis as created from the shared experiences of researcher and participants and the researcher's relationships with participants' (Charmaz 2002: 677).

The identification of grounded theory with the interpretivist paradigm resulted in quite a degree of controversy between Glaser and his followers in the one camp and Strauss and Corbin and their followers in the other. The most open controversy centred on Glaser's rejection of what he saw as Strauss and Corbin's (1992) over-codification of explicit procedures for qualitative data analysis. Anyone interested in the nature of the controversy would do well to read the account of it presented by Atkinson *et al.* (2003: 148–52). This, however, is not the place to enter into a discussion of the pros and cons of either position. Rather, the stance adopted here is that the fundamental approach common to both positions is most appropriate when a study is designed within the interpretivist paradigm, and particularly where the theoretical foundation is that of symbolic interactionism; a position upheld by Chenitz and Swanson (1986: 3–15).

Fundamental to grounded theory is that it is an inductive approach to data gathering and analysis. It is oriented, as Taylor and Bogdan (1998: 7–8) put it, to developing 'concepts, insights, and understandings from patterns in the data rather than collecting data to assess preconceived models, hypotheses, or theories'. 'A theory', they hold, 'may be said to be grounded to the extent that it is derived from and based on the data themselves'. On this, they refer to Lofland (1971), who described this kind of theorizing as 'emergent analysis' and who pointed out that the process is one which is creative and intuitive as opposed to being mechanical. At the same time, Taylor and Bogdan (1998: 8) are not naive enough to claim that pure induction is possible. As they put it, 'We can never escape all of our assumptions about the world. Even an interest in social meaning directs our attention to some aspects of how people think and act in a setting and not to others'. The goal, they conclude, 'is to make sure the theory fits the data and not vice versa'.

With whom, then, do we commence our largely inductivist-oriented research? The standard approach is to first of all imagine the ideal research setting. This, in the words of Taylor and Bogdan (1984: 19), 'is one in which the observer obtains easy access, establishes immediate rapport with informants, and gathers data directly relating to the research interests'. Being 'ideal', of course, means that the situation to which we would like to gain access never fully exists, but one should do one's best to approximate it as much as possible. Having done so, one then commences one's research usually by interviewing one participant. It is hardly possible to be more inductivist than this! Once the first interview has been completed analysis can commence.

At this juncture it is helpful to consider Crabtree and Miller's (1992) observation that four major analysis styles tend to be used by the wide range of qualitative researchers. These are termed the 'quasi-startistical style', the 'template analysis style', the 'immersion/crystallization style', and the 'editing analysis style'. The following summary of each of these is based on extracts from the very useful overview provided by Polit *et al.* (2001: 382):

> *Quasi-statistical analysis style*: The researcher reviews the content of the narrative data, searching for particular words or themes that have been specified in advance. The result of the information is information that can be analysed statistically. For example, the analyst can count the frequency of occurrence of specific themes, or can cross-tabulate the occurrence of certain words.
>
> *Template analysis style*: The researcher develops a template or analysis guide to which the narrative data are applied. The units for the template are typically behaviours, events, or linguistic expressions (e.g. words). A template is more adaptable than a codebook in the quasi-statistical style. Although the researcher may begin with a rudimentary template before collecting any data, it undergoes constant revision as more data are gathered. The analysis of the resulting data, once sorted according to the template, is interpretive and not statistical.
>
> *Immersion/crystallization*: This style involves the analyst's total immersion in and reflection on the text materials, resulting in an intuitive crystallization of the data.
>
> *Editing analysis style*: The researcher acts as an interpreter who reads through the data in search of meaningful segments. Once segments are identified and reviewed, the interpreter develops a categorization scheme and corresponding codes that can be used to sort and organize data. The researcher then searches for the patterns and structure that connect the thematic categories. The grounded theory approach typically incorporates this style.

While there may be occasions when students engaging in research of the type which is the focus of this book may draw upon the first three styles outlined above, the concern is almost totally with the fourth style. Here, as concepts are generated they are compared and clustered – 'the constant comparative method' – until categories are formed. This process is assisted by asking oneself constant questions of the data, particularly the question, 'What is this an example of?' – 'the method of constant questioning'.

The processes of constant comparison and constant questioning are referred to by Polit *et al.* (2001: 385) as follows:

The researcher asks questions about discrete events, incidents, or thoughts that are indicated in an observation or statement, such as the following:

What is this?
What is going on?
What does it stand for?
What else is like this?
What is this distinct from?

Important concepts that emerge from close examination of the data are then given a label that forms the basis for a categorization scheme. These category names are necessarily abstractions, but the labels are generally sufficiently graphic that the nature of the material to which it refers is clear.

Operating in this manner, one moves on to the next participant and the next one, in each instance building analysis upon analysis. In other words, the researcher is regularly involved in generating hypotheses about categories and about their relationships and interrelationships, and then testing these hypotheses with data. In this way, the process is also deductive. Equally, it means that data collection and data analysis occurs in parallel and repeatedly, rather than consecutively as a one-off set of activities.

The next question then is, on what basis is each subsequent participant chosen? The grounded theory response to this is captured in the notion of 'theoretical sampling'. Taylor and Bogdan (1984: 83) summarise this notion as follows:

In theoretical sampling the actual number of 'cases' studied is relatively unimportant. What is important is the potential of each 'case' to aid the researcher in developing theoretical insights into the area of social life being studied. After completing interviews with several informants, you would consciously vary the type of people interviewed until you had uncovered the full range of perspectives held by the people in whom you are interested. You would have an idea that you had reached this point when interviews with additional people yielded no genuinely new insights.

Adopting a theoretical sampling approach facilitates the generation of the full range and variation in a category. Also, as a category is being developed in this manner it is constantly tested against new data as it is collected. A particular strategy utilised in this regard is that of seeking out negative cases in order to disprove hypotheses and thus further refine emerging theory.

The idea in grounded theory, then, is that data collection and analysis continues until categories become saturated. Saturation refers to the inability to develop categories further in terms of their properties and dimensions no matter how much new data are collected. Experienced researchers adopting this approach appreciate that they may stop at any level of analysis where saturation has been reached in relation to just some categories, and then report their findings. They are also comfortable with Burgess' (1985) notion that researchers may formulate and reformulate their research, developing it out where they judge that it is yielding a poor return for effort and contracting it where it appears to be too broad in scope.

A beginner, however, quite understandably, often seeks from the outset to work within a clearer set of parameters, not least so that a reasonable prediction can be made regarding the length of time which will need to be spent on the study. There appears to me to be at least two main ways in which such parameters can be established. The first is to harness Stainback and Stainback's (1984: 299) notion of 'modified analytic induction'. They elaborate on this notion as follows:

> ... a modified analytic induction strategy has been developed for practical purposes. In the modified approach, the researcher may tightly define a population, thus limiting the applicability of the description of theory to a specifically defined group. Or, a researcher may determine the number of cases he/she has the resources to handle in an investigation and simply base the theory and testing of the theory on those cases, making no claim that the theory is inclusive beyond the defined set.
>
> (Stainback and Stainback 1984: 299)

This is somewhat akin to Adelman *et al.*'s (1976: 141) notion of a case as a bounded system 'within which issues are indicated, discovered or studied so that a tolerably full understanding of the case is possible'. Within the bounded system chosen, of course, one still has to theoretically sample. An example of one case study undertaken along such lines is presented in the next chapter.

Another slightly different way to narrow the focus of study is to define the area of interest so tightly from the beginning that the full population which could be studied is so small that all can be participants in the research. An example of a study undertaken along such lines is presented in Chapter Six. Before proceeding to these chapters, however, a short exposition on the value of generating theory of the type which they report is now offered.

What is the value of this kind of theory?

The next obvious major question to be posed from considerations so far is, 'What is the value in theory developed through studies of the types being proposed here which are idiographic and are based on data collected from relatively small populations?'. For some, this sort of question is irritating and they are inclined to retort with the question: 'What is the value in historical studies or philosophical studies?'. What they imply through such a response is that within the academic world there are great bodies of work which are considered of value for reasons other than that of having practical relevance. In particular, the contention is that such work can be academically and intellectually relevant in its own right. While the same contention can be made in regard to studies of the type which are the focus of interest in this book, it is instructive to consider that an extensive set of arguments regarding their practical value have also been articulated for many years. What this final part of the chapter now outlines is an overview on these practical arguments. It does so under three main headings: (i) arguments for the value of the theory developed in terms of its importance for bringing about change in the situation studied; (ii) arguments for the value of the theory developed in terms of its potential for contributing to professional development programmes; (iii) arguments for the value of the theory developed in terms of its generalizability to situations other than the ones studied. There is, however, quite a degree of overlap in the three groups of arguments.

The value of the theory generated for bringing about change in the situation studied

The necessity of understanding people's contextual realities before introducing changes in the hope of improving the quality of education in any context is well summarized by Fullan (1982: 149) as follows:

> … in order to effect improvement, that is, to effect an introduced change which has the promise of increasing success and decreasing failure, the world of the people most closely involved must be understood.

This position has also been taken up by others, including Dove (1986: 212). What they emphasize is that the first step in the process of improving the quality of education should be to aim at understanding the contextual reality. Hargreaves (1993) has considered this matter in some detail and what he had to say can be summarized in the following short account.

Hargreaves (1993: 149) spoke of the 'immunological capacity' of interpretivist studies, and especially symbolic interactionist studies. He contended that many social policies fail and nowhere is this more evident than in education where, he held, innovations frequently fail quite disastrously. The one common reason for this, he argued, is as follows:

> … in grafting new ideas onto schools, we do it with so little knowledge about the nature of the everyday world of teachers, pupils and schools that our attempted grafts (and various forms of major and minor surgery)

merely arouse the 'anti-bodies' of the host which undermine our attempts to play doctor to an educational patient.

(Hargreaves 1993: 149–50)

He went on to argue that symbolic interactionist studies can help provide us with the necessary understandings, 'for only when we understand the precise nature of the host body can we design our innovatory grafts with any confidence that they will prove to be acceptable' (Hargreaves 1993: 150). Fullan (1982) made a similar argument in his contention that central-level bureaucrats who are trying to promote change could benefit from reflecting on interpretivist studies. This, he argued, is because to effect improvement, that is to introduce change that promises more success and less failure, the world of the people most closely involved in implementation must be understood.

There is also another aspect to this argument. Theory in the form of detailed description can function to familiarize policy makers with how those who are expected to implement change understand their world. Hargreaves (1993: 149), however, has reminded us of the importance of also generating concepts, categories, propositions, models and typologies to this end. At its most basic, this involves *naming* features 'of the complex commonsense knowledge of members of society'. Through this process, he argued, we are provided with 'a language for speaking about that which is not normally spoken about: the ineffable is rendered articulate' (Hargreaves 1993: 149). He concluded with an example from the world of education as follows:

> Recent interactionist work in the field of education shows the extent to which teacher skills rest upon ... tacit knowledge. Teachers have no explicit conceptual apparatus in which to express and communicate these skills – and they reject the traditional language of the educational sciences to that end. By its designatory function, symbolic interactionism...can provide such a language.
>
> (Hargreaves 1993: 149)

Finally, he argued that the 'language' produced through analysis can also be put before the research participants, acting as a mirror which 'reflects man (*sic*) back to himself'. This can provide the participants with 'an opportunity to judge and appraise the reflection' they see and, perhaps as a result, seek to change themselves and their professional world.

The relevance of the theory generated in one setting for professional development programmes in other settings

Theories of the sort being considered in this book are usually developed in just one setting. However, they can also have relevance for professional development programmes, not only for those in this setting, but also for those working in other settings. Indeed, they can be instructive to an international audience. As Sultana (1991) puts it, they can expose stakeholders involved in similar circumstances in various other parts of the world to material which could help them in clarifying and sharpening their own perspectives. Another way of putting this argument is that the insights provided by a theory can provide a framework for developing enlightenment and guiding activity since it can 'speak' to others in similar and related contexts who share some of the same concerns.

This position also serves to highlight another point, namely, that many uninformed readers can have unrealistic expectations of what a good theory can offer, in particular in terms of expecting clear directives for practice from theory. Such expectations, as Entwistle (1971: 98) pointed out over 30 years ago, often betray a misunderstanding of the very nature of theory. He developed this point as follows:

> Demands are made of theories for guidance which, in their nature, it is impossible for them to supply. There never can be a one-to-one relationship between theory and practice if by this we mean theory which predicts every contingency in a practical situation. A theory gains its relevance to every conceivable situation by being an exact account of none of them ... The fault for the theory-practice gap may lie not in the theory but in the unrealistic expectation of practitioners.

The same point regarding the limitations of theory was made by William James (1958: 15) back in 1892, when he commented as follows regarding the function of the study of psychology for educationalists:

> You make a great mistake if you think that psychology, being a science of the mind's law, is something from which you can deduce definite programmes and schemes and methods of instruction for immediate classroom use. Psychology is a science, and teaching is an art. An intermediary inventive mind must make the application, by using its originality. The science of logic never made a man reason rightly, the science of ethics never made a man behave rightly. The most such sciences can do is to help us catch ourselves up, check ourselves, if we start to reason or behave wrongly; and to criticise ourselves more articulately if we make mistakes. A science only lays down lines within which the rules of the art must fall, laws

which the follower of the art must not transgress; but what particular thing he shall positively do within those lines is left exclusively to his own genius ... and so while everywhere the teaching must agree with the psychology, it may not necessarily be the only kind of teaching that would so agree; for many diverse methods of teaching may equally well agree with the psychological laws.

For many decades this position was overlooked as research in the professions, including education, became preoccupied with attempts aimed at the invention and discovery of sure-fired prescriptive models which would lead to easily generalisable solutions in each area (Hopkins 1993). Eisner (1983), for one, however, became instrumental in providing compelling arguments which enabled educational scholars and practitioners to question such preoccupation. He made the case that due to the changing uniqueness of the practical situations that make up the educational domain, only a portion of professional practice can be usefully treated in the manner of a prescriptive science. The gap between general prescriptive frameworks and successful practice is, he held, dependent more on the reflective intuition, the craft, and the art of the professional practitioner than on any particular prescriptive theory, method or model. To apply this position to considerations on professional development programmes for participants other than those who take part in studies leading to the generation of ideographic theory is to argue that such theory can, in the language of Stenhouse (1975), aid in the development of the capacity of educationalists to understand relationships and make judgements by constituting frameworks for others within which they can think. In similar vein, symbolic interactionist studies of the sort being discussed in this book may constitute one source to assist us in breaking away from a notion of continuing professional development as being concerned only with instrumental ends achievable through 'the recipes of tried and true practices legitimated by unexamined experiences or uncritically accepted research findings' and towards one of 'developing reflective practitioners who are able to understand, challenge and transform' (Sachs and Logan 1990: 479).

Generalisability of theory developed in one situation to other situations

No claim can be made for the 'generalisability' of interpretivist theories, including those developed in symbolic interactionist studies, in the sense in which researchers working within the positivist paradigm can claim generalisability for their theories. At the same time, this is not to argue that they have no generalisability. Stake (1978), for example, has argued that interpretive studies undertaken with small populations may be in harmony with the reader's experience and thus a natural basis for generalisation. In other words, readers can relate to the study and perhaps gain an understanding of their own and others' situations. This is what is referred to when it is stated that a theory can have 'reader or user generalisability'. As Kennedy (1979), in the same vein, put it, generalisability is ultimately related to what the reader is trying to learn from such studies.

Lancy (1993: 165) has provided a different angle on this yet again in stating that such an approach 'is comparable to the law where the applicability of a particular precedent case must be argued in each subsequent case. The reader must decide whether the findings apply or not'. This is similar to the argument of Strauss and Corbin (1994: 279) when they state:

> Grounded theories ... call for exploration of each new situation to see if they fit, how they might fit, and how they might not fit. They demand an openness of the researcher, based on the 'forever' provisional character of every teacher. For all that, grounded theories are not just another set of phrases; rather, they are systematic statements of plausible relationships.

A related argument is that insofar as theory that is developed through this methodology is able to specify consequences and their related conditions, the theorist can claim predictability for it, in the limited sense that if elsewhere approximately similar conditions obtain, then approximately similar consequences should occur (Strauss and Corbin 1994: 278).

On the latter matter, Lincoln and Guba's (1985) notion of 'transferability' is instructive. They have contended that unlike researchers operating in the positivist tradition who strive for high levels of 'external validity', those who operate in the interpretivist, or what they call the 'naturalistic paradigm' cannot specify the external validity of an inquiry. Rather:

> ... he or she can provide only the thick description necessary to enable someone interested in making a transfer to reach a conclusion about whether transfer can be contemplated as a possibility.
>
> (Lincoln and Guba 1985: 316)

Consequently, emphasis is placed on the concept of 'transferability' and the associated responsibility for providing an accurate and comprehensive 'data base' that would make transferability judgements possible on the part of potential 'appliers' (Lincoln and Guba 1985). For this reason, the presentation of any theory developed should, as much as possible, be both conceptually 'dense' and interlaced with relevant extracts from the data.

Interpretivist studies can also be seen as having generalisability in the sense outlined by Uhrmacher (1993: 89–90). Building his ideas on those of Eisner (1985), he has argued for the production of cases which describe school life, interpret that life by exploring the meanings and consequences of educational events, and assess the educational significance of events described and interpreted. This 'thematics' approach, Uhrmacher (1993) states, is related to generalising in social science research. He goes on to argue that rather than make formal generalisations, one can provide the reader with an understanding of the major themes that run through the cases under study. In turn, these themes can provide the reader with theories or guides for anticipating what may be found in other situations; 'these theories provide guidance, not prediction' (Uhrmacher, 1993: 90). Thomas (1997a) offers a similar view in his identification of four broad uses of theory in educational inquiry. Finally, Hargreaves (1993) makes the point that micro-theories of the sort produced in symbolic interactionist studies are 'a potential source of correction to macro theories, which frequently oversimplify, underestimate or ignore the complexity of the detailed operation of relevant factors in actual social settings'. To put it differently, there is much scope for using symbolic interactionist studies 'as a basis for a critical reading of a macro theory, and then actively to seek out the micro implications' with a view to undertaking the necessary empirical work to 'provide an empirical testing ground' (Hargreaves 1993: 150).

Chapter 5

An example of a 'perspectives' study

So far this book has emphasized that two main types of studies can be conducted where the central underlying principles are those of the symbolic interactionist theoretical approach within the interpretivist paradigm. The first of these types consists of studies where the central research question is formulated in terms of participants' perspectives on 'things'. This chapter now presents an exemplar of one way of presenting theory generated within a study of this type.

The background to the study is the restructuring of school systems which took place throughout much of the educational world in the 1990s, with deregulated decentralized systems replacing central control and supervision. The specific concern was with investigating the perspectives of primary school teachers in a school district in the Perth metropolitan area in Western Australia regarding the impact of such restructuring on their work. It emerged that, in general, teachers' perspectives on restructuring were largely in terms of what they saw as its influence on their curriculum work. In particular, it emerged that teachers evaluated developments associated with restructuring using at least three related frames: (1) the extent to which what was happening did not take into consideration the complexity of the teacher's curriculum role; (2) the extent to which what was happening was not empowering teachers to engage in curriculum decision-making; and (3) the extent to which what was happening was affecting teachers' classroom work. The report on the study which is about to be presented is organized in a manner aimed at providing a detailed exposition on this central proposition with its three component parts.

The structure of the report is one which is logical and coherent. It is not being argued, however, that it conforms to one correct standard reporting pattern. Rather, the contention is that the notion of such a pattern is to be eschewed since its adoption would be likely to lead to a practice of generating all of the types of theory outlined in the previous chapter simply as a matter of course. In other words, there could be some 'forcing' of theory out of one's data rather than a generation of theory through following such grounded theory procedures as theoretical sampling and the seeking of negative cases.

Instead, the challenge to the researcher who shows fidelity to the latter procedures is to take stock of the types of theory generated and then make a set of judgements regarding the best way of presenting them.

The judgements made regarding the reporting format for the theory generated in the particular study about to be presented were very straight-forward. Firstly, because of the ideographic nature of the study it was deemed essential to provide a contextual overview. Secondly, the decision was taken that the approach which had the greatest potential for communicating the theory generated was to focus on the three 'frames' outlined in the central proposition, present them as themes and provide an exposition on each theme. This exposition, it was considered, would be enriched by making comparisons, where appropriate, with the previous empirical works of others on similar and related issues. Finally, it was decided to engage within the exposition on a certain amount of 'thick description' with a liberal use of quotes in order to 'give voice' to the views of the participants and facilitate a sense of empathy on the part of the reader.

It is also important to note that not all of the types of theory outlined in the previous chapter are represented in the report. In particular, there is no outline of concepts generated and the relationships between them (Strauss and Corbin 1990: 29). This simply is because no theory generation of this type was conducted. Also, no propositions were developed apart from the central one which is at the core of the presentation. This, however, is not to highlight weaknesses in the study. Rather, it is to highlight other possibilities which could have been pursued. Equally significant is that research of this type is often undertaken in order to provide teachers and other educationalists with studies for deliberation and reflection regarding challenges in the work place. Within the present context this means that if one had pursued other possibilities in the interest of creating a greater density and sophistication of theory the potential of the study for sharpening the insights of practitioners in order to contribute to their professional development could have been weakened by appearing to be too removed from reality.

The impact of restructuring on teachers' understandings of their curriculum work

Since the 1980s, restructuring of school systems has been taking place in much of the world, with a deregulated, decentralized system replacing central planning, control, and supervision (Cistone 1989). This change has been associated with such notions as school-based management, school-based budgeting, and the community management of schools (Lawton 1992). The process took on different forms in different contexts, having been enacted at the national level in the United Kingdom and New Zealand, at the state level in Australia, and at the district level in Canada (Pricket et al. 1991). No shortage of explanations exists for the widespread emergence of restructuring or of prescriptive theories as to why educational systems *should* be restructured. These explanations have been offered in various countries either to initiate restructuring processes, or to legitimize those already begun (Purkey and Smith 1985; Caldwell and Spinks 1988; Derouet 1991).

Restructuring in some countries has also involved significant curriculum changes. In the United Kingdom, for example, the administrative changes reflected 'the deregulatory, market-oriented solutions economists might dictate, even to the point of allowing schools to opt-out of their local education authorities and to collect funds from the central government', while concurrently, a core National Curriculum was introduced that provided the central government with control over the subject-matter content of education (Lawton, 1992: 143). In New Zealand, on the other hand, where economists rather than educationists initiated the major educational reforms, 'new-right' influence was not reflected to the same extent in pedagogy, the curriculum, and assessment, though it was strongly evident in the administrative restructuring of education and the accountability mechanism (Gordon 1992).

Very little is known about the impact of these and other aspects of the restructuring movement on the classroom teacher. This omission must be rectified, because most educational improvement takes place through the work of teachers. As Lipsky (1980) has said, teachers often play the role of street-level bureaucrats, influencing the actual implementation of policies. Accordingly, to paraphrase Floden and Huberman (1989), research aimed at understanding what teachers think and feel is necessary, because the success of educational innovations relies on their commitment.

The remainder of this report outlines the results of a study that sought to determine the perspectives of primary school teachers in a school district in the Perth Metropolitan Area of Western Australia regarding the impact of restructuring on their work. First, the context is detailed. The focus then moves to the outcomes of the study proper in which state primary school teachers were interviewed to determine their perspectives on the impact of the process on themselves.

For the purpose of educational research, Western Australia is usually divided into four major geographical divisions: Perth Metropolitan, Rural City, Rural Town, and Rural Country. Constraints of time, finance, and accessibility dictated that the study be located within the Perth Metropolitan area. In keeping with the goal of probing a wide variety of perspectives, a district was selected that contained a school in a predominantly middle-class area, a school in an educational priority area, a school in an area of mixed social class, and a school with a multicultural student population. A purposive sampling approach in selecting teachers within the schools for interviews further enhanced the possibility of accessing as wide a variety of perspectives as possible (Merriam 1988). As a result of this approach, each group interviewed consisted of a teacher with 3 years or less experience, a teacher with between 3 and 10 years experience, and a teacher with 10 years or more experience. Five groups were interviewed in each school, resulting in a total sample of 60 teachers – 30 females and 30 males.

The semi-structured in-depth interview was chosen as the most suitable method for gathering data (Taylor and Bogdan 1984). The researcher spoke with groups of teachers rather than individuals. In this type of interview, people talk about their lives and experiences in free-flowing, open-ended discussions, and the researcher can interpret their views. Each interview lasted, on average, one hour. The conversations were tape-recorded with the teachers' consent and transcribed. The transcribed material was then analyzed.

The context

A trend toward greater participation in educational decision-making by local school communities began in Australia in the early 1970s. By the mid-1980s, administrators became the focus of interest, as state departments of education were instructed to examine their own organization and operational efficiency. Then, in the 1990s, in the context of the deteriorating economic situation and associated unemployment, many people looked at education primarily in terms of its potential to contribute to providing a solution for Australia's economic malaise. Accompanying this view was a 'fascination ... with the cult of management' (Angus 1992: 389), and parents, teachers, and administrators throughout the country were charged with developing plans for the collaborative administration of schools.

To note this development on the national scene is not to ignore the fact that under the Australian constitution education remains 'a residual constitutional power of the states'. But negotiated consensus at the Australian Education Council – the intergovernmental body consisting of the federal and state education ministers – was used to arrive at a national approach to the development of policy for Australian schooling and 'at the same time to circumvent politically the constitutional and financial realities of Australian federalism' (Lingard 1991: 85). The outcome was that restructuring proceeded in all of the states, albeit at a different pace in each of them.

A significant landmark in educational developments in Western Australia, as in the rest of the country, was the establishment of the Quality of Education Review Committee by the federal government in 1985. A signal of the end of growth in federal spending, the committee was to assure that federal expenditures were appropriately spent and to gear the education system more closely to labour needs (Quality of Education Review Committee 1985). Following the publication of the committee's report, a number of states, including Western Australia, produced policy documents reflecting its economic rationalist and corporate managerialist approach. In 1987, the Western Australian Ministry of Education, which reigned over one of the most centralized state education systems in the country, published *Better*

Schools in Western Australia: A Programme for Improvement (Ministry of Education (Western Australia) 1987). This report established the overall plan for restructuring schools and devolving administrative authority and responsibilities from a previously centralized ministry to the school level. Underpinning the plan was the need to reach maximum effectiveness by achieving goals, while assuring efficient, economical use of resources. However, as Robertson and Soucek (1991) reported, various interest groups, including the State School Teachers' Union of Western Australia (SSTUWA), became suspicious because they, along with other key stakeholders, were not invited to participate in the discussions that led up to the report

The response of the SSTUWA took the form of a call to members to refuse to implement the proposals, to not take part in drawing up school development plans, and to do nothing in their own time. Relations between the union and the ministry deteriorated and were further complicated in July 1989 when the ministry withdrew support for a wage claim by the teachers. This led to a four-month union protest that eventually resulted not only in a compromise on the salary issue, but also 'in feelings of alienation from the profession' (Robertson and Soucek 1991). Nevertheless, in 1990, what has been termed 'a landmark industrial agreement' was reached between the Ministry of Education and the SSTUWA (Australian Education Council Review Committee 1991). It contained an in-principle agreement to the full implementation of devolution over a five-year period and a detailed plan for the first phase of implementation. The plan focused on school-based decision-making groups, school development planning, and the monitoring and reporting of school performance.

Developments centred largely on the first two aspects of the plan, though a Monitoring Standards in Education Project completed the writing of benchmarks and of associated assessment materials to measure student performance in English and Mathematics system-wide. The state still issued requirements and guidelines for the whole curriculum at primary and post primary levels; however, teachers were encouraged to select their own content and methods within these so-called 'non-negotiables'. In this respect, it appears that developments closely paralleled those undertaken in the Netherlands, Sweden, and Norway (Lindblad 1984; Alvik 1991; Creemers 1993).

A change in 1993 from a Labor to a Liberal government in Western Australia led to the appointment of a new education minister. A discussion paper prepared for the minister proposed that school communities set and collect fees in 1994, manage their own budgets by 1995, and choose their own staff by 1996. The paper was leaked to the press, and the resultant outcry from the SSTUWA led to the publication of a modified document. However, the level of trust between the union and the ministry was once again severely damaged.

In addition to the events outlined above, teachers in Western Australia, as in all of the other states in Australia, were also being exposed to national curriculum developments. These had been on the nation's political and educational agendas since 1960, but had gained momentum with the signing of the Hobart Declaration. This declaration, agreed to by state and territory ministers for education, articulated a common set of educational goals across the nation (Piper 1992). Concurrently, the Finn Report (Australian Education Council Review Committee 1991) addressed issues dealing with employment-related competencies, the report of the Mayer Committee (1992) outlined structures of a set of key competencies, and the Carmichael Report (Employment and Skills Formation Council 1992) argued for a national framework of competency-based vocational training.

Overall, then, teachers not only in Western Australia, but nationally, faced great uncertainties. Participating in restructuring at the administrative level meant they had to redefine their professional lives. Further complicating matters was the fact that their future role in curriculum decision-making was unclear because of continuing uncertainties at the state level and because they had been excluded from the debate taking place on the possible introduction of a national curriculum. Accordingly, many observers argued that teachers were very unhappy with their situation (Knight 1990; Porter 1990; Skilbeck 1990). However, little evidence was put forward to substantiate this claim. The next section of this report details the results of a study which sought to respond to this situation by focusing on the impact of the devolution process on their work.

The participants' perspectives on the impact of restructuring on their work

The analysis indicated that, in general, teachers' perspectives on restructuring were largely in terms of what they saw as its perceived influence on their curriculum work. Furthermore, teachers evaluated particular developments associated with restructuring using at least three related frames: (1) the extent to which what was happening did not take into consideration the complexity of the teacher's curriculum role; (2) the extent to which what was happening was not empowering teachers to engage in curriculum decision-making and (3) the extent to which what was happening was affecting teachers' classroom work. Each of these frames is considered in turn.

Frame No. 1: Teachers' views on the extent to which the restructuring process did not take into consideration the complexity of their curriculum role

The findings of the study concurred with those of Robertson and Soucek (1991), namely, that although the teachers did not look at the past through 'rose-coloured glasses' and although they disliked much about the old bureaucratic Department of Education with its rigid rules and inflexible resourcing and staffing policies, they missed the days of certainty in which one knew exactly where everything fitted into the scheme of things and one had a sense of direction. One of the teachers in the study expressed it as follows: 'We had a very good system with good back-up'.

Not all teachers, however, opposed change. In fact, the majority favoured it, but stated a belief that it was taking place too quickly. In the words of one teacher: 'People used to say schools were too slow to adapt to the changing needs of society. Now we are going like lightning, but the trouble is no one seems to know where we are going'. One of the interview groups explored this matter further. It pointed out that while the literature from the Ministry of Education and from the schools' administration teams continually stressed that what was taking place was a process that should not and need not be rushed, this was not reflected in practice: 'We have to rush around all of the time. The administration teams are rushing us so much that we cannot possibly give our best to the children'. Others put it differently, stating that they were left with the impression that they were 'running around in circles'. Furthermore, the vast majority of the teachers were adamant that the call for change did not originate from within the teaching force and that those promoting restructuring had no appreciation of the complexity of the teacher's role.

The teachers viewed restructuring as a process imposed on them and, as with much of educational policy, as an area in which they had no input: 'As usual, nobody sought the voice of the classroom teacher'. Accordingly, those responsible for restructuring appeared to pay little attention to that aspect of the 'change' literature that demonstrates that teachers who have no input into an innovation will have no sense of ownership of it and, consequently, little commitment to it (Pratt 1980: 428).

However, the situation was not just one of an absence of motivation, but also of the presence of a certain degree of antagonism. In this respect, teachers were particularly incensed by much of what they saw as the dehumanizing language of restructuring emanating from the Ministry of Education. In particular, they objected to being referred to as 'human resources' and viewed such a notion as not being consistent with the concept of 'caring' that they saw as central to the definition of their role.

The importance that teachers in the study attached to the caring aspect of their work was evident in a number of ways. For example, it constituted the major criterion by which they evaluated the ministry's present stress on competencies and outcome statements. One teacher put it as follows:

You can't pay a teacher to be a more caring person. The intangibles are what matter, not just immediate competencies. What about 20 years down the track? What type of person will the pupil be? What about the emotional and social side of development?

Another, focusing on the large number of competencies being outlined by the ministry, put it thus:

> The danger with outcome statements is that they will turn into a curriculum; that is what is going to be evaluated, this is what you have to teach, this is what is going to be used to make you accountable. To achieve such a massive number you will work the kids harder, and so Pastoral Care goes out the window. My early reaction when I saw all those sheets is that you can kiss goodbye to Pastoral Care as you have so much else to do. You won't have time to sit down and establish personal relationships with the kids.

This comment echoed Feiman-Nemser and Floden's (1986: 517) point regarding developments in the United States, where many teachers want student learning to be based on individual needs, yet their schools expect them to improve standardized test scores, cover prescribed curricular at a prescribed pace, and maintain an orderly classroom.

Certainly not all of the teachers in this study were opposed to schools adopting outcome statements to guide the planning of work. As many of them saw the situation, 'outcome statements have the advantage of giving a distinct focus to your work'. Rather, the teachers seemed to be developing the notion that outcome statements are useful so long as they did not, as one teacher said, 'become the engine that drives your curriculum work, with teachers having to teach towards them solely, since they might become the measure of teacher performance'.

Central to what the majority of the teachers in the study said in this respect was the belief that those promoting restructuring appeared not to appreciate that the number and diversity of students in any one classroom created a wide variety of individual and group needs. The only group that showed little concern in this regard was that composed of four special education teachers. As one of the four explained, their position was understandable because they had much smaller classes, were under much less stress, and 'worked at a leisurely pace'.

The teacher population as a whole expressed great annoyance at what they perceived as a lack of consideration by those promoting restructuring of the fact that many students did not come to school willingly and that teachers could not count on students being motivated to learn. In particular, they believed there was no appreciation of the 'caring' role that teachers need to adopt in order to deal with this situation by, as one teacher put it, 'meeting children where they are at'. The importance of the 'caring' perspective was particularly evident in the language the teachers used when describing their pupils. They spoke regularly of 'my kids' and 'my class', and about the fact that although they were not pleased about much that they were now requested to do, they would do it because they were 'committed and love the children'. In fact, their references to their pupils' parents as 'my parents' and 'my mums' indicated that they saw themselves almost as part of extended families.

The great importance that the teachers placed on their caring role became evident in a number of other ways. They alluded regularly to situations in which they were unable to concentrate fully during school-based decision-making meetings because they were 'too worried about the poor kid who is sick or the poor kid who is being beaten up or the poor kid who is being abused'. More than one teacher apologized for arriving late for the research interview because of the need to attend to a sick or worried child during recess. They also spoke of the importance of their dealing, as appropriate, with a pupil's grief and emotional trauma as a result of the break-up of the parents' marriage. As one teacher summarized, 'You are the sounding board for the kids. They often have no one else to speak to, so you listen and you get emotionally involved'.

Teachers, then, were largely operating within the Australian education culture fostered in the 1970s, with its concern for equity and community. That decade, as Angus (1992: 389) has written, fostered 'a sense that, by educating the 'whole child', schools would develop individuals to their full potential while socializing them into communities of enquirers who would contribute to a just society'. The Schools Commission and the Curriculum Development Centre (CDC), both established by the Federal government, actively promoted the notion of school-based curricular decision-making and supported it through research and funding. The CDC, in its commitment to a social reconstruction philosophy, also advocated the introduction of a core curriculum (Marsh and Stafford, 1988: 55). These developments, with their concern for the personal growth of the individual and for social justice, arguably won the support of teachers since the associated social reconstructionist and child-centred philosophies articulated by policy makers were consistent with the 'caring' language teachers use when speaking about their work.

The teachers in the study reported here also clearly articulated a justification for continuing to place great importance on their caring role in the 1990s. They asserted that as Australian society is characterized more and more by situations in which children's personal relationships outside the classroom are unsatisfactory, the need increases for students to have a good relationship with their teacher. One teacher put it as follows: 'The academic stuff is still important for the kids, but it's almost a lesser priority than [their] feeling good about themselves and all those attitudinal things'. This understanding suggested the teachers were ascribing an *in loco parentis* role to themselves. The important thing, as they saw it, was for the children to have available an adult with whom they could maintain a good relationship. The teachers saw themselves as being that adult, as desiring such a role for themselves, and as being best placed to fulfil that role:

You know what's important. You teach those kids every single day. You know how they tick. The administration team and the school psychologists see the kids in a once-off situation. We teach 32 kids, see them interacting with other kids, see a totally different side of them. We need to meet those kids' needs over and above the curriculum, especially when it comes to social issues, values issues, health issues, because we see that every single day.

As the teachers viewed it, the breakdown of the family unit is the most serious issue that should concern teachers, and to deal with it, the teacher must be 'psychologist, nurse, mum and dad, social worker, and teacher'. However, they felt that those promoting restructuring in Western Australia did not place a high value on this issue, and it would be even less valued in the future.

The teachers also considered that 'the real reasons' for restructuring revealed a lack of respect for the complexity of teaching. The most frequently cited of these 'real reasons' was that the Ministry of Education believed that financial savings would occur if schools were given budget responsibilities. However, teachers were not annoyed so much by this cost-saving agenda as by the perception that those promoting devolution were not open about this matter and sought to legitimize their actions by arguing that their proposals would lead to a better education for the pupils in the state.

The teachers' other stated 'real reason' for restructuring was more cynical in nature, namely, that the politicians in power were promoting change so they could be seen to be politically active, or, as one teacher said, 'seen to be doing something'. Once again, the issue for teachers was that this move had curriculum implications. Their attitude is captured very well in Sutherland's (1985: 226) observation, made in relation to developments in the United Kingdom in the previous decade, that

> ... fashions succeed each other and teachers – theirs not to reason why – are expected to change content and methods of their work in due conformity, following and climbing on each successive bandwagon as it comes along.

Teachers in this study echoed these sentiments in a number of ways. One teacher alluded to the experience of going through a stage when she and her peers were told not to stress the learning of multiplication tables, only to be told the opposite later on, with no consultation on either occasion. Another noted:

> It all comes from outside the system. Someone has done a study or a brainstorm. Take handwriting, for example. We are now on the third method we have had to use. Similarly, parents point out that pupils

cannot spell and say, 'It's the bloody teacher's fault'. But why is it? We were discouraged from doing it.

Finally, a small number of teachers argued that 'the motivation is to put the school in the front line'. What they were referring to corresponds with Weiler's (1989) argument with regard to developments in Norway, namely, that because the policy domain was so heavily contested, the Ministry of Education was anxious to 'diffuse the sources of conflict, and to provide additional layers of insulation between them and the rest of the system', while at the same time keeping ultimate control over the content of the curriculum. The teachers in this study expressed this notion in such terms as, 'Before, if you had a problem you got in touch with the ministry; now you are in the firing line', and 'Before, the ministry was there to soften the blow. Now you are on your own while the ministry dictates the parameters within which you can work'.

Frame No. 2: Teachers' views on the extent to which they were not being empowered to engage in curriculum decision-making

Nearly all of the teachers agreed that their respective school administration teams had gone to great lengths to establish communication networks within the school community. A typical comment was along the following lines: 'There are a lot more committees in the schools. We have committees for everything – textbooks, language, curriculum, maths, budget, science, social studies, music, and so on'. However, they also made clear that their experience confirmed that achieving consensus and promoting action were much more complex than simply having many committees. They offered a number of examples to substantiate this proposition: 'There is no mechanism for the textbook committee to liaise with everyone else'; 'You may not be on the same committee next year even if you want to'; 'New staff come each year, and you go back over the same ground with them, explaining the rules of the committee structures and trying to win their support for them'.

The majority of the teachers favoured the concept of collegial decision-making. This view was aptly summarized in the words of one teacher: 'We feel it is right we should have a say in the running of the school and in curriculum decision-making'. What was frustrating for them, however, was their perception that, although they were encouraged by the principals of their schools to participate in decision-making, the principals could and did occasionally disregard their decisions: 'You get a consensus and it is not overruled immediately, but later down the tract a totally opposite decision comes across where something totally different is put in place'.

Some teachers were annoyed by what they viewed as the contrived nature of the decision-making process. They spoke of the process being 'a big cover-up to make it look like we are all having a say'. Three of the teachers in the study stated that they had decided not to participate in any more decision-making meetings because of the meetings' 'fabricated nature'. They argued that decisions were predetermined and that they would take no part in such a 'questionable process'. An equally small group argued that the latter perception was correct and pointed to inconsistencies in the process: 'Nobody asks what are our ideas for professional development. We are told what will take place'. Unlike their more radical peers, however, they stated that they were not prepared to make 'an equally principled stand', because involvement in meetings was necessary for their professional advancement and 'to ensure that we are not penalized by being transferred to teach at unfavourable locations'.

Most teachers perceived that the principals regularly disregarded their decisions because devolution of decision-making had not been underpinned by legislation delineating with whom authority lay: 'There must be boundaries to what the principal and we can do, but we do not know what the boundaries are'. Their explanation of this situation was that 'because the management bears the final responsibility, it has the final say'. One teacher voiced the understanding as follows: 'We don't know how far we can go in decision-making, but if you get down to the legal nitty gritty, I still think you cannot go past the principal'. Another stated: 'Now there is this freedom, but your freedoms are not down in black and white, so the principal has the final say'.

One outcome of this situation, as the teachers saw it, was that no fundamental changes took place. They described the decisions that were made as ones concerned with such 'trivial issues as what kind of flowers to have around the school, where they are to go, how the grounds should be laid out, and what kind of choir uniforms we should have'. Of most concern to the teachers, however, was that the curriculum decision-making process in which they were being asked to participate was bounded by 'system imperatives'. As one teacher expressed it, 'We can only make decisions as to what we value within the syllabus. The school encourages adapting the existing curriculum, not developing a new one'. Overall, teachers in this study clearly recognized that schools were not free to design their own generic curriculum from first principles. Rather, schools had to make decisions within the broad frameworks provided by the Ministry of Education, and teachers who wished to develop alternative programmes had to justify their intention to the ministry's regional office, which might grant approval. As teachers understood it, this process detracted greatly from the credibility of the argument that decision-making was being devolved to empower teachers.

A number of other factors exacerbated teacher frustration on this matter. One of these factors was, as a teacher said, the fact that 'so much is being plonked in the curriculum and nothing is being taken out'. An example chosen to demonstrate this conclusion was the desire 'to mainstream more and more disabled students with no drop in the overall teacher–pupil ratio and no increase in financial or human support'. Equally frustrating was the knowledge that the ministry continued to set limits on the decision-making powers of teachers in curriculum matters. An example regularly chosen to illustrate this conclusion was that 'handwriting is set down. You can make decisions but not about handwriting'. Furthermore, teachers held that even their limited freedom within the curriculum frameworks laid down by the ministry was being eroded by the introduction of outcome statements: 'If you don't do the outcome statements on which you are soon likely to be evaluated, how are you going to look at the end of the day?'.

The possible role of parents in decision-making in the future also emerged as a major fear. Although teachers spoke of the need for parents to continue to be involved in fund-raising and to take a greater interest in their children's education, they also expressed great concern that they were entering an era in which parents would have 'too much of a say' in the hiring and firing of staff and in such curriculum issues as choice of subject matter content and teaching strategies. Their main argument was that parents were not sufficiently informed to have input on such matters. One teacher stated her concern as follows: 'You could have a very pushy minority of parents in schools who might take a dislike to a teacher because of how he dressed or because he rode a motorbike to school'.

Associated with this concern was a fear that students' performances on outcome statements could be 'used to hold teachers accountable for the students' progress and, thus, to sack you if they want to get rid of you'. The only group that openly welcomed the possibility of greater parental involvement in the schools were the four special education teachers. They very much favoured inviting parents to the school and involving them in the planning of programmes so that, as they confidently put it, 'we could do even better what we already do very well'.

The majority of the teachers, however, did not display such confidence. Some, in fact, argued that they were beginning to think that they were not as good teachers as they used to be, that they were losing confidence in their own ability, 'trying to cope with everything and cope with the class'. They offered examples to illustrate this concern. One teacher noted:

> You may have a timetable worked out for your class for the year, then other things outside of your control cause you to change it, such as an all-school decision to emphasize some subject. You had no say in that, but you mist fit it in.

Ball (1993: 117) made a similar observation about developments in England and Wales. He argued that school development planning had replaced teacher planning with head teacher/governor planning. He went on to say,

> Teacher participation relates not to involvement for its own sake, as a collegial, professional or democratic concern, but for the purposes of the management of motivation. The School Development Plan signifies and celebrates the exclusion and subjection of the teacher ... they are the objects of management relegated to the status of human resources.

However, a small but significant cohort of teachers in the study reported that their feelings of incompetence had forced them to rethink their professional standing, and an emerging outcome was a reaffirmation of their professional competence: 'I go into the classroom and teach in the manner I consider best. That, now, is when I feel empowered'. Another stated: 'I go into the classroom and engage in passive resistance. They never come and check up on you. They don't check to see if you understand or can do what they tell you to do. That's when I am finally empowered'. This group of teachers appeared to be developing an attitude that all they needed was to have patience, to put up with what was happening, and that perhaps, when the government changed, they would return to where they were before the current restructuring. For these teachers, developments seemed to have drawn them together as professionals, with the older teachers in particular giving their younger colleagues advice and, as it was put, 'telling you to take it easy, things come and go, just go along with it at the time'.

Frame No. 3: Teachers' views on the extent to which the restructuring process was affecting their classroom work

Teachers in the study tended to view as a distraction any activity that did not contribute directly to the tasks of classroom teaching. This finding corresponded with those of Campbell and Neill (1990), who studied British primary school teachers. When asked how they would use more time if it were available, the British teachers said they would dedicate it almost exclusively to within-class contact. Such a response is, of course, to be lauded, given the well-documented relationship between effective teaching and the proportion of time teachers actually spend engaging pupils with learning tasks (Anderson 1990; Myers 1990). It is also understandable given the long-established finding that classrooms are complicated and busy settings, serving a variety of purposes and incorporating a variety of processes and events, including managing groups, dealing with individual needs, maintaining records, promoting learning, and formally and informally evaluating student abilities (Jackson 1968).

In this respect, what was particularly annoying to teachers in this study was the number of decision-making meetings held during class time. This schedule required that the class teachers be replaced by 'relief' teachers. The class teachers believed that these interruptions affected the quality of pupil learning. Furthermore, they believed that the meetings had not resulted in any significant contribution to what they described as their 'real job', namely, teaching pupils.

Many of the teachers believed that the time and energy devoted to the meetings could be invested more profitably in classroom teaching. As one teacher said, 'We were trained as teachers. We are here for the kids. The more time we put into meetings and so on, the less time there is for the kids'. They also asserted that administrative tasks took up much time. Teachers on school-subject committees had to sort out budgets, find out about equipment and order it, and fill out invoices. For one teacher, these new demands meant that he now did 'things which work rather than experiment with teaching ideas'. Another teacher commented about the situation as follows: 'Because I haven't time … I haven't time to think through this whiz-bang science experiment, so I decide to do magnets, as I've mastered that and can get through it without much preparation'.

This situation, it was concluded, could prove to be troubling if one accepts Shulman's (1985) contention that quality teaching requires teachers to work at elucidating subject-matter knowledge in new ways; recognize and partition it; and clothe it in activities, emotions, metaphors, exercises, examples, and demonstrations. Such activities require the availability of what is clearly becoming more and more unavailable: significant amounts of teacher time. Teachers in this study regularly closed their statements with the comment: 'We appear to have less and less time to prepare our lessons properly and give our best to the children'.

Another consequence of the new demands on teachers was that they no longer had free time during lunch breaks, time that was once occasionally used to do extra work with pupils. A similar situation in England and Wales alarmed the teachers unions, which had judged it 'unhealthy' that teachers had to devote so much of their spare time to their jobs (Assistant Masters and Mistresses Association 1991). Accordingly, what appeared to be happening internationally was a proliferation of the circumstance recognized by Wise (1979) nearly 15 years earlier in the United States, namely, a tremendous increase in the administrative work of teachers that constrains them and takes time away from teaching.

Teachers' time, then, is a commodity which was in short supply. Time was of major concern to the teachers in this study. Not only were they required to perform more non-teaching duties during school hours, but they also found they have to do many things after school that once were done by the deputy principals. The consequence of this circumstance was simple. Teachers believed that they could not give their best to the children because, as they regularly stated, 'everyone is stressed out'. One teacher put it as follows:

> If teachers aren't in a state to teach kids properly and effectively because they are worked out, it's all a waste of time. You start to get tired. You

cannot think and be as creative as you would like to be because of all the new pressures and things to be done.

Another observed:

I'm so far behind in my marking it's awful. That's the biggest thing for me that suffers. I'm marking more on the spot than ever before, not just over the shoulder marking, but 'let's stop 10 minutes before the end and mark it together as a class' stuff in, let's say, social studies. Otherwise I'd have that plus math, science, and project work at night.

This frustration was accentuated when teachers requested help on matters related to curriculum. Restructuring meant that educational support was either not available, or was available in such a superficial way as to be considered of little value.

The teachers also had a gloomy view of what the future held because of what they saw as a trend toward ignoring issues of equity. In particular, they were concerned that further devolutionary thrusts would result in compulsory payment of fees by parents and that consequently some schools would be truly disadvantaged. One teacher aptly summarized this concern as follows: 'Better schools will employ better teachers. They will be able to afford their higher salary demands, while the lower socioeconomic schools will only employ first-year-outs'.

Teachers also feared the possibility that each school would be given a capitation grant based on the number of pupils in the school and that this grant would be insufficient for the purchase of a wide variety of equipment such as reading materials and computer software for pupil enrichment. The wealthier areas, unlike the poorer areas, they argued, would be able to provide these extras through local fund-raising, but the system would not ensure that resources are shared among different social groups. The teachers spoke passionately about this concern time and time again, suggesting that relegating the issue of equality of educational opportunity to a place of secondary importance would betray what the nation represents. This view was exemplified by a teacher who nodded enthusiastically after listening to a colleague argue that there was a great danger that current restructuring could lead to severe disadvantages for children in lower socioeconomic groups, even at the primary school level. The supportive teacher then responded, 'Good on you, that's very Australian of you, mate'.

Conclusion

The widespread restructuring of school systems throughout much of the world constituted the broad context for this study. At the time it was conducted some Australian educators were contending that restructuring was having a major negative impact on teachers, but very little evidence was available to contest or to substantiate such claims. The research described in this chapter explored the matter by studying the perspectives of primary school teachers in a school district in the Perth Metropolitan Area in Western Australia regarding the impact of restructuring on their work.

The research revealed that teachers viewed and assessed the restructuring process largely in terms of what they saw as its influence on their curriculum work. They saw this influence as being very negative. Furthermore, they could not foresee improvement in the future and in some respects they anticipated a deteriorating situation. The overall result was low teacher morale. Findings of this study also suggested that those responsible for restructuring took little cognizance of that aspect of the 'change' literature that demonstrates that teachers who have no input into an innovation will have no sense of ownership of it and, consequently, little commitment to it. Even those who would like to proceed on the assumption that education is a business cannot afford to ignore findings such as those of Peters and Waterman (1982) and Ouchi (1981). These findings show that, although the most successful companies are characterized by a lean head office with power and authority devolved to subsidiaries in the field, further improvements in production and success depend on the existence of human relations among management and the work force that are based on trust, subtlety, and intimacy. In other words, productivity will improve if people feel that they have more control over their destiny, are trusted while having the opportunities to contribute to decision-making and, as a consequence, feel better about themselves. The study described in this chapter indicates that this desired situation has not been reached.

To effect improvement, that is, to introduce change that promises increasing success and decreasing failure, the world of the people most closely involved must be understood. Studies of the type reported here, which aim to understand what teachers think and feel, are important in facilitating such understanding. At the same time, no attempt should be made to generalize from the findings of this particular study. Rather, it demonstrates the need for similar studies both in Australia and in other nations. Insights from such studies can be used to develop a framework that better explains the process of enlightened restructuring and that 'speaks' to others in similar and related contexts who share some of the same concerns. The findings offer a challenge for deliberation and reflection and thus constitute a source of power to promote professional growth and to lead to transformative action.

Chapter 6

An example of a study on how participants 'deal with' a particular phenomenon

This chapter presents an exemplar of the write-up of the second main type of study which can be conducted where the central underlying principles are those of the symbolic interactionist theoretical approach within the interpretivist paradigm, namely, studies where the research question is formulated in terms of how participants 'deal with' 'things'. The background to the study is the trend over the last 25 years towards the 'inclusion' of students with intellectual disabilities into the mainstream of education rather than having them educated in the separate environment of the special class or special school. This development has posed challenges for teachers and has generated an associated research agenda for educational researchers. The particular focus of the study, undertaken with Dr Ron Chalmers, was on the 'inclusion' of children with severe or profound intellectual disabilities into the 'regular' classroom setting in the state of Western Australia (WA). The aim was to generate theory on how teachers in rural and remote schools in WA who had no specific training for the education of children with disabilities 'dealt with' their classroom work when they were placed in the position of including a student with a severe or profound intellectual disability in their class.

The range of this particular chapter extends over a wider canvas than the previous one. The research approach is outlined in some detail. This provides an opportunity to demonstrate how the interpretivist paradigm, the symbolic interactionist theoretical position, grounded theory methodology, and the methods of semi-structured interviewing, observations and document study all interconnect within a logical research plan. Also, the focus within the study on theory generation was greater than in the study reported in the previous chapter. Once again, a certain amount of 'thick' description is used in the presentation, with a liberal use of quotes so that 'voice' can be given to the views of the participants and to give the reader a sense of what it would be like to be in a similar situation. However, much attention is also given to presenting the wide range of concepts developed and to the relationships between them. Furthermore, it is demonstrated how the theory generated was such that propositions emerged and a typology was constructed.

The implementation of the research plan

The research question and the guiding questions

In framing the aim of the study in terms of how teachers 'deal with' their classroom work, a concept which has been clearly articulated within the symbolic interactionist tradition in social theory was being adopted. Herbert Blumer (1969) has argued that this particular social theory is based on three principles: human beings act towards things on the basis of the meanings those things have for them; the meaning of such things is derived from, or arises out of social interaction that one has with others; and meanings are handled in and modified through an interpretive process used by the person in dealing with the things encountered. Adopting these principles as a foundation for the present study meant that it was important to explore teachers' perspectives on the phenomenon of 'inclusion', how they act towards it, how they act towards others in relation to it, and how their perspectives and actions change over time. It is from an understanding of these dimensions of the phenomenon of 'inclusion' that we can arrive at an understanding of the basic social process, or processes, involved.

The following illustrates the types of guiding questions which were formulated in the light of the above-mentioned principles and which formed the basis of the first round of interviews with each of the 11 classroom teachers in the study:

- What do you hope to achieve over the year in terms of including John in your classroom? Why?
- What effect, if any, do you think having John in your class is going to have on your life? Why?
- What do you think will be the outcomes for John from having him included in the classroom? Why?
- What do you think will be the outcomes for you from having John included in the classroom? Why?
- What do you think will be the outcomes for the other members of the class from having John included in the classroom? Why?
- Have you given any thought to the task of developing an appropriate educational programme for John? Why?

This list was not as comprehensive as that which could have been developed if the procedure outlined in Chapter Three had been followed. Nevertheless, it did facilitate an extensive canvassing of the perspectives.

The research setting

WA occupies approximately one third of the Australian continent. Within the state, the Education Department is responsible to the State Minister for Education for the operation of approximately 800 schools. School-age children are educated in a variety of settings ranging from one-teacher schools located in remote rural locations, to large senior secondary schools with student populations of up to 2000 or more. In all major respects, this system is similar to school systems operating in other Western societies in that it has well-trained teachers, modern school facilities and educational resources, and highly developed curricula. The 10 schools which were involved in the present study are primary schools in rural and remote areas of WA. These schools are located hundreds of kilometres from each other and from the state capital city, within eight education districts in the southern half of WA, namely Albany, Manjimup, Bunbury North, Bunbury South, Narrogin, Northam, Moora and Merredin.

While there was significant variation in the school settings of each of the 11 teachers in the study, the 'support' provided by the Education Department to assist with 'inclusion' was similar for all. In each situation a teacher assistant was appointed to support the classroom teacher and, in the majority of cases, this support was provided for 90 percent of the time that the student with the disability attended school. A visiting teacher service, which operated from the central office of the Education Department, provided specialist advice to the teachers about a wide range of issues associated with the 'inclusion' of children with disabilities into regular classes. These visiting teachers also conducted professional development activities with the staff of each school in an attempt to increase the knowledge of teachers about the education of children with intellectual disabilities and to gain the support of the whole school for the policy of 'inclusion'.

Participants

All of the 11 participants were classroom teachers in WA rural state schools who had a student with a severe or profound intellectual disability 'included' in their class. Throughout the state there were 25 government primary school teachers in that situation. Of these, 22 had no previous experience of teaching a student with a severe or profound intellectual disability. Eleven of the 22 were located in the south-western portion of the state, which is the most densely populated rural district in WA and covers an area of about 360,000 square kilometres. When approached they all agreed to participate in the study. The other 11 teachers were located in the remainder of the state and it was not possible to include them in the study as they were scattered over a sparsely populated area which constitutes about six times the area of the United Kingdom.

The level of teaching experience of the 11 teachers selected varied significantly. The year the study commenced was the first year of teaching for one of the teachers. This contrasted with another teacher who had been teaching for 25 years and was in the twenty-first year of teaching at the same school. A more detailed profile of the teachers can be displayed in Table 6.1.

Here it will be noted also that 10 of the 11 teachers were female, thus reflecting the ratio of female to male teachers in the WA education system in rural areas.

Interviews

Data gathering took place in the 10 study schools over a 12-month period, commencing in the latter half of the 1990s. Three semi-structured interviews (Jones 1991) were conducted with each of the classroom teachers and the first round of interviews commenced in the week prior to the start of the school year. By scheduling the initial interviews for this time, it was possible to examine the perspectives and actions of the teachers about 'inclusion' as close to the start of the school year as possible before they had much, if any, direct experience of 'inclusive education'.

The duration of the first interviews with each teacher was approximately two hours and they consisted mainly of open-ended questions. The *aide-memoire* for these interviews, which was developed directly from the study's guiding questions, comprised 36 data-collection questions. These questions were designed to gather information from the teachers about their background in education, the knowledge they had about issues related to disability, the current arrangements for the 'inclusion' of a student with a disability in their class, the expectations they had about the 'inclusion' initiative and the plans they had in this regard for the year ahead.

Table 6.1 A profile of the teachers in the study

School enrolment nos	Teacher	Grade level taught	Male/female	Years of teaching experience	Years in current school
110	Mary	2	F	18	9
230	John	4	M	10	0
105	Joan	2	F	3	3
312	Kelly	4	F	1	0
90	Liz	2	F	4	2
180	Jodie	3	F	0	0
60	Amie	5	F	25	21
260	June	4	F	2	1
145	Heather	6	F	13	0
270	Becky	3	F	25	6
320	Lily	4	F	16	2

During the two months that followed the first round of interviews, each of the teachers in the study was contacted by telephone. The purpose of the calls was to gather more data and to make arrangements for the second round of interviews. Telephone interviewing was a productive supplementary data-gathering strategy. Seven positive features of telephone interviews identified by Dinham (1994), Borg and Gall (1983) and Groves and Kahn (1979) were evident in the interviews conducted for the study, namely, they allow coding and analysis to begin almost immediately, they assist respondents to clarify their perspectives, they promote reflection and 'stream of consciousness' responses, they are cost-effective, they result in minimal cost if interviews need to be re-scheduled, they can be cathartic in certain cases, and they promote greater relaxation because there is less threat posed by the 'faceless researcher'. The telephone interviews also enabled the teachers to report incidents related to the phenomenon of 'inclusion' near to the time they were experienced rather than having to wait until the next face-to-face interview.

The second round of face-to-face interviews was held over an extended period between March and June. The teachers were invited to nominate a suitable date and time for the interview so as to minimize disruption to their teaching programmes. Each teacher interview during the second round lasted approximately three hours. These interviews were used to gather additional data about the concepts which emerged from the analysis of the transcripts of earlier interviews and to identify the experiences the teacher had been having with 'inclusion' since the last round.

Also, during this second round of visits to schools, unstructured interviews were conducted with principals, teacher aides and other school personnel. These interviews were held during lunch-breaks or after school and varied in duration from fifteen minutes to one hour. Without exception, teachers, assistants and principals were cooperative and positively disposed to the informal interview process. In most cases they were eager to give their views about the 'inclusion' policy and to offer advice about the manner in which they thought 'inclusion' should be carried out in their school.

Informal telephone contact continued throughout the year. The teachers were invited to initiate telephone conversations at any time to discuss any matters related to 'inclusion' or the research process. Four of the teachers were particularly interested in elaborating on key issues or critical incidents related to 'inclusion'. This information became another source of data for the study.

The final round of interviews was held during November and December. Each interview again lasted for approximately three hours and was conducted in a variety of settings. Interviews were often punctuated by lunch breaks or walks in the school grounds. By this stage of data gathering the teachers were at ease and information about their experiences of 'inclusion' flowed with little prompting. Again, these interviews with teachers were used to gather additional data about the concepts that emerged from the analysis of the transcripts from earlier interviews, to establish the experiences the teachers had been having with 'inclusion' since the last round of interviews, and to involve the teachers in a process of testing and verifying data which had been gathered and analyzed from previous interviews. Furthermore, during the third round of interviews teachers were encouraged to critically analyse the full range of conceptual relationships which had been developed as components of the emerging theory, a strategy deemed by Lincoln and Guba (1985: 314) to be 'the most crucial technique for establishing the credibility' of qualitative studies.

Funding was provided to each of the schools in the study to employ replacement teachers – known in WA as 'relief teachers' – for the periods in which the 'inclusion' teachers were participating in interviews. This ensured that the teachers in the study were not required to be interviewed outside regular school hours and it also allowed the teachers to participate fully in the interviews without being concerned about the management of their classes. Altogether, over 100 hours of teacher interviews were conducted. Each interview was tape recorded and all recordings were transcribed for coding and analysis.

Classroom observations

Classroom observations were another important source of data for the study. The decision to gather data through the observation of the teachers in their classroom situations was influenced by the second major symbolic interactionist principle, namely, that people act towards things on the basis of the meanings they have for them (Blumer 1969). In other words, classroom observations facilitated clarification and elaboration on the perspectives that teachers held about 'inclusion'. This was done by observing the actions of each teacher and the situations in which they occurred. Furthermore, observations facilitated an uncovering of the strategies that teachers used to respond to the phenomenon of 'inclusion'.

Classroom observations were conducted on two occasions in each of the schools in the study. The first round of observations coincided with the second round of semi-structured interviews with teachers, and the second round of observations coincided with the third round of interviews. Typically, a full day was spent in each school, with half the day devoted to classroom observations and the rest of the day spent conducting a teacher interview.

What is important in the case of studies like this formulated within the symbolic interactionist research tradition is that perspectives and actions are consistent. As stated above, people respond to things on the basis of the meanings they have for them (Blumer 1969). Accordingly, standardized inventories and checklists as used within observational studies formulated within the positivist tradition were not appropriate for this study. Rather, a major purpose was to observe how teachers' perspectives get translated into strategies which are practised in the classroom. Where observed actions seemed to indicate inconsistencies with stated 'perspectives' it was important to allow the teachers the opportunity to explain why this was not the case. This was achieved by engaging them in further 'conversations' to unearth nuances to perspectives which had been misunderstood.

Analysis of data

This study utilized 'grounded theory' methods of data analysis as outlined in the work of Strauss and Corbin (1990) to generate 'substantive theory' regarding how teachers 'deal with' their classroom work when they are placed in the position of having a student with a severe or profound intellectual disability included in their class. These methods are consistent with symbolic interactionism. Their use involved three major types of coding, namely, open coding, axial coding and selective coding (Glaser 1992; Strauss and Corbin 1990). While each of these is a distinct analytic procedure, it is often the case that the researcher will alternate between the three modes of analysis, a practice which was followed within the present study. At the same time, from the early days of the data gathering and analysis phase of this study of 'inclusion', cognisance was taken of the fact that, despite the explicit nature of these coding procedures, they are not mechanical or automatic, nor do they 'constitute an algorithm guaranteed to give results' (Diesing 1972: 19). Accordingly, the coding procedures were applied flexibly and in accordance with changing circumstances throughout the two-year period of data gathering, analysis and theory formulation. The three types of coding and how they were used in the study will now be considered in turn.

Open coding

Open coding is the process of 'breaking down, examining, comparing, conceptualising, and categorising data' (Strauss and Corbin 1990: 61). It is the process whereby concepts, drawn from data, are identified and developed in terms of their properties and dimensions. During open coding, the data are broken down or 'fractured' (Strauss 1987: 55; Strauss and Corbin 1990: 97) into concepts 'to be closely examined and compared for similarities and differences, while constantly asking of the data the following question: What category or property of a category does this incident indicate?' (Glaser 1992: 39). Through the process of open coding, one's own and others' assumptions about a phenomenon are analysed, questioned or explored. This, in turn, leads to new discoveries (Strauss and Corbin 1990: 62).

In this study, open coding continued throughout the school year. Each of the transcripts from all of the teacher interviews was coded on a line-by-line and, in some cases, word-by-word basis. Code words were written in the right hand margins of the interview transcript sheets (Schatzman and Strauss

1973), as illustrated in Table 6.2, taken from the fourth transcribed interview from the first round of semi-structured interviews.

Similarly, Table 6.3 provides an example of open coding from notes made during the first round of classroom observations.

Documents provided by teachers and school administrators were also the subject of open coding procedures. On this, Table 6.4 provides an example of open coding of a school document made available during the research.

Throughout the coding process two basic analytic procedures were used. These were: asking questions of the emerging categories of data (Strauss and Corbin 1990) and making comparisons between the data, concepts and categories (Glaser 1978). These two procedures, as Strauss and Corbin (1990) point out, help to give the concepts in grounded theory their precision and specificity. Code notes and memos were also prepared to represent the questions asked of the data, and the comparisons and relationships between concepts and categories as they emerged from the data.

Code notes and theoretical memos were written throughout the data analysis and theory generation phases of the study. Code notes are a specific type of memo prepared to describe and explain the conceptual labels which emerge from the data (Strauss and Corbin 1990). Theoretical memos are developed to keep track of coding results and to stimulate further coding (Strauss 1987). They also contain the products of inductive and deductive thinking about relevant and potentially relevant categories of concepts (Strauss and Corbin 1990).

Table 6.2 Open coding of interview transcript extract

Interview transcript	Coding
T01: We have two aides. One has a strong personality. I anticipate that we will have some interesting tussles this year. There have been some practices I've observed in the past which I wish to discontinue. I think there will be a battle of wills. The other one (aide) is OK as long as things are explained and why you want them done she's quite amenable. As programmes have developed over the past five years they have sort of had a free reign and they have almost had ownership of S01 rather than it being the classroom teacher's responsibility, and one of them is now used to that situation. It is going to be a bit of a battle. At the same time, to be fair to the person, I think they will come around. It will just be a little bit of adjustment for both of them.	*assessing staff;* *predicting the future;* *expectation of conflict;* *classroom practices;* *observing; looking back;* *change; expectation of conflict;* *stubbornness; assessing staff;* *conditions; clarifying;* *open-mindedness;* *developmental approach;* *long-term view;* *control; decision-making power;* *ownership; alternative approaches;* *responsibility;* *familiarity with process;* *expectation of conflict; strong willed;* *even-handedness;* *positive expectation, confidence;* *minor adaptation.*

Table 6.3 Open coding of classroom observation notes

Observation notes	Coding
10.00am	
Teacher Aide (TA) helps S09 to stand and move towards the 'time out' area. TA tells the researcher that S09 usually gets a bit of free time to 'catch her breath' at the end of the maths session.	*TA: Physical assistance; Mobility Use of time-out area; Pattern/routine; Recovery; Physical impact;*
S09 selects a small blackboard from the shelves at the side of the classroom and walks slowly towards the TA.	*Selecting/choosing; Mobility; Relationship with TA;*
TA instructs S09 to get some chalk. TA: 'Ask Mrs xxx (T10) for some chalk'.	*TA instructing; TA controlling;*
S09 walks slowly to the front of the room.	*Compliance;*
10.02am	
Teacher directs class to work on a word activity book. Teacher says: 'S09, go and draw; sit down and draw!'	*Teacher instructing; Teacher instructing;*
S09 moves away from the main group; she moves towards the side of the classroom.	*Separation;*
All students appear completely undistracted by S09 walking through the middle of them. S09 stops to tap one girl gently on the top of the head. the student looks briefly at S09 and then continues with her work.	*No distraction; Mobility; Proximity; Physical contact; Gentleness Recognition; Reaction;*
10.05am	
TA moves to where the Year 2 students are working and helps them with their workbooks. S09 sits on her own at the side of the classroom. She starts to 'draw' on her small blackboard.	*TA mobility; TA assists class; Initiation; Isolation; Initiation;*
10.08am	
S09 stands and moves about the shelves. TA talks quietly, but directly, across the room: 'S09, sit down and do your drawing'.	*Initiation; Mobility; TA instruction; TA direction;*
S09 sits for a minute and then resumes her walk around the shelves, looking and touching various objects.	*Compliance; Initiation; Mobility; Sensory contact;*
Teacher: 'Who has got on their contract to read S09 a story? (Two hands are raised). 'John, would you please read S09 the story?'	*Teacher questioning; Contract; Student response; Teacher request;*

(continued ...)

Table 6.3 (… continued)

TA helps S09 to sit on the floor where the other students are sitting. John sits next to S09 with a reading book and starts to read.	*TA assistance; Student initiates contact; Student assistance/tutoring;*
10.15am S09 stands up and starts to open the door of the classroom. John stands and gently closes the door. S09 starts to walk to the other side of the classroom. Teacher: 'S09, go and sit down'.	*Initiation; Mobility; Student initiative; Gentleness; Initiation; Mobility; Teacher direction;*

Table 6.4 Open coding of school documents: extract from teacher diary – week 3, term 3

Document	Coding
Monday 7/8/95 AM – Toilet times as for yesterday, wet but no results on toilet. Bike ride, TA walking behind bike letting him pedal which he did (allowed his feet to propel as it is free wheel), kept his hand on handlebars and at one stage when the bike stopped (hit the side of the garden) he turned the handles slightly to get away but didn't look where he was going. Rest of the time not very co-operative and quite noisy.	*Routine; Expectations; Lack of performance; TA assistance; Empowering; Achievement;* *Persistence;* *Initiating; Intent? Failure to perform/conform? Non-compliant; Noisy;*
PM Was good outside. Toilet – sat on, got off and did wee on the floor! Went on swing and let children push him. NB: The children in class are willing to try to interact but don't get any response at this stage.	*Judgemental; Routine; Not meeting teacher routines; Giving permission; Control; Attempted interaction; Lack of response; Undiminished expectations;*

An example of a code note written in the early stages of data analysis is presented in Table 6.5.

Theoretical memos were written with a similar degree of detail.

Axial coding

While the primary purpose of open coding is to identify categories of data and their related properties and dimensions, in axial coding the aim is to make connections between each of the identified categories and its sub-categories. According to Strauss and Corbin (1990: 97), the focus in axial coding is on:

> … specifying a category (*phenomenon*) in terms of the conditions that give rise to it; the *context* (its specific set of properties) in which it is embedded; the action/interactional *strategies* by which it is handled, managed, carried out; and the *consequences* of those strategies.

Table 6.5 Code note

Code name:	expectation of conflict
Related codes:	minor adaptation
	responsibility
	planning for improvement
	establishing territory
	confidence in managing change

Code note: Teacher anticipation of conflict with the teacher aides over specific classroom practices. The teacher is clearly expecting to have 'tussles' and a 'battle of wills' with one or more of the teacher aides (expectation of conflict). The teacher anticipates that this will be an issue that she will have to deal with at some stage in the school year. This is a task that the teacher would not have to deal with if the child with the disability had not been placed in her class. It will be important to explore the reasons why the teacher anticipates the conflict and the resources available to deal with it. The working relationship between the teacher and the aides will be an important area to explore throughout the year. How does the relationship develop? What changes in the relationship over the year? What factors cause any changes which may occur? This could be a critical aspect of the way the teacher deals with the situation of having a student with a severe disability in their class.

Questions: What caused the teacher to anticipate conflict with the aides?
Does the teacher relish the prospect of conflict?
Is the potential for conflict a source of stress for the teacher?
What experience has the teacher had in handling conflict situations – generally?, with teacher aides?
Does the teacher plan to wait until conflict situations arise, or will she initiate the conflict on particular issues?
What strategies will the teacher employ to deal with the 'tussles' when or if they arise?
Has the teacher spoken with her colleagues about this situation?

Dimensions of conflict: positive/rewarding experience ↔ negative only

What study are these data pertinent to?:

Conflict analysis
Conflict resolution
Team building
Personnel management
Job description analysis

In this study of 'inclusion', axial coding was engaged in by constantly moving between inductive and deductive analysis in an attempt to build up a 'dense texture of relationships around the axis' (Strauss 1987: 64) of categories which were generated from the data analysed through open coding. Hypotheses were generated about the relationships between each category and its sub-categories. These were then tested by re-examining data previously gathered or by analysing new data about the phenomena represented by the categories and sub-categories.

Throughout this process of axial coding, code notes and memos were prepared to represent the relationships between categories and their sub-categories. Table 6.6 is an example of an axial coding memo which pertains to the category entitled 'committing', which emerged as a major process in the theory of 'selective adaptation'.

The coding model utilized in this research is recommended by Strauss and Corbin (1990) and is very much based on symbolic interactionism.

Selective coding

During the early months of the year of the research, the task of integrating the categories generated and developed through open and axial coding into a theory about how teachers 'deal with' their classroom work in situations where one member of their class has a severe or profound intellectual disability

Table 6.6 Axial coding theoretical memo

Theoretical memo – Committing (to a particular perspective on 'inclusion')	
Causal Condition	*Phenomenon*
Critical incident	Committing
Properties of a critical incident	*Specific dimensions of committing*
single event	extent – total
school 'work' based	intensity – high
multi-dimensional	duration – ongoing
deviation from the norm	potential for consequences – high
relevance for teacher	boundaries – class, school and general life

Context for committing
Under conditions where teacher commitment to a particular perspective on 'inclusion' is intense and ongoing, and where the potential for consequences in class, school and general life are high, then:

Action/interaction strategies for committing
teacher verbalises her 'commitment' to her perspective on 'inclusion'
teacher seeks out examples to support her perspective on 'inclusion'
teacher seeks out information to justify her perspective on 'inclusion'
teacher finds fault in alternative perspectives on 'inclusion'

Intervening conditions
Conflicting 'expert' opinion on aspects of 'inclusion'
Advice and/or direction from others

Consequences (for the teacher)
Greater 'certainty' in class, school and general life
Increased confidence in the teacher's approach to 'inclusion' and managing class work
Increased assertiveness in the relationship with teacher assistant(s)

was begun. This process of integrating categories, with particular reference to a central or 'core category' (Strauss 1987: 69) is known as 'selective coding' (Glaser 1978: 61). According to Strauss and Corbin (1990), selective coding is the process of selecting the core category, systematically relating it to other categories, validating those relationships, and filling in categories that need further refinement and development.

The process of selective coding was commenced by developing a 'general descriptive overview of the story' (Strauss and Corbin 1990: 119) which represented the emerging theory. The main story seemed to be about:

> ... how regular teachers in rural and remote schools who have had no specific training for the education of children with disabilities deal with their classroom work when they are placed in the position of having a student with a severe or profound intellectual disability included in their class. In general, the 'inclusion' of such students impacts widely on the teacher both in terms of their in-school life and their out-of-school life. For all teachers, 'inclusion' has a significant impact on their classroom work.
>
> There are three types of teachers in terms of the 'areas of life' in which the phenomenon of 'inclusion' is significant: the 'technician', the 'strategist' and the 'improviser'. 'Technicians' (type A) deal with their classroom work by focusing on classroom organisation issues. They 'selectively adapt' aspects of their teaching classroom organisation practices in response to the impact of 'inclusion'. For the 'technician', 'inclusion' has an impact primarily on their in-school life. 'Strategists' (type B) deal with their classroom work by focusing on classroom organisation and teaching methodology issues. They 'selectively adapt' aspects of their teaching methods and teaching techniques in response to the impact of 'inclusion'. For the 'technician', 'inclusion' has an impact on their 'in-school life' and their 'professional' life at home. 'Improvisers' (type C) deal with their classroom work by focusing on classroom organisation, teaching methodology and curriculum content issues. They 'selectively adapt' the content of the curriculum in response to the impact of 'inclusion'. For the 'improviser', 'inclusion' has an impact on their 'in-school life', their 'professional' life at home, and their general life.
>
> While all teachers initially focus on and selectively adapt aspects of their classroom organisation and management, type B teachers widen their focus and begin to adapt their teaching methods. Type C teachers take the additional step of selectively adapting the curriculum.
>
> Selective adaptation is a complex theory which is constructed of five distinctive categories: (1) receiving, (2) accepting, (3) committing, (4) adapting, and (5) appraising. Each of these categories, in turn, are comprised of processes and sub-processes.

This 'story' was used as the basis for generating the fully integrated theory about how teachers 'deal with' their classroom work in an 'inclusive' classroom.

Throughout the process of selective coding, theoretical coding notes of ever increasing theoretical abstraction were prepared. The aim was to ensure that the integrity of the theoretical framework would withstand close scrutiny and at the same time provide a high level of conceptual density and conceptual specificity. An example of a theoretical coding note written at the selective coding level is provided in Table 6.7.

Such theoretical memos were developed throughout the study to capture the 'frontier of the analyst's thinking' (Glaser 1978: 83) in relation to the data, concepts, codes and categories. In this way, a substantive theory (Glaser and Strauss 1967: 32) was generated.

Recording and storage of data

Within the context of theory generation, the labelling of concepts and the creation of categories is a complex process which requires an orderly and efficient system for data coding, storage, and retrieval (Corbin 1986: 102). Through the consistent and rigorous application of coding protocols and data storage methods, it became possible to ensure that all data were accessible and readily retrievable for coding and theory generation. All data were stored in hard copy and computer files. Interview recordings were transcribed, coded and filed. Classroom observation notes and school documents were

Table 6.7 Selective coding theoretical memo: processes and sub-processes of the category 'receiving'

Selective adaptation is a complex theory which is constructed of five distinctive categories: (1) *receiving*, (2) *accepting*, (3) *committing*, (4) *adjusting*, and (5) *appraising*. Each of these categories, in turn, is comprised of processes and sub-processes.

Receiving is the first in a series of processes in which teachers are engaged prior to making changes (adjusting) to their classroom practices as a consequence of 'inclusion'. The teacher who is *receiving* is engaged, alternately, in *clarifying, scrutinising* and *checking*. *Clarifying* refers to finding out about 'inclusion'. This may be a passive process or a process initiated by the teacher. In other words, some teachers actively seek out information about a wide range of practical and/or 'philosophical' matters relating to 'inclusion'. The extent to which teachers seek out information about 'inclusion' varies depending upon teacher 'type'. While some teachers demonstrate a 'hunger' for information about 'inclusion', others seek to *clarify* specific issues when they arise (linked with teacher typology). Once a particular matter or issue has been *clarified* to a point where teachers are satisfied that they have enough information to 'deal with' it, the process of *scrutinising* commences. *Scrutinising* is a process engaged in by teachers which involves detailed analysis of the issue or matter at hand and/ or the broad range of issues associated with 'inclusion'. Teachers engaged in *scrutinising* may, from time to time, engage in the related process of *checking*. *Checking* occurs when the teacher seeks out information from multiple sources and compares responses.

also coded and filed. Lists of conceptual labels and categories were generated and filed separately from the data. Code notes and memos were referenced and filed, and were easily retrievable for sorting and cross-referencing.

As well as assisting in analysing the data efficiently, the systematic coding of transcripts, documents and observation notes, and the methodical storage of code notes, categories and memos led to the generation of a theory in which the core category, categories, sub-categories and concepts can be traced back to the data. This 'audit trail' (Lincoln and Guba 1985: 319) is a key component in the demonstrated credibility and dependability of the study. All data associated with the study, from the interview transcripts to the constructed categories, sub-categories and processes, are readily accessible and available for others to check and for use in further research.

Trustworthiness of the grounded theory of 'selective adaptation'

Given that this was an interpretivist study in the symbolic interactionist tradition, it was deemed appropriate to use the criteria of the interpretivist to evaluate the study in terms of trustworthiness. The 'trustworthiness' criteria are credibility, transferability, dependability and confirmability and are most clearly articulated by Lincoln and Guba (1985). They are concerned with determining the extent to which we can have confidence in the outcome of the study and the extent to which we believe what the researcher has reported (Maykut and Morehouse 1994).

Credibility

Credibility refers to the truthfulness of the data. It is enhanced when research activities are used which make it more likely that 'credible findings and interpretations will be produced' (Lincoln and Guba 1985: 301). Credibility is also enhanced when strategies are put in place to check on the inquiry process and to allow for the direct testing of findings and interpretations by the human sources from which they have come.

The credibility of this study was enhanced by the extended period of data gathering, the prolonged engagement with the participants in the study, the use of multiple data-gathering methods, and the involvement of the teachers in critiquing the conceptual relationships and theoretical propositions as they emerged during the process of data analysis. Furthermore, regular 'peer debriefing' (Lincoln and Guba 1985: 308) sessions with colleagues were utilized throughout the planning and data-gathering phases of the study.

Transferability

According to Lincoln and Guba (1985), transferability, in a strict sense, is impossible in qualitative inquiry. However, it is possible when operating in this paradigm to generate theories which incorporate working hypotheses together with descriptions of the time and context in which they were found to hold. If this incorporates appropriate 'thick description' then judgements can be made about the possibility of transfer to other situations.

Strategies used in this study which enable judgements to be made about the transferability of the findings to other contexts include the detailed analysis of interview transcripts, observation notes and documents, the use of theoretical and purposive sampling, and the logical and concise presentation of theoretical propositions accompanied by relevant examples from the data.

Dependability

Dependability refers to the criterion of rigour related to the consistency of findings (Guba 1981). The development of an 'audit trail' has become an accepted strategy for demonstrating the stability and trackability of data and the development of theory in qualitative studies. The permanent 'audit trail' created in this study allows one, if required, to 'walk readers through' the work from beginning to end so that they can understand the path taken and the trustworthiness of the outcomes.

Confirmability

Confirmability refers to the 'extent to which the data and interpretations of the study are grounded in events rather than the inquirer's personal constructions' (Lincoln and Guba 1985: 324). In this study, the availability of a clear 'audit trail' was the major strategy which was used to ensure that confirmability was achieved. The audit trail enables the study to be evaluated in relation to the following questions: Are the findings grounded in data? Are the inferences which are based on the data logical? Does the category structure have explanatory power and does it have fit to the data? Furthermore, throughout the research process, and particularly during the writing of the study, guidance was provided by a series of seven questions developed by Strauss and Corbin (1990) which can be used to assess the extent to which grounded theory studies are empirically 'grounded':

Criterion #1   Are concepts generated?
Criterion #2   Are the concepts systematically related?
Criterion #3   Are there many conceptual linkages and are the categories well developed? Do they have conceptual density?
Criterion #4   Is much variation built into the theory?

Criterion #5   Are the broader conditions that affect the phenomenon under study built into its explanation?

Criterion #6   Has process been taken into account?

Criterion #7   Do the theoretical findings seem significant and to what extent?

Ethical considerations

Approval was obtained from the principals in each of the study schools to interview teachers and conduct classroom observations. Teachers signed a consent form before participating in the study. The consent form contained a description of the purpose of the study, details of the data-gathering methods, a description of the potential benefits of the research, and an assurance that participants could withdraw from the study at any time without prejudice. Furthermore, before data gathering commenced, officers from the Education Department's Disabilities and Learning Difficulties Branch were informed about the aims of the study, the research timetable and the proposed data-gathering techniques.

All data were treated in a way which protected the confidentiality and anonymity of the teachers involved in the study as well as the students and their parents. Coding was used during the gathering and processing of interview notes, tapes and transcripts. Teachers were informed that their identity would remain confidential and would not be disclosed either verbally or in publications based on the study. Pseudonyms are used throughout this report

How teachers 'deal with' their work in inclusive classrooms

The theory of selective adaptation

The theory of 'selective adaptation' which emerged from the data represents the basic social-psychological process by which regular classroom teachers deal with their classroom work when one member of their class has a severe or profound intellectual disability. The theory is now presented in two parts. The first part is an outline of what is meant by selective adaptation. This provides a background to the second part, namely, a 'grounded typology' of teachers with regard to how they deal with their classroom work in an 'inclusive classroom'.

The meaning of 'selective adaptation'

The data indicated that teachers tend not to make radical changes or trans-formations to their classroom organization, teaching methods or curriculum content when responding to the challenges of managing their classroom work in an 'inclusive' classroom. Rather, where changes are made, they tend to be carefully considered modifications of existing teaching practices. In other words, teachers 'deal with' their classroom work in an 'inclusive' classroom by 'selectively adapting' aspects of their 'normal' practices. Each of these categories will now be considered in turn.

CATEGORY 1: RECEIVING

Once teachers become aware that they will have a student with a severe or profound intellectual disability as a member of their class they begin to gather information about 'inclusion'. The processes that teachers use in this regard are categorized within the theory of 'selective adaptation' as 'receiving'. Kelly gave general expression to this notion of 'receiving' as follows:

> I spent a lot of time with the deputy discussing the whole thing. I wanted to find out everything I could about the whole deal, about what I was entitled to and what was expected of me. This was a whole new ball game for me and I just wanted to know the rules.

Teachers engage in the processes associated with 'receiving' with greatest intensity at the start of the school year. However, they also utilize the processes at subsequent times to deal with situations which arise in relation to specific aspects of managing their classroom work.

Within 'receiving' there are three distinct but inter-related processes: *clarifying*, *analysing* and *checking*. *Clarifying* is the term that has been given to the process by which regular classroom teachers find out about 'inclusion' and its myriad elements. A comment made by Lily captures what is involved:

> I wanted to know my rights in this area. I wanted to know if I had to take a child with such problems. I even thought about contacting the union to get some advice about inclusion. I knew that more and more of these children were moving into regular classes, but I didn't know very much about it at all.

Teachers in the present study used a wide range of strategies when 'clarifying'. The more 'formal' of these strategies were discussions with representatives of the Education Department and union officials. Other 'formal' strategies included participation in training programmes and professional development programmes designed to increase teachers' skills in the education of students with disabilities. 'Informal' strategies included discussions with colleagues and school administrators, and casual conversations with friends and family members.

While the combination of strategies used to gain information varied amongst teachers, the overall outcome was that during the course of the year each of the teachers received a substantial amount of information about all aspects of 'inclusion'. Teachers used this information as the basis for making decisions about how they would respond to the new conditions which they would encounter in their 'inclusive classroom'. In particular, the information was used to guide their decision-making in relation to what they saw as the main facets of classroom work: classroom organisation, teaching strategies and curriculum content.

Scrutinising is the process through which teachers examine closely the information they receive about all aspects of 'inclusion'. In particular, it is the process through which they analyze individual pieces of information and then reconcile them with their current overall understanding of 'inclusion'. As Joan put it:

> I was given conflicting advice about where Nola [disabled student] should be seated in the class. On the one hand, I was told that she must be in with the other kids and then I was told that for practical and safety reasons she should be at the desk on her own. It was up to me to balance the principles of inclusion with the practical task of running the class.

This process can be likened to the construction of a jig-saw puzzle whereby each piece of information has significance for the whole picture of 'inclusion' and the emerging picture has significance for each of the pieces.

As a direct result of engaging in 'scrutinizing', teachers' overall understanding about 'inclusion' can change significantly over a school year. The process of closely examining information about a wide range of specific issues associated with 'inclusion' tends to have a cumulative effect on their overall understanding of the phenomenon. In the words of one teacher in the present study, 'the big picture about inclusion kept changing as the year wore on because I was forced to think about all aspects of it very thoroughly'.

Checking is the process used by teachers to compare and contrast the information they receive about 'inclusion'. Amie explained as follows how she engaged in this process:

> Already I've got a few ideas about how to 'take advantage' of having Sophie in the room. It will be a good opportunity to teach the others about acceptance and tolerance, and being thankful for what you've got. But I am not sure how far you can take it. I am not sure if I should be drawing attention to Sophie [disabled student] or not. I'll have to check this out with the visiting teacher.

'Checking' stems from a reluctance on the part of teachers to accept any information, advice or suggestions about the broad range of issues associated with 'inclusion' without corroboration. It can relate to a single issue or situation, or it can be a lengthy process involving complex issues and multiple sources of information. In this regard, the teachers in the present study frequently sought the views of the principal, other teachers and teacher-aides about very specific matters related to the student with the disability. Also, each of the responses was considered and compared with the teachers' prevailing views about 'inclusion'. As with 'clarifying' and 'scrutinizing', the intensity with which teachers in the present study engaged in the process of 'checking' was greatest at the commencement of the school year. However, they also continued to engage in 'checking' well into the second half of the school year.

The majority of teachers in the study recognized early in the school year that there was no specific source of information from which they could obtain answers to many of their questions about inclusion. Schools were particularly lacking in this regard. As a result, they tended to seek out and compare the views and opinions of school administrators, 'experts', colleagues and friends about matters related to 'inclusion'. The advice and opinions of 'experts' such as specialist teachers, therapists and psychologists constituted a particularly important element of the 'checking' process.

The regular visits to schools by professional staff enabled the teachers in the study to compare and contrast information from an external source with the school-based information about 'inclusion'. 'Checking' of this type between external and internal sources was done for a variety of purposes. On most occasions, the advice of visiting professional staff was sought by teachers to support their own understandings about 'inclusion' or to endorse their current classroom practices. The advice of 'experts', however, was used by some of the teachers to question or challenge the advice or instructions given by the principal or other school administrator. There were also occasions when the views of one visiting 'expert' were used to challenge the advice of others. For example, therapists, psychologists and members of the visiting teacher service reported that they felt the information and advice they provided was often manipulated or used in ways that would suit the specific purposes of teachers or school administrators. To avoid becoming the 'pawns' in the 'checking' processes which were occurring in particular schools, they became somewhat guarded in the release of information and sensitive to the processes they would use to offer advice in school.

CATEGORY 2: ACCEPTING

Once teachers have satisfied themselves that they have developed an understanding of the broad conceptual underpinnings of 'inclusion' and that they have received useful information about specific aspects to this approach to the education of students with disabilities, they begin to consider the implications of this new educational phenomenon for themselves and for others. They do this through *assessing impact, values clarifying* and *reconciling*.

Assessing impact is the process through which teachers make initial judgements about the overall impact that 'inclusion' will have on their classes. Jodie voiced her thought patterns in this regard in the following manner:

> There's no doubt that I'm going to be spending a lot of extra time developing individual educational plans and thinking up new ways of teaching.

Teachers 'assess impact' by creating a mental image of what the year ahead will look like and by visualizing the changes that they believe they will have to make to their existing classroom work-practices.

A significant feature of 'assessing impact' is that it tends to be based on information 'received' by teachers rather than on the outcome of their direct experience of 'inclusion'. In other words, the initial judgements that teachers make about 'inclusion' are strongly influenced by what they find out about this educational phenomenon from outside the classroom. As a result, the outcome of 'assessing impact' is largely dependent upon the accuracy and reliability of information that has been 'clarified', 'scrutinised' and 'checked' by the teachers; major processes which, it will be recalled, constitute the first major category within the theory of 'selective adaptation', namely, 'receiving'.

Values clarifying is the process through which teachers examine 'inclusion' within the values framework they hold in relation to the education of students with intellectual disabilities. Mary was engaging in this process when she stated:

> I have no doubt that inclusion is the right thing to do. The days of segregating children with disabilities are behind us. But teachers are going to need a lot of support and advice to make sure that all kids in the class get a fair deal.

In 'values clarifying' teachers ask themselves two types of questions. The first type is along the following lines: Does 'inclusion' fit with my own values in relation to human rights, equity, ethics and social justice? The second type of question they ask is along the following lines: Does the practice of 'inclusion' fit with my own values about education?

The outcome of the process of 'values clarifying' influences significantly the extent to which teachers 'selectively adapt' their classroom practices in an 'inclusive classroom'. It was found that teachers who were generally supportive of the practice of including students with intellectual disabilities in mainstream schooling tended to be more prepared to adapt their classroom practices than were teachers who either did not support 'inclusion' or who were uncertain about 'inclusion'.

Reconciling is the process through which teachers examine 'inclusion', or specific aspects of it, in relation to their existing personal and professional frameworks. June used the term when reflecting on her experiences at the commencement of the school year:

> I found it difficult to reconcile 'inclusion' with my life at this time. Up until the start of this year I had my teaching career on track and I knew where I was heading. This was a big change for me in many respects. I had to think carefully about it [inclusion] to see how it would influence my life.

She went on to give a detailed account of the aspects of her life she considered may have been influenced by having a student with a severe intellectual disability as a member of her class. In analyzing this account a series of recurring questions which she asked herself became clear: How will this 'inclusion' affect my career? Will the experience increase or decrease my opportunity for transferring to another school? Will it enhance my opportunity for promotion within the education system? How will 'inclusion' affect my relationship with colleagues? What impact will it have on my personal life? Consideration of these and other questions led the teacher to make an overall assessment of the likely impact of 'inclusion' on her professional and personal life.

Significantly, the outcome of the process of 'reconciling' also influences the extent to which teachers 'selectively adapt' their classroom practices in an 'inclusive' classroom. In cases where teachers form the view that 'inclusion' will have a positive overall impact on their personal and professional lives, the extent to which they are willing to adapt their existing classroom practices is greater than it is for those teachers who form negative views about the impact of 'inclusion'. As in the case of 'assessing impact', however, the outcome of the process of 'reconciling' is influenced significantly by teachers' experiences of 'inclusion'. Initial judgements made by them about the likely impact that 'inclusion' will have on their personal and professional lives will tend to be amended after they have had experience with managing an 'inclusive' classroom.

CATEGORY 3: COMMITTING

The third major theoretical category of 'selective adaptation' is 'committing'. 'Committing' is a category comprised of three processes: *deciding, rationalising* and *explaining*. Through these processes teachers develop a consistent 'point-of-view' about 'inclusion'. This then leads them to engage in a range of actions and interactions aimed at justifying the particular point-of-view they have taken about 'inclusion', both to themselves and to others. In this regard, John made the following comment:

> I gave a lot of thought to my teaching during first term. Towards the end of term I realised that I would have to make some decisions. Was I going to make 'inclusion' work or was I going to fight against it. I felt I had to become more definite in my approach. So I decided to give it my best shot. But I could easily have gone the other way. I can see how some teachers become negative and say it can't work. I didn't. I decided to make it work.

Through the process of *deciding* which is exemplified in this extract, teachers adopt a particular stance in relation to 'inclusion' which, in turn, influences the nature and extent of the adaptations they make to their classroom work practices.

The stance taken by teachers in relation to 'inclusion' after engaging in the process of 'deciding' can vary significantly from one teacher to the next. While some teachers develop a strong commitment to 'inclusion' based either on axiological or educational grounds, others reject this approach to the education of children with disabilities and, as a result, spend the remainder of the school year implementing a policy to which they have little or no commitment. Perspectives which range between these two 'points-of-view' can also develop as the outcome of the process of 'deciding'.

The time it takes to reach the point of 'deciding' upon a particular 'point-of-view' in relation to 'inclusion' also varies significantly between teachers. In some instances teachers engage in the process of 'deciding' during the first few days in which they have responsibility for an 'inclusive' classroom. Other teachers, however, will not develop a firm position on 'inclusion' until mid-way through the school year.

Rationalising is a process in which teachers justify to themselves the particular stance they have adopted about 'inclusion'. Liz was engaging in this process when she stated:

> I was quite open with the deputy principal. I told him that I was setting up the classroom and establishing routines that would take care of Jane's needs, but that I would be relying heavily on the teacher aide to work with her. I am happy to put time into preparing her programme, but I can't take time away from all the other kids during class time.

Through engaging in such 'rationalising', teachers use information, advice from others and personal experiences which support their stance. Also, they tend to downgrade, trivialise or reject information or advice which conflicts with the stance they have taken.

While teachers talk with their friends and colleagues, particularly in the early part of the school year, to 'clarify' and 'check' information about 'inclusion', they also use these discussions to *explain* the stance they have taken. A typical 'explanation' was along the lines of that offered by Joan:

> I think there will be more gains than losses for me in this. I've already learnt a lot of new things about my teaching so far this year. By making changes to the way I teach I am going to get more satisfaction and the class is going to work more effectively.

As with 'rationalising', teachers tend to use the process of 'explaining' to criticise or reject viewpoints about inclusion which conflict with their own. Also, as they gain experience with 'inclusion' they tend to speak with increased conviction about their own views, interlacing their contributions to conversations with examples drawn from their own experiences in managing an 'inclusive' classroom.

CATEGORY 4: ADJUSTING

'Adjusting' is the 'core category' of 'selective adaptation'. Thus, it represents the central phenomenon around which all the other categories are integrated. It consists of three major processes: *selecting*, *reacting* and *initiating*.

Selecting involves teachers identifying aspects of their classroom work practices they are going to change in response to 'inclusion'. As Lily put it:

> I knew that I would have to give my teacher assistant a lot more responsibility, far more than I would normally allow. I made a conscious decision to give her a more direct and responsible role.

For all teachers the 'selecting' process tends initially to be focused on classroom organisational practices. Some teachers then move beyond this somewhat narrow focus and 'select' elements of their teaching strategies for change. Yet another group of teachers takes the additional step of 'selecting' particular aspects of the content of the curriculum for change.

Reacting is the process whereby teachers make changes to their classroom practices in response to a particular experience or set of experiences they have had when teaching in an 'inclusive' classroom. In this regard, John explained how he was preparing himself for what was to come:

> There is no doubt that this will be a big learning year for me. It will be a real opportunity to learn more about teaching kids with disabilities. I am already booked in for two training programmes in Perth.

Through 'reacting', teachers attempt to change particular classroom practices with which they are dissatisfied and make adjustments which they believe will improve the way the classroom is operating. The overall aim of the process is to make a positive change in current practices which, in turn, will enhance the capacity of the teachers to deal with their classroom work.

The time taken for teachers to 'react' to particular classroom situations can vary significantly from one teacher to the next. While some teachers are prepared to make significant changes across a broad range of their existing teaching practices in a short period of time, others take a more measured approach and attempt to consolidate one change before moving on to the next. Also, while factors such as professional and life experiences, and the capacity and willingness to implement change, have a significant influence on the time taken for teachers to 'react' to classroom situations with which they are dissatisfied, the 'point-of-view' that teachers adopt towards 'inclusion' through engaging in the processes of 'deciding' 'rationalising' and 'explaining' will also have an influence on the pace of change. This notion of 'point-of-view', it will be recalled, was considered under 'deciding', the first major process of the third category of the theory of 'selective adaptation'.

Initiating involves teachers making pre-emptive changes which are based on the information they have received about 'inclusion' through the processes of 'clarifying', 'scrutinising' and 'checking', or on the 'point-of-view' they have adopted in relation to the education of students with intellectual disabilities in regular classrooms. The following comment from Becky indicates what is involved in this process:

> It took a lot to implement the friendship roster for Kelly [disabled student]. My lunch breaks and recess times were taken up with this. I gave it my best shot because I had been told that it would have positive results.

Through engaging in this process, teachers make changes on the basis of the conditions they anticipate they will experience in the 'inclusive' classroom.

Motivation for teachers to engage in 'initiating' can stem from a range of sources. There were many examples in the present study where teachers made changes to their regular practices, especially in relation to classroom organisation, as precautionary measures to increase safety for the student with the disability, for other students, or for adults in the classroom. Other changes were motivated by the concern of the teachers to ensure that they were implementing classroom practices consistent with current practices in relation to 'inclusion'. In most cases, however, 'initiating' was motivated by the desire to establish an effective classroom environment which would result in productive outcomes for all students in the class.

CATEGORY 5: APPRAISING

The fifth and final category of the theory of 'selective adaptation' is 'appraising'. It consists of two major processes, namely, 'assessing' and 'judging'.

Assessing is the process used by teachers to estimate the magnitude or quality of the outcomes of the adjustments they have made to their regular classroom practices in response to 'inclusion'. Heather gave the following example of such an adjustment:

> The change we made to the arrangement of desks and equipment has been very successful. I've been able to set up a reading corner and the kids can move about without falling over things. It also feels as though we have more space. The room seems bigger.

'Assessing' can be a simple process in which teachers examine the direct effects of specific changes they have made to the classroom. However, this is rarely the case. The complex and dynamic environment of classrooms is such that most changes made by teachers have a number of interrelated consequences. Therefore, it is often the case that the process of 'assessing' involves an examination of the impact of changes on and between the disabled student, the other students, the teacher aide and the teacher. Teachers use a variety of strategies to 'assess' the outcomes of the adjustments they make to their normal classroom practices. These range from 'objective', statistically-based techniques such as counting the number of times the student with the disability will engage in a particular type of behaviour, through to 'subjective', intuitive methods of assessment.

The present study also indicated that teachers tend to use their own observations of what is happening in the classroom as the basis for 'assessing' the outcomes of adjustments they have made. However, the observations of colleagues, school administrators, and in some cases students, can also have an impact on their 'assessments'. Most teachers in the present study were eager to engage their colleagues in discussions about the changes they had made in their classroom practices and sought their views about the impact of the changes.

Judging is the process through which teachers draw conclusions about the value of the outcomes of the adjustments they have made to their current classroom practices. The following was June's 'judgement':

> When I look back to the start of the year and think about how the classroom was operating, I know that the new approach was worth the pain in making the changes. I was very uncertain about my capacity to teach all the students in the class and to keep things under control if I chose to spend a lot of time with Michelle each day. I know that the experts might be saying that I am relying too heavily on the teacher aide, but I really don't think there is any better way of going about it.

When they engage in this process they are asking: Have the adjustments I have made in my normal classroom practices increased my capacity to deal with my classroom work? The judgements they make in this regard lead them to consider whether to persist with the changes, revert to their previous classroom practices, or implement alternative adjustments. The findings from this study clearly show that in situations where teachers 'judge' that the changes they have made have not resulted in an increased capacity for them to deal with their classroom work, they either make new changes or revert to previous practices. Where changes have been 'judged' by the teacher to be effective they are retained or, in some cases, modified in an attempt to gain further improvement in classroom operations.

A 'grounded typology' of teachers regarding how they 'deal with' their classroom work in an 'inclusive classroom'

A major outcome of the study being reported here was the generation of a 'grounded typology' (Glaser 1978) of teachers with respect to how they deal with their classroom work in an inclusive classroom. The typology is based on three propositions which build upon the meaning of 'selective adaptation' outlined in the previous section. The first proposition is that teachers can be classified into three 'types' in relation to the extent to which they 'selectively adapt' aspects of their classroom work in an 'inclusive classroom'. The second proposition is that the 'inclusion' of a child with a severe or profound intellectual disability into regular classrooms can have a significant impact on the professional and personal lives of teachers. The third proposition is that there is a correspondence between the degree to which teachers 'selectively adapt' aspects of their classroom work and the extent to which their lives are affected by 'inclusion'. Each of these propositions will now be considered in turn.

Proposition one

The extent of 'selective adaptation' varies amongst teachers. For some teachers, labelled 'the technicians', the adaptation is limited to the area of classroom organisational matters. This includes, for example, making changes to the regular layout of the classroom or implementing new routines or procedures. Other teachers, labelled 'the strategists', move beyond this somewhat narrow focus and 'selectively adapt' their teaching strategies and methods. For a third category of teacher, the 'improvisers', 'selective adaptation' also extends to the content of the curriculum.

All teachers tend to focus initially on and 'selectively adapt' aspects of their classroom organisational practices in response to 'inclusion'. There are many examples in the data which indicate that teachers are eager to attend to the technical aspects of 'managing' the 'inclusive' classroom before turning their attention to other areas to 'adapt'. As Amie remarked: 'it's like anything in teaching, you've got to attend to the basics before you can move on to the fancy stuff'.

The time taken for 'strategists' and 'improvisers' to shift their focus to 'selectively adapting' beyond classroom organisational matters varies from one teacher to the next. Some of them move beyond this narrow focus within a few days of the school year commencing, while others make the transition many weeks or even months into the year. Similarly, the time taken by the 'improvisers' to commence 'adapting' the content of the curriculum also varies amongst the teachers in this category. The situation with regard to the present study can be illustrated as shown in Table 6.8.

Proposition two

For some teachers, the 'inclusion' of a student with a severe or profound intellectual disability in their class has a significant impact on their 'in-school' life. For other teachers, 'inclusion' has an impact both on their 'in-school' life and their 'professional work at home'. For a third category of teachers, 'inclusion' has an impact on their 'in-school' life, their 'professional work at home' and their 'general life'.

(A) THE IMPACT OF 'INCLUSION' ON TEACHERS' 'IN-SCHOOL' LIFE

For each of the teachers in the present study the 'inclusion' of a student with a severe or profound intellectual disability in their class had an impact on their 'in-school' life. At various times during the working year issues associated with 'inclusion' dominated their working lives. Conversations with colleagues were frequently interlaced with discussions about disability issues, principals frequently sought information about the students with disabilities, parents frequently asked questions about the implementation of 'inclusion',

Table 6.8 Teachers classified by type and the approximate timing of their transition through the stages of 'selective adaptation' in the 41-week school year

Teacher	Teacher type	Selective adaptation of classroom organisation	Selective adaptation of teaching methods	Selective adaptation of curriculum content
Joan	technician	Week 3		
John	technician	Week 2		
Jean	technician	Week 2		
Becky	technician	Week 3		
Mary	strategist	Week 1	Week 2	
June	strategist	Week 5	Week 5	
Lily	strategist	Week 2	Week 3	
Heather	strategist	Week 5	Week 7	
Liz	improviser	Week 1	Week 2	Week 8
Amie	improviser	Week 1	Week 2	Week 18
Kelly	improviser	Week 2	Week 2	Week 12

and non-teaching staff often offered opinions about the 'new approach' to educating students with disabilities. While for some the impact was minor, for others their exposure to 'inclusion' resulted in a significant change in the regular pattern of their lives at school. They spoke often about the increased demands on their time which resulted from managing an 'inclusive classroom' and the restrictions this placed on their ability to participate in the regular activities of the school.

Throughout the course of the year most of the teachers in the study reported that the task of managing an 'inclusive classroom' had affected in some way their relationships with their colleagues. For example, mid-way through the school Becky made the following comment:

> I've really noticed a change in my relationship with the others. There seems to be a bit more distance between me and them and I'm still trying to work out why. It may just be my imagination, but I think they may be giving me more consideration because of the extra work involved in looking after Angela [disabled student]. Even the boss seems to be treating me with kid gloves. It's very subtle but it's also a bit spooky.

Other teachers attributed their changed relationships with colleagues to the increased workloads associated with managing an 'inclusive classroom'. As Joan put it:

> I don't have the same amount of time to mix with the staff during breaks. I used to spend a lot of time in the staffroom during recess and lunch but I can't do that any more. I am not moaning about it. It's just a fact of life. But it's got to have an effect on my role with the staff. That's OK.

The teachers also spoke about how the increased demands on their time which resulted from managing an 'inclusive classroom' placed restrictions on their ability to participate in regular activities at school.

There were also, however, a number of positive features in the relationships between the teachers and their colleagues as a consequence of 'inclusion'. Diane was particularly pleased that her status in the school had been enhanced because of the increased responsibility which was associated with teaching a student with very high support needs. This highlights another general area in which 'inclusion' has an impact on the 'in-school' lives of regular teachers. Indeed, most of those in the study provided examples to illustrate the increase in the overall level of responsibility and accountability which is associated with 'inclusion'.

A final area in which 'inclusion' has an impact on teachers 'in-school' life is related to the attention focused on the 'inclusive classroom'. Joan spoke of 'operating in a goldfish bowl' when referring to the many visits she received from therapists, psychologists and visiting teachers. Similarly,

Mary was concerned about the ongoing attention her class received during discussions at staff meetings as a result of 'inclusion'. Yet again, John spoke of the inordinate amount of time spent during 'Parent and Citizens' meetings discussing the operation of his classroom and, in particular, matters pertaining to 'inclusion'.

(B) THE IMPACT OF 'INCLUSION' ON TEACHERS' 'IN-SCHOOL' LIFE AND THEIR 'PROFESSIONAL WORK AT HOME'

While the impact of 'inclusion' is felt in a myriad of ways by all teachers in relation to their 'in-school' life, others also feel the impact on their 'professional work' which is done at home. The following examples from the data illustrate the impact that 'inclusion' has on teachers in this regard:

> I'm thinking a lot more about why I am planning to do things. It takes a lot more time but I think it's making things easier at school. (Mary)
> I learnt early on that you cannot skip a week of planning and preparation and run on automatic. You can't wing it and you can't just rely on last year's programmes. You have to think about things carefully, especially at home in the evenings. (June)
> I'm a lot more disciplined in my preparation at weekends. This inclusion has got me into a good routine. (Heather)
> My husband and the kids said a few things at the start of the year. They noticed how much more time I was spending on preparation at home at night and at the weekends. (Lily)

One of the most common changes to a teacher's professional work at home is an increase in the overall amount of time spent planning and preparing. A general view held by the teachers in the present study is that this additional planning and preparing is required to ensure they can deal with their classroom work effectively. At the same time, however, while some of them were concerned initially about this increased time commitment, as the year progressed they were generally pleased with their own abilities to reduce the amount of additional planning and preparation time required. Also, despite the additional time spent, it was possible for some teachers to stop 'inclusion' impacting beyond this realm of their lives.

(C) THE IMPACT OF 'INCLUSION' ON TEACHERS 'IN-SCHOOL' LIFE, THEIR 'PROFESSIONAL WORK AT HOME' AND THEIR 'GENERAL LIFE'

For a third group of teachers within the present study, the impact of 'inclusion' was felt in their 'general lives', including interactions with their families and friends, leisure pursuits, hobbies, holidays and entertainment activities. The following examples from the data illustrate this:

Inclusion dominated my home life for a while. It is one of those things that we as a family tended to talk about over meals, on week-ends, any time. (Liz)

It is a routine topic of conversation with my friends. They are really interested because of Sophie's [disabled student] degree of disability. Sometimes I raise the topic and sometimes someone else will. I guess it is because I have started to think a lot about social justice issues. My mind goes to it all of the time. (Kelly)

During the first few weeks I was worried about the safety issues. I kept on thinking about my responsibilities and what would happen if anything went wrong. I used to wake up at night worrying. (Amie)

While these and other extracts from the data illustrate the impact that 'inclusion' can have on the 'general lives' of teachers, the study also found that the extent of this impact declined during the latter half of the school year. The following comment made towards the end of the school year by Liz was typical of the explanations given to account for this decline in the impact of 'inclusion': 'It's like anything in teaching, after a while you just get used to it'.

Proposition three

Considerations so far have focused on the classification of teachers according to the extent to which they 'selectively adapt' their classroom work and on the classification of teachers according to the extent to which their lives are affected by 'inclusion'. What now follows is an exposition on the correspondence which was found to exist between these two series of classifications.

For 'technicians' – teachers who tend to restrict the 'adjustments' they make in their regular classroom practices to the area of classroom management – the impact of 'inclusion' tends to be confined to their 'in-school' lives and does not impinge to any significant extent upon either their 'professional work at home' or their 'general life'. There are very few examples in the data which indicate that teachers classified as 'technicians' are particularly concerned about, or give special consideration to, issues associated with 'inclusion' either during their planning and preparation time at home or during the general course of their lives. An exception in this regard was voiced by Becky as follows:

This inclusion stuff nearly destroyed a dinner party we gave last term. I was really surprised by the passion it stirred up amongst a couple of my friends. They took opposing views on the practice of having really disabled kids in our schools and I had to become the umpire. Everyone joined in, everyone had an opinion. I was really surprised.

Becky was surprised by the incident because, as she commented, 'it was the first time that inclusion ever became an issue for me outside school'.

For 'strategists' – the teachers who 'selectively adapt' both their regular classroom organizational practices and their teaching strategies – the impact of 'inclusion' extends beyond their lives at school to also affect their 'professional work at home'. Teachers in this category regularly spend periods of time at home on matters related directly to 'inclusion'. However, like the 'technicians', the 'general lives' of the 'strategists' tend not to be affected by 'inclusion'. For 'improvisers' – the teachers who 'selectively adapt' their regular classroom practices, their teaching strategies and the content of the curriculum – the impact of 'inclusion' is felt across three areas of their lives, namely, 'in-school life', 'professional work at home' and 'general life'. As the following comment made towards the end of the school year by Amie, an experienced teacher, illustrates, the lives of teachers in this category can be affected significantly by 'inclusion':

> Even my mother noticed a change in me during the first few months. She said she was concerned about me. Maybe it was because I was talking a lot more about my work than I did in previous years. But she knew that I had been very keen to make this [inclusion] a success and she also knew that it was taking a lot of my time and energy.

Amie's deputy principal also noticed the impact that 'inclusion' was having on her:

> It's become a big part of her life this year. She's certainly given 100 per cent to make sure that Marnie gets the best chance in school.

These and other examples from the data support the finding that teachers who tend to make the widest range of adjustments to their classroom work practices are also the teachers most widely affected by 'inclusion'. The situation within the present study can be illustrated as shown in Table 6.9.

Conclusion

The emergence of 'inclusion' as a central concept underpinning much of the policy direction regarding the education of students with severe or profound intellectual disabilities has generated considerable attention in recent years (Erwin and Soodak 1995). The associated research agenda incorporates an extensive range of topics and issues, and there have been calls for the undertaking of a variety of empirical studies from both the quantitative and qualitative research perspectives. In particular, there have been calls for studies which will increase our understanding of the phenomenon of 'inclusion' from the perspectives of the people involved, including teachers, parents, school

Table 6.9 Teachers classified by the extent of 'selective' adaptation and the impact of 'inclusion'

		Extent of 'selective adaptation'		
		Selective adaptation of classroom organisation	Selective adaptation of teaching methods	Selective adaptation of curriculum content
I M P A C T	In-school	Joan John Jean Becky		
O F	Professional Work at home	Mary June Lily Heather	Mary June Lily Heather	
I N C L U S I O N	General Life	Liz Amie Kelly	Liz Amie Kelly	Liz Amie Kelly

administrators and students. On this matter, Haring (1996: 7) contends that in the field of 'inclusion' for people with severe disabilities, there is a need for studies which:

> .... more completely and honestly describe behaviour and contexts that are naturally occurring and that are more directly tied to the needs and the problems in people's lives.

The study reported in this chapter is one contribution to this call.

Part II

Extending the range of interpretivist studies

So far the focus of this book has been on the two main types of studies that arise directly out of the central principles of the symbolic interactionist theoretical approach within the interpretivist paradigm, namely, studies where the aim is formulated in terms of participants' perspectives on 'things' and studies where the aim is formulated in terms of how participants 'deal with' 'things'. To pursue such questions is to engage in research which was defined in Chapter One as 'big theory' research. In Chapter One also, it was pointed out that other types of 'big theory' research can be undertaken within the interpretivist paradigm by adopting other theoretical approaches, including phenomenology and ethnomethodology. Furthermore, it was argued that the position adopted throughout this book is one which does not favour an approach based on the argument that symbolic interactionism, phenomenology and other theoretical positions within the interpretivist paradigm can be combined loosely to underpin an eclectic research approach. Neither does the development of such a research approach by combining theoretical approaches from various paradigms find favour. This is not to argue against eclectic research approaches in principle; rather, it is to maintain that in order for any such research approach to be put forward as defensible, rigorous logical arguments need to be mounted to make crystal clear what is involved. The latter, of course, would necessitate a separate book.

At the same time, it is not being argued that the only types of interpretivist studies which can be undertaken using symbolic interactionism as the underpinning theoretical approach are the two main types outlined at the commencement of this chapter. In recent years I have either engaged in research projects of my own, or in supervising students' research theses, conceptualised within the parameters of five related types. The first four of these types are Policy Studies, Life History Studies, Retrospective Interactionist Longitudinal Studies and Interactionist Historical Studies. Recalling the point made in Chapter One that along with 'big theory' questions and related studies, we can also engage in research based upon 'concept-driven' ideas and 'problem-focused' ideas, what these four types of research have in common is that while they are 'concept-driven', they can also be ultimately mapped back to an interpretivist foundation, with symbolic interactionism as the underpinning theoretical position. The fifth type of study is of the 'problem-focused' variety. Here again such studies can be mapped back to give them interpretivist and symbolic interactionist foundations. It is recognised, of course, that the substantive areas which are the focus of these proposals could also have led to proposals to engage in research conceptualised within other paradigms. For example, it is not too difficult to imagine policy studies being undertaken within the critical theory paradigm, or life history studies being conceptualised within the poststructuralist paradigm.

This part of the book, Part Four, contains five chapters. Each chapter outlines a research proposal related to one of the five types of research outlined above. While all of these proposals deal with issues which were investigated within Western Australia, they could be adapted quite easily for a large variety of contexts around the world. Within each proposal a research topic is identified and is located both contextually and within a body of research literature. The emphasis then shifts to detailing a research plan demonstrating how the research topic can be conceptualised within the interpretivist paradigm. Overall, such a plan is useful as it allows one to see how each of the component parts could possibly be developed so that they could become the early chapters of a thesis. At the same time, it is recognised that as a study unfolds there could be good reasons for structuring a thesis differently.

While the general pattern noted above holds for all five proposals, there are also certain ways in which the proposals deviate from each other. Some of these differences will now be highlighted to emphasise a belief that not only is there room for flexibility in proposal development, but also that such flexibility may be necessary and is to be encouraged. First, there is the idiosyncratic matter of some researchers favouring certain terms over others, even though what is meant is invariably the same. Thus, we find 'the background' being used as a heading in Chapter Seven, but what is being indicated is no different than what is outlined under 'the research context' in Chapter Eight and 'the context' in Chapter Eleven.

Some of the headings used in Chapters Eight and Ten also deviate from those in the other chapters for another reason, namely, they were those which were required at the time of proposal development by the grant-awarding bodies to whom the proposals in question were submitted for funding. In particular, the early headings of 'aims and background' and 'significance and innovation' introduce a different way of making one's case. In similar vein, 'significance' is substituted for 'literature review' in Chapter Ten. A feature of Chapter Ten also is that it addresses the requirement in proposals submitted to grant-awarding bodies to provide justifications as to why tax-payers' money should be spent supporting such a project. This is done through an exposition on how the proposed research is seen as having the potential to contribute to understanding the nation and to promoting social and economic development.

The proposals also vary in the length of the expositions given on such matters as selection of participants, approaches to be adopted in data gathering, and the modes of data analysis to be utilised. Again, I would argue that there is no hard-and-fast rule about this. Sometimes the decision is made in the light of required word-lengths by student research committees in universities, or by grant-awarding bodies. Other times, a judgement is made by the researcher as to the extent to which he or she thinks those assessing the proposals may need to be educated on issues of method, particularly if there is a suspicion that judgements may be made by using criteria other than those used by interpretivists. Finally, before moving on to the chapters on the proposals in question it is necessary to make one other point, namely, that there would appear to be further 'types' of studies which could be added to the five considered. To date, however, I have not explored them in any detail and so I will not dwell on them here.

Chapter 7

Policy studies and the interpretivist paradigm

In recent years there has been a burgeoning of educational research in such specific fields as educational leadership, educational management, educational administration, curriculum studies, and teaching and learning studies. Concurrently, there has been an increasing recognition that these areas do not exist in a vacuum. Rather, they are located within a context which is shaped by historical and cultural conditions. Major lenses for studying this context have been provided by a number of research approaches. Prominent amongst these are those approaches centred on policy-analysis frameworks. The outcome has been a growth in educational policy studies. Furthermore, regardless of the underlying definition of policy and the nature of the frameworks utilised, these policy analysis studies are all concept-driven, the central concept being that of 'policy' itself.

At the same time, the concept of policy is not a straightforward one. Indeed, its contested nature has led to a myriad of definitions. It is because of this that there are various approaches to policy analysis. Ozga (2000) describes three approaches that have developed over time. The first approach is the 'social administration project', where the researcher is concerned with the needs of the clients of the policy. This is well summarised by Majchrzak (1984: 12):

> Policy research … is defined as the process of conducting research on, or analysis of, a fundamental social problem to provide policy makers with pragmatic, action-oriented recommendations for alleviating the problem.

The second approach is the 'policy analysis project', which is concerned with the 'efficient and effective delivery of social policies irrespective of their content' (Ozga 2000: 39). This approach is therefore preoccupied with the outcomes of policy. Ozga's third approach is the 'social science project' and here the concern is to:

> ... find out how things work, rather than putting them to work.... The social scientist is not oriented towards a client's definition of the problem. The problem is defined by the nature of existing theory; that is, a better understanding of how things work. The orientation is towards the academic discipline...and the rules of the discipline, and its principles of enquiry guide research practice, rather than a framework of strategic planning requirements and possibilities.
>
> (Ozga 2000: 40)

In adopting this position Ozga would appear to be at one with Ham and Hill (1993: 2–5) in highlighting a traditional distinction between analysis *of* policy and analysis *for* policy.

This chapter outlines a proposal to conduct a research project conceptualised as an 'analysis of policy' project, illustrating that one useful approach to such a policy analysis is where it is viewed as being closely aligned to the interpretivist paradigm. The proposal is also informed by a conceptualisation of policy analysis as a 'trajectory study' (Ball 1993: 1994), which involves a definition of policy as a cyclical, freewheeling, dialectical process. For Ball, the process has three dimensions or contexts: the context of influence, the context of text and the context of consequences. It was concepts such as these which constituted the major influences on the thinking of Dr Anthony Curry when he began to prepare his Doctor of Education thesis proposal with me in the late 1990s in the Graduate School of Education, The University of Western Australia. His particular interest centred on the policy of the Catholic Education Commission of Western Australia with regard to the education of students with disabilities from 1982 to 1997. The proposal which was eventually developed and which will now be outlined was based on a realisation of a need to anchor the informing concepts and the emerging methodology in a paradigm's base, and the paradigm chosen as being most appropriate was that of interpretivism.

Title

An analysis of the policy of the Catholic Education Commission of Western Australia with regard to the education of students with disabilities, 1982–1997.

The background

The education of students with disabilities has been a significant international educational issue over the last 20 years (Hall 1997). Western Australia (WA), like the other states in Australia, has not been immune to this trend. Here the impact has been not only on the state's public education system, but also on the various non-government education systems, including the Catholic system. Between 1982 and 1997, a series of changes occurred in the policy of the Catholic Education Commission of Western Australia (CECWA) with regard to the education of students with disabilities. CECWA is the administrative body which overseas the provision of education in the great majority of Catholic schools throughout the state. The particular concern of the study being proposed here is to analyse the CECWA policy regarding the education of students with disabilities for the period 1982–1997. The study, located within the interpretivist tradition, will involve the use of qualitative research methods of data gathering and analysis.

The general background to the proposed study is the increasing interest in the education of children with disabilities. During the last quarter of the twentieth century, major attitudinal changes have taken place in Western society with regard to this cohort. These attitudinal changes have been part of broader historical changes originating in the civil rights movement of the 1960s. While there was considerable diversity in some countries, the trends in the USA and the UK during the two-decade period following the mid-1970s signalled that the disability-rights movement was becoming stronger and more influential in public life. In the period to be examined in the proposed study, namely 1982–1997, the validity of the rights of people with disabilities, pushed by the social forces emphasising the importance of autonomy and justice, continued to be recognised. Consequently, de-institutionalisation and greater autonomy became the norm for people with disabilities throughout the world, including Australia.

The latter development also needs to be viewed within the broad context of Australia's educational history. Here the nature of educational institutions was changed dramatically with the introduction of compulsory education into all of the states in the last decades of the nineteenth century. Up to this point in time children with learning difficulties were often denied access to formal education, thus limiting their future opportunities (Casey 1994). On this, of course, Australian society was simply mirroring other societies that also had periods in which the rights of people with disabilities were considered less legitimate than those of others.

The history of Western ideas, attitudes and service delivery to people with disabilities has been summarised in terms of four motivating considerations, namely 'threat to survival, superstition, science and service' (Hewett and Forness 1984). Casey (1994: 7) contends that to these four variables 'could be added a fifth variable, "rights", that has substantially influenced the social acceptance of, and delivery of services (including education) to, people with disabilities'. Internationally, it was the social justice movement that prompted a radical change in mainstream attitudes towards several minority or disadvantaged groups in the 1960s. As this movement gathered momentum, the concern for the rights of minority groups began to include a widespread acceptance of the right of all persons to participate fully in the mainstream community (Fulcher 1989; Cocks et al. 1996).

Stemming from the social justice movement was the increased worldwide awareness of the rights of people with disabilities. Despite the 'battles' fought, however, the gaining of rights for people with disabilities seemed to be progressing quite slowly until about two decades ago, when a number of important legislative decisions were made. In some countries, legislation was enacted to address the discrepancies between opportunities in the community available to the able-bodied and people with disabilities. The *Declaration on the Rights of Mentally Retarded Persons* (United Nations 1971) and the *Declaration of the Rights of Disabled Persons* (United Nations 1975) were followed in the USA by the Education for All Handicapped Children's Act (1976) (Doenau 1984). In the UK, the British Education Act (1981) legislated many of the recommendations of the report entitled *Special Educational Needs: Report of the Committee of Inquiry into the Education of Handicapped Children and Young People* (1979), known also as the Warnock Report. This report had examined the state of education and schooling for children with disabilities in the late 1970s. In Australia at this time the Federal and state parliaments began to promulgate anti-discrimination legislation that highlighted the needs of children with disabilities (Casey 1994).

In the period which is the focus of the study being proposed here, namely, 1982–1997, there was also an increased awareness internationally of the rights of people with disabilities. This awareness was heightened by the United Nations declaring 1981 as the *International Year of the Disabled Person* (Doenau 1984). The declaration signalled an international belief about accepting the basic rights of people with disabilities (Casey 1994). Viewed from a wider perspective, the period was also one of great change in education in general. Against this background, the push for greater access and opportunity for students with disabilities took place as economic rationalist governments attempted to restructure education in many Western countries (Goddard 1992; Clark *et al.* 1997). This restructuring of mainstream education produced, in turn, intense pressure to restructure education for students with disabilities.

Many of the international trends that emerged in Australia during the period 1982–1997 reflected very different attitudes to those which existed 50 years earlier (Gow 1989). People with disabilities began to be seen as consumers with equal rights. This, in turn, resulted in service providers extending and individualising services more than they had in the past. In this context, governments, system administrators and school administrators, along with teachers and parents, began to look critically at the educational provisions, facilities and infrastructures and to suggest improvements and alternatives (Clark *et al.* 1997). A worldwide educational argument gaining prominence during this 16-year period centred on the right of students with disabilities to be educated within regular school settings. Supporters of this practice, known variously as 'inclusion', 'mainstreaming' or 'integration' (Chalmers 1994; Thomas 1997), argued that all students, irrespective of the degree of sensory, physical or intellectual disability, have the right to learn in the most educationally enhancing environment.

Although there is evidence to suggest that students with disabilities were attending Catholic schools in WA as early as the 1940s, the first policy document that acknowledged the enrolment of such children, *Pupil Enrolment Policy and Practice* (CECWA 1983), was formulated only in 1983. This policy document demonstrated cognisance of the many initiatives in Catholic schools with regard to the enrolment and education of students with disabilities. However, it also recognised that there were many limitations in the education offered. Three issues in particular that concerned many people associated with Catholic schools in WA at this time were highlighted. These were as follows: the restricted availability of services to students with disabilities; an ignorance of the number, location and type of disability of the students in WA Catholic schools; and a lack of funding.

In the period that followed the release of *Pupil Enrolment Policy and Practice* (CECWA, 1983), many formal and informal changes in the organisation of services for students with intellectual and physical disabilities in WA Catholic schools took place. However, the official written policy with regard to such students was reformulated on just two occasions. In 1988, *Special Education Policy* (CECWA 1988) was produced, followed by *Students with Special Needs – The Enrolment and Integration of Students with Disabilities* (CECWA 1992) in 1992. Each of these two policy documents, along with the original document of 1983, constitute key focal points for engaging in an analysis of the policy of the CECWA with regard to students with disabilities during the period 1982–1997.

As the titles of the CECWA policy documents signify, CECWA policy with regard to students with disabilities underwent a gradual transformation between 1982 and 1997. The emphasis in the study proposed here, however, will extend beyond an analysis of these documents only. It will take the position that since policy is best thought of as a relational practice at all levels of the educational hierarchy (Fulcher 1989), the significance of the documents needs to be considered within a broader context which keeps three considerations in mind:

1 The first consideration relates to the need for an identification of the initial reasons behind the development of each of the policy documents.
2 The second consideration relates to the need for an investigation into the relation between the policy documents and what was actually occurring with regard to students with disabilities in Catholic schools in WA.
3 The third consideration relates to a need for an evaluation of how influential the documents were in affecting school change.

Overall, the notion is that such policy analyses of aspects of Australian education can contribute to an understanding of the relationship between schools, society, and the realisation of the human potential (Prunty 1984). Also, they can enable us to examine the links between government and bureaucratic policy and practice within educational institutions (Crump 1993).

Overview of the conceptual framework

In the last decade researchers have generated much literature on the issue of how policy should be examined and theoretically considered. Although Wildavsky (1979: 15) believes that 'it is more important to practise policy analysis than to spend time defining it', it is likely that research would lack direction without an agreed understanding of what is meant by policy. On this, Ranson (1996) believes that the idea of policy remains under-conceptualised and that education policy studies must focus on the policies themselves. He describes 'policy' in the following way:

> Policies are statements which are typically expressed both in utterance and in textual form. They have a distinctive and formal purpose for organisations and governments in codifying and publicising the values that are to inform future practice and thus encapsulate prescriptions for reform. Policies ... project images of the ideal (and) are thus oriented to change and action, providing public intent of transforming practice according to ideal values.
>
> (Ranson 1996: 265)

This approach is consistent with Beetham's (1987) contention that the formulation of public policy is an intrinsically political exercise. Therefore, as he sees it, one of the important reasons for organisations to clearly enunciate policy is to enable a struggle to take place between different interest groups as they contest ideas and resources (Ranson 1996).

Various theorists have tended to focus on specific aspects of policy. Foster and Harman (1992: 310–11), for example, distinguish between what they identify as two important aspects of policy work. The first of these is the collection of data that are needed to obtain an adequate picture of the past and the present with regard to a particular policy. Foster and Harman's second function of policy work (1992) is concerned with the efficient implementation of the policy decisions. In this regard, the ideas of Crump (1993: 15–23) are also informative. He describes eight models of policy which vary from the *rational* model, popularised in the 1950s, with an emphasis on the strong links between economic and social policy, to the *problem-solving* model, which is based on a premise that public policies are responses to, and sources of, problems. Crump concludes that while policy models are helpful, any one model struggles to accurately convey the policy process as it takes place in the real world. Crump (1993) also believes that a plurality of policy models that define policy as 'process' rather than 'product' are the most accurate in describing the cyclical nature of policy.

This, of course, is not to argue that focusing on process is a relatively new development. Over 20 years ago, Dye (1976: 1) considered the process aspects of policy models when he stated that a study of policy means 'finding out what governments do, why they do it, and what difference it makes'. More recently, Ham and Hill (1993: 11) argued that the main aim of policy analysis is 'to interpret the causes and consequences of government action, in particular the processes of policy formulation'. Ball (1994: 10) was even more explicit on this when he described policy as 'both text and action, words and deeds; it is what is enacted as well as what is intended'.

While the accommodation of process into models of policy analysis is to be welcomed, many models still do not reflect the fluid nature and considerable complexity of educational institutions. Nevertheless, there has been a strong focus in recent years on the acceptance that there are multiple, and often conflicting, influences on the policy process. Such a focus gives much attention to the role of individuals at the local level. In this regard, Ham and Hill (1993) offer a useful model of policy-making that combines the decisional top-down perspectives on policy with action-oriented perspectives. They settle on the term 'policy analysis' to describe policy studies because they believe that it assists in making the important distinction between analysis 'of' policy and analysis 'for' policy. They state:

> This distinction is important in drawing attention to policy analysis as an academic activity concerned primarily with advancing understanding and policy analysis as an applied activity concerned mainly with contributing to the solution of social problems.
>
> (Ham and Hill 1993: 23)

They argue that the policy debate by academics has intensified in the period since the 1960s, believing this has been due to 'studies which had originally developed out of the work of political scientists, economists and others (being) embraced by the emerging policy analysis perspective' (Ham and Hill 1993: 2). They then go on to compare and contrast various definitions of policy analysis. These include the relatively basic idea that the role of analysis is sometimes to locate problems where solutions might be tried (Wildavsky 1979). At other times it is simply concerned with the description and explanation of the causes and consequences of government action (Dye 1976).

Furthermore, Ham and Hill (1993) argue that by drawing on a range of disciplines, policy analysis is useful in interpreting the causes and consequences of government action. They also concur with Fulcher's (1989) idea of policy-making being very much a web of decisions when they state:

> ... a decision network, often of considerable complexity, may be involved in producing action, and a web of decisions taking place over a long period of time and extending far beyond the initial policy-making process, may form part of the network. A second aspect is that even at the policy-making level, policy is not usually expressed in a single decision.
>
> (Ham and Hill 1993: 12)

In addition, Ham and Hill (1993) and Hill (1997) have no doubt that the political agenda often means that analysis of policy is rarely value free. The fact that policy research is regularly funded by one of the parties with a vested interest in the outcome means that the beliefs and assumptions of the researcher inevitably influence the research.

Ranson (1996) has considered a great variety of policy analysis models in order to develop his own comprehensive model. In doing so, he has identified four major traditions of policy analysis, namely *pluralist, neo-marxist, new right*, and *neo-pluralism*, and has identified these in terms of how they have emerged chronologically. The *pluralist* tradition, which emerged in the post-Second World War era and remained dominant until the 1970s, is one based on partnerships between different tiers of government and the stakeholders within the administration. However, although partnerships are a key part of this tradition, this is not to say that the power is evenly distributed between the various groups (Ranson 1996). The weakness of a *pluralist* tradition is that it assumes equality within the partnership. Another way of putting this is to argue that the pluralist tradition is not fully cognisant of the power wielded by the state in either policy formulation or implementation (Ranson 1996).

In attempting to address the lack of interest on the part of the *pluralist* tradition in understanding the state's role in policy-making, the *neo-marxist* tradition emerged in the 1970s. This tradition is one that recognises the dominant role of the state in the system of education (Prunty 1984; Ranson 1996). During the 1980s, a new tradition yet again, namely *new right*, emerged (Ranson 1996). This tradition recognised that policy formulation was a messy and complex process (Ball 1990). Moreover, the *new right* tradition argued that the *neo-marxist* understanding of policy was too simplistic and did not take into account all of the complex elements involved in formulating policy. The *new right* tradition, on the other hand, recognised that it is often difficult, if not impossible, to control or predict the effects of policy. On this, Ball (1990: 3) states:

> Policy-making in a modern, complex plural society like Britain is unwieldy and complex. It is often unscientific and irrational, whatever the claims of the policy-makers to the contrary.

It follows from this that the reasons for formulating a certain policy may be lost or appropriated very differently to what is intended by the policy.

A fourth tradition of policy formulation, namely, *neo-pluralism*, emerged in the 1990s. The main thrust of the *neo-pluralist* tradition is that although partnerships are a focal part of any policy formulation, the state is the most powerful player and, through its power, is capable of wielding a tremendously strong influence. Therefore, although the results of policy can result in very different outcomes to those originally intended, Ranson (1996) believes that for any effective analysis of policy there must be a strong focus on the state. On this he goes on as follows:

> While policies, like texts, cannot be controlled at the level of discourse, they can, unlike texts, be regulated at the operational level of practice. Although age-weighted pupil formulas may have allowed much interpretation at the level of discourse, in practice their implementation is tightly regulated at the level of local discretion.
>
> (Ranson 1996: 263)

He then draws from each of these four traditions to develop a comprehensive framework for conceptualising educational policy. In doing this, he identifies some important dimensions. Firstly, he states that the researcher must decide whether the policy process focuses on a particular issue or is part of a much bigger question encompassing a larger part of the organisation. Secondly, he states that understanding the policy process requires cognisance of the 'moments' of policy, namely *generation, formulation, implementation* and *evaluation*. Furthermore, the researcher is required to discover if and how each of these 'moments' interrelate, as well as discover the information and resources available to the participants in the policy process. Finally, he argues that for effective policy analysis to occur, an understanding of the organisation's control and regulations are needed. This enables the researcher to identify whether the policy change arose as part of a 'policy cycle' or whether it was prompted by another decision or event. It also enables the participants in the policy process, and the type of management of the organisation, to be identified.

Ranson's policy model is most comprehensive. Accordingly, it was deemed an appropriate model to underpin the research plan being proposed here. The non-linear nature of the model also calls for a qualitative approach to research. Such an approach tends towards the descriptive rather than the numerical. In other words, data would include field notes and interview transcripts rather than questionnaires and statistics. Qualitative research is also concerned as much with process as with product, and the setting of the study is usually the natural one, such as a school. Furthermore, it focuses not just on assessing what occurs, but also explaining 'why'.

In order to understand the reasons for a particular phenomenon, qualitative researchers believe it is crucial to explore the perspectives which participants have of aspects of their lives. Capturing these perspectives accurately allows the qualitative researcher to generate a theory about what is being studied. The particular qualitative approach deemed appropriate for the research project being proposed here and underpinned by Ranson's approach to policy studies, is that based on interpretivism. Interpretivist studies assume that people act for a variety of reasons. These reasons are based on the meanings the people have of certain others, events and 'things'. Proponents of the interpretivist viewpoint share the goal of understanding the complex world of lived experience from the point of view of those who live it (Schwandt 1994). Interpretivism is based on a belief that social actors construct a world of lived reality by attaching specific meanings to local situations. Interpretivist procedures and practices give structure and meaning to everyday life. This is because interpretivists believe that knowledge is always local, situated in a local culture and embedded in organisational sites (Denzin and Lincoln 1994).

Underpinning interpretivism are Blumer's (1969) three central propositions of symbolic interactionism:

1   Human beings act toward 'things' on the basis of the meanings that the 'things' have for them.
2   This attribution of meaning to objects through symbols is a continuous process. The symbols are gestures, signs, language and anything else that may convey meanings.
3   The meanings are handled in, and modified through, an interpretative process used by the person in dealing with the things he or she encounters. (Blumer 1969: 2)

These three propositions shaped initial thinking regarding the nature of the guiding questions to be asked in this proposed study. These guiding questions have been developed in terms of understandings of policy at the 'process' stage, at the 'content' stage, at the 'output' stage and at the 'evaluation' stage (Hogwood and Gunn 1981). Also, they will be focused on the three major CECWA policy documents pertaining to students with disabilities in Catholic schools in the period 1982–1997, namely *Pupil Enrolment Policy and Practice* (CECWA 1983), *Special Education Policy* (CECWA 1988) and *Students with Special Needs – The Enrolment and Integration of Students with Disabilities* (CECWA 1992).

In summary, the following set of guiding questions will be posed around each of the above-mentioned documents:

1   In the period leading up to the emergence of each major policy document, what were the different perspectives that the various stakeholders had with regard to the education of students with disabilities in WA Catholic schools?

2 What were the characteristics of the CECWA policy in each of its major policy documents on the education of students with disabilities in WA Catholic schools?

3 Which stakeholders dominated – and why – with regard to the eventual written policies?

4 During the implementation phase following the publication of each main policy document, what, if any, were the changes in the stakeholders' perspectives of CECWA policy with regard to the education of students with disabilities in WA Catholic schools?

However, it is also recognised that as the study unfolds, other questions are likely to suggest themselves. This is why the above are outlined as guiding questions rather than as specific research questions. The manner in which these guiding questions will be pursued through the use of particular data-gathering methods will now be considered.

Data-gathering methods

Two of the three methods central to most qualitative studies, namely, document analysis and interviews (Taylor and Bogdan 1984), will be used in the study. The third approach, participant observation, involves entering the field of the participants with the hope of establishing open relationships. Due to the retrospective nature of this study, it will not possible to use participant observation strategies to collect data.

The interviews

Interviews will be used to gather data to assist in formulating hypotheses pertaining to policy formulation. They will be semi-structured interviews. By semi-structured interviews is meant a 'face-to-face encounter between the researcher and participants' perspective on their lives, experiences or situations as expressed in their own words' (Taylor and Bogdan 1984: 76). Semi-structured interviews allow 'greater depth than is the case with other methods of data collection' (Cohen and Manion 1989: 308).

In conducting interviews, the researcher will take cognisance of Kerlinger's (1970) point that while the purpose of the research determines the questions asked, their content, sequence and wording are completely in the hands of the interviewer. Accordingly, the interviews will be carried out in a flexible manner. However, while being focused by the guiding questions already noted, neither the wording nor the ordering of specific questions to be asked will be fixed. Trial interviews will be conducted with people known to the researcher in order to refine questioning techniques and question structure prior to the formal interviews beginning.

The aim of the semi-structured interview format is to ensure an open, non-threatening atmosphere and to create a relaxed atmosphere for discussion rather than that usually associated with more formal 'question and answer' interview sessions (Taylor and Bogdan 1984). The first contact with each participant will be through a letter outlining the purpose of the interview and an abbreviated copy of this proposal will be included. Those to be interviewed later in the process will receive additional information in the form of a restatement of the proposal as it evolves. Following the initial letter, personal or telephone contact will be made with each person to set an interview date. It will be made clear to each interviewee that the principles of anonymity and confidentiality are to be observed at all times.

Each participant will be informed that the interview will have two parts. The first part will be an explanation of the study. The participant will be invited to discuss any aspects of the study during this time. The second part will be the semi-structured interview itself. The time and place of each interview will be determined by each participant. Every interview will be audio-recorded, fully transcribed from the tape, and taken back to the participant. Each participant will then be invited to make additions, alterations, or deletions, with any changes being transferred to the original. The interviews will be conducted with a series of people defined as having specific knowledge regarding the various aspects of the relevant policies under study, particularly those who motivated, developed and implemented policy during the period in question. This group includes the Directors of Catholic Education in WA, members of the CECWA, senior consultants, Catholic Bishops, principals of primary schools, primary school teachers associated with the education of students with disabilities, and parents.

Document to be studied

Appropriate documentation will also provide data for this study. Crump (1993) believes that analysing documents is useful because it:

> ... allows an identification of the spaces, gaps, accidents and missed opportunities in policy-making and, therefore, to make some comment on the role of the state in this context. This strategy should thus avoid rhetoric of solutions as well as avoiding a deterministic pessimism.
>
> (Crump 1993: 33)

Documents on Catholic education in WA from 1982 to 1997 are one source of data. In particular, the policies released by the CECWA, entitled *Pupil Policy and Practice* (CECWA 1983), *Special Education Policy* (CECWA 1988), and *Students with Special Needs – The Enrolment and Integration of Students with Disabilities* (CECWA 1992) are key documents. The minutes of CECWA meetings, reports, press releases and other public documents will also be perused and analysed. Also to be examined are a series of reports released in the 16-year period by both government and non-government organisations. The *Report of the Committee of Inquiry into Education in Western Australia* (Beazley 1984) and *The Education of Students with Disabilities and Specific Learning Difficulties* (Shean 1993) are two examples of state government-sponsored reviews which have had a profound influence on the education of students with disabilities in public schools. Such reports also had some influence on the policies with regard to students with disabilities in the Catholic school sector in WA.

Data analysis

The process of data analysis is an ongoing process in qualitative research and can take place by developing, testing and changing of propositions through:

> ... the process of systematically searching and arranging the interview transcripts, fieldnotes and other materials ... to increase your own under-standing of them and to enable you to present what you have discovered to others.
>
> (Bogdan and Biklen 1992: 153)

The constant comparative method of data analysis will be used in this study to generate and verify theory (Glaser and Strauss 1967). This method will be used by the researcher simultaneously to code and analyse data in order to generate propositions (Taylor and Bogdan 1984). As the data collection progresses, these propositions will be refined, discarded or fully developed. This method of data analysis offers a systematic approach to collecting, organising, and analysing data from the empirical world in question.

Analysis will progress through the stage of open coding. This type of coding is described by Taylor and Bogdan (1984: 126) as follows:

> ... the researcher simultaneously codes and analyses data in order to develop concepts. By continually comparing specific incidents in the data, the researcher refines these concepts, identifies their properties, explores their relationships to one another, and integrates them into a coherent theory.

During open coding, the data are broken down into concepts (Strauss and Corbin 1994). These concepts are then closely examined and compared for similarities.

The first stage of the analytical process will necessitate gathering all of the data, namely, the documents and the interview transcripts, and organising it chronologically. The analysis of each interview will begin with its transcription. After the transcribing process, the interview will be re-read several times to identify the major categories contained in the transcript. Data will be simultaneously read thoroughly and appropriate notes, comments, observations and queries will be made. Each of the transcripts and interviews will be coded on a line-by-line or paragraph-by-paragraph basis. The aim of this exercise is to produce concepts that fit the data. Code notes will be written throughout the data analysis, mainly in the right-hand margins of the interview transcript sheets (Schatzman and Strauss 1973).

Cross-interview analysis will then be undertaken to locate those concepts relating to phenomena which occur regularly within the interviews and to make comparisons with those concepts that have already emerged from the other documents. A number of substantive concepts are likely to be identified. Referring back to the data and making comparisons should refine the coding of the substantive concepts. In this way, concepts underpinning most of the data will be developed and the research themes and propositions generated will be refined until they are ready to be integrated into an exposition.

Chapter 8

Life history studies

I became interested in the possibility of relating interpretivism to life history studies through a major research project in which I was involved with my colleague, Professor Clive Dimmock. Our specific focus of research was on trying to account for why some high school principals were successful managers of change within the context of the educational restructuring movement taking place in Australia in the 1990s. Exploring the concept of the 'life history' and associated life history research approaches presented fruitful avenues for pursuit in this regard. We recognised that biographical and life history approaches in educational studies are not new. Thirty years ago Abbs (1976) demonstrated the value of autobiographical approaches in teacher education. Later, Evetts (1989: 89) argued that life history accounts and biographies had become 'an increasingly popular source of sociological data'. She went on to highlight Plummer's (1983) contention that in sociology, research which highlights the actual human subject must provide the necessary counterbalance to positivistic emphases on structure and systems.

Having canvassed the field we settled on the edited topical life history approach as holding out much potential for the study of principals who were promoting restructuring initiatives in the areas of curriculum, teaching and learning. This, as we saw it, could allow us to take one step further Ribbins and Sherratt's (1992: 153) proposal that studies of the principalship can benefit from adopting a biographical and autobiographical approach. What we sought was not only to develop accounts of schools and the role of the principals within them which integrate the perspectives of both the principals and the researchers, but also to examine the socializing influences relevant to the formation of the principal over the full life experience. Such an approach, as Sikes *et al.* (1985: 13) put it, 'is holistic, that is to say, concerned with a teacher's total life and career, and not just a segment or aspect of it'. These authors concluded by arguing that 'for a full understanding of teacher interests and motives, we need as complete a biographical picture as we can acquire' (Sikes *et al.* 1985: 13).

A number of cases for adopting this approach in studying the lives of teachers have been made over the last 25 years. Waring (1979) argued that an understanding of curriculum innovation is not possible without a history of context and she alerted us to the importance of considering the extent to which the interpretation and execution of curriculum briefs reflect the background and personalities of the curriculum organizers chosen. Goodson (1992: 6), in examining the literature on teacher socialization, also made a convincing case by highlighting the fact that the period of pre-service training and early in-service teaching has been designated as the most formative socializing influence. An alternative tradition, he argued, has insisted that the situation is far more complicated than this:

> Many studies in the 1970s and 1980s have focused on the teachers' own experience as pupils which is seen not only as important as the training period but in many cases more important. One way to follow up on this alternative tradition in teacher socialization research requires that we examine those socializing influences relevant to the formation of the teacher over the full life experience.

Elsewhere Goodson (1991: 144) has also argued as follows: 'There are critical incidents in the teachers' lives and specifically in their work which may crucially affect perception and practice'. More recently, he has again articulated this position in a major work published with Sikes (Goodson and Sikes 2001).

In conclusion, a consideration of such positions led us to develop the following proposal where an explicit link is established between the symbolic interactionist theoretical position within the interpretivist paradigm and the concept of life history in order to develop a specific life history research approach appropriate for investigating our substantive area of interest. The outcome was a book entitled *Innovative School Principals and Restructuring: Life History Portraits of Successful Managers of Change* (Dimmock and O'Donoghue 1997).

Project title

School restructuring initiatives and principals' biographies: An edited topical life history study.

Research aim

Restructuring of school systems has been taking place in much of the world. It is widely acknowledged that the part which the school principal can play in managing associated processes is a crucial factor in ensuring their successful implementation. At the same time, however, research on the principalship has failed to keep pace with this changing context. Accordingly, there is a need for studies aimed at understanding the various aspects of principals' work as part of current restructuring.

The focus of restructuring research to date has largely been on the administrative dimension of the phenomenon rather than on initiatives aimed at improving teaching and learning, the core activities of schooling. There is a growing acceptance internationally that there is a need to address this imbalance. Such research also needs to take cognisance of various contextual conditions. Thus, while the proposed research will focus on the principalship within the unique Western Australian (WA) context, it will also complement the research of those who are examining other contexts and make a contribution to studies aimed at illuminating similarities and differences on the wider international stage.

The specific aim of the proposed study is to adopt the edited topical life history research approach to generate theory regarding the relationship between innovative WA principals' activities aimed at improving teaching and learning and their life histories. A number of cases have been made for adopting this approach in studying the lives of teachers (Goodson 1992). These cases can also be made for the study of school principals.

Significance

In the immediate post-Second World War period, leadership studies focused on searching for traits which apparently successful leaders, including principals, displayed. The value in this research was that it led in the 1960s and 1970s to the emergence and widespread acceptance of two dimensions of leadership recognised by Blake and Mouton (1964), namely, task- and person-orientations. From this was spawned a host of theories about leadership styles. Most of these theories were developed with corporate leaders in mind, but they soon proved a rich source of ideas for application to the school principalship. Concurrently, the 1960s and 1970s witnessed an expansive literature, largely of a sociological nature, which focused on the roles that principals were expected to play. The research agenda of the 1980s shifted again, focusing strongly on the conception of the principal as instructional leader. This thrust of principal leadership research aligned closely with the emergence in the late 1970s and early 1980s of the school effectiveness movement (Purkey and Smith 1985). Principals who were instructional leaders were recognised as crucial agents in the effectiveness of their schools.

In Australia, the work of Chapman (1987) has been noteworthy in highlighting the relationship between the changing nature of the principalship and the restructuring context. As the 1980s drew to a close, two further developments in research on the principalship were discernible, both of which aligned with a shift in research emphasis from school effectiveness to school improvement and restructuring. One was the distinction between transactional and transformational leadership which highlighted the growing importance of leaders as managers of change, itself an endemic feature of improvement and restructuring; the other was the emergence of a socio-psychological oriented approach exemplified in cognitive studies of principals (Hallinger *et al.* 1993).

In evaluating the body of literature on the principalship at least four major trends are identifiable. Firstly, much of it is prescriptive with surprisingly few sound empirical studies of principals. Secondly, a significant amount of the empirical work which exists has been generated using research methods and conceptual frameworks in the positivist tradition. Thirdly, the studies tend to be of a general statistical nature dealing with samples of populations rather than being individual case studies. Fourthly, research on the principalship has tended to ignore both particular contextual conditions and the holistic standpoint which would take cognisance of the dynamic between the principal and the particular environment.

The research context

The phenomenon of educational restructuring is taking place in much of the world, with deregulated, decentralised systems replacing central planning, control and supervision. This change is placing expectations on schools either to become self-managed, or to function under devolved authority from their central offices. These conditions have led to the development of the notions of school-based management, school-based budgeting, and the community management of schools (Lawton 1992). The process can assume different forms in different contexts, having been enacted at the national level in the United Kingdom and New Zealand, at the state level in Australia and at the district level in Canada. It has also involved significant curriculum changes in some countries.

Two related policy initiatives have been shaping change in Australian schools. The first centres on the restructuring of school systems and involves a shift from centralised governance to decentralised school-based management. The focus is on change at the whole-school level, primarily affecting governance, management and administration, rather than classroom activities of teaching and learning (Chadbourne and Clarke 1994). In the early stages of restructuring in Australia it was argued that such macro initiatives which involve a shift from centralised governance of decentralised school-based management would, on their own, lead to the achievement of enhanced learning for all students. However, while changes in the administrative and organisational contexts were targeted to create an environment conducive to improving teaching and learning, micro reforms were also necessary to bring about such improvement. Accordingly, the second policy initiative shaping change in Australian schools concerns school restructuring aimed at introducing more flexible, responsive and student-oriented service delivery by targeting change in work organization, pedagogical practices and learning processes.

The National Project on Quality Teaching and Learning (NPQTL) (1993) was launched by the Federal government in February 1991 to restructure the teaching profession, deal with low teacher morale, and improve the quality of teaching and learning. The National Schools Project, whose aim was to investigate how changes to work organization could lead to improved outcomes in student learning and school leadership, was initiated in association with the NPQTL. This project recognised the crucial part principals have to play in school restructuring aimed at the improvement of teaching and learning. At the same time, while there is no shortage of advice to principals on the role they should play in this regard, relatively little of it has been based on contemporary studies. This is not to deny the existence of a significant body of literature on the principalship. Rather, research on the principalship has failed to keep pace with the changing restructuring context.

Ribbins and Sherrat (1992: 160) pointed to one way forward in outlining a research agenda involving an in-depth longitudinal study of the headship. This was close to being an action research project, with the role of the experienced researcher approximating that of a consultant. A challenge now for other researchers is not only to adopt the approach of Ribbins and Sherratt, but also to adopt other approaches in a range of leadership and other contexts. The work of Leithwood *et al.* (1994) can be seen as an attempt to meet the challenge through their pioneering research on principals' problem-solving capacities.

This research proposal details a plan to meet the challenge of Ribbins and Sherratt in three respects. Firstly, the approach is that of the edited topical life history. Secondly, the project focuses on principals who are considered by educational administrators, peers and staff to be undertaking adventurous change programmes to improve the quality of teaching and learning in their schools. Finally, the context of the project is Western Australia (WA).

The research plan

The aim of the study proposed here is to contribute to the existing knowledge base by using the edited topical life history approach to generate theory regarding the relationship between principals' life histories and the initiatives they are taking to improve curriculum, teaching and learning in their schools. The theoretical framework underpinning such a research approach is now outlined.

Theoretical framework

This proposal highlights the need at a time of educational restructuring to develop in the case of principals a tradition which owes its origins in educational research to a movement of the late 1970s which 'fully opened up the question of how teachers saw their work and their lives' (Goodson 1992: 3–4). Accordingly, when initially deciding to study the work and effect of a number of principals in WA who are undertaking change programmes to improve the quality of curriculum, teaching and learning in their schools, particular consideration was given to the need to generate a richness of data. This, it was felt, would be necessary so that patterns which exhibited the interaction between the creativity of the principals as agents and the structure within which they operated could, if they existed, be identified. Thus, the study will take its theoretical impetus from that stream of qualitative research known as symbolic interactionism.

Meltzer *et al.* (1975: 1) summarize symbolic interactionism as being:

> ... the interaction that takes place among the various minds and meanings that characterize human societies. It refers to the fact that social interaction rests upon a taking of oneself (self-objectification) and others (taking the role of the other) into account.

They go on to argue that the most basic element in this image of human beings is the idea that the individual and society are inseparable units; that while it may be possible to separate the units analytically, the underlying assumption is that a complete understanding of either one demands a complete understanding of the other. They then highlight the following:

> In the interactionist image, ... the behaviour of men and women is 'caused' not so much by forces within themselves (instincts, drives, needs, etc) but by what lies in between, a reflective and socially derived interpretation of the internal and external stimuli that are present.
>
> (Metzen *et al.* 1975: 2)

Ritzer (1983: 301) developed the position of Blumer, one of the originators of modern symbolic interactionism, as follows:

> To Blumer, behaviorism and structural functionalism both tended to focus on factors (for example, external stimuli and norms) that cause behavior. As far as Blumer was concerned, both ignored the crucial process by which actors endow the forces acting upon them, as well as their own behaviors, with meaning ... In addition to behaviorism, several other types of psychological reductionism troubled Blumer. For example, he criticised those who seek to explain human action by

relying on conventional notions of the concept of 'attitude' ... what is important is not the attitude as an internalized tendency, but the defining process through which the actor comes to define his act. Blumer also singled out for criticism those who focus on conscious and unconscious motives. He was particularly irked by their view that actors are impelled by independent, mentalistic impulses over which they are supposed to have no control.

Ritzer concluded by arguing that Blumer was also opposed to sociologistic theories that view individual behaviour as determined by large-scale external forces. In short, he was opposed to any theory that ignores the processes by which actors construct meaning.

Woods (1993: 450) makes the following case which would appear to clarify the connection between the theoretical position of symbolic interactionism and the life history method of research:

> The present has a living connection with the past. Current meanings and interpretations are shown to have grown and developed over time. In tracing teachers' own histories, we acquire a fuller, deeper and richer understanding of them. Examining the interrelationships of incident, thought, people and place that underpin the current person provides a context that is just as relevant as, if not more than, the prevailing social, institutional and situational.

We find an illustration of this process in Aspinwall's (1992: 254) account of her study of one teacher's professional life:

> It was impossible for Sarah to speak of her professional life without referring to her personal experiences. Significant figures and incidents from her childhood, her time at university studying politics, her children's own unhappy time starting school were all deeply influential in her decision to enter teaching and to her image of the kind of teacher she aspired to be. Her life experiences and her personality combined to give her an idealistic and demanding vision of teaching and teachers. This made her present colleagues particularly hard for her to understand and work with.

Minichiello *et al.* (1990: 152) highlight the arguments of Schwartz and Jacobs (1979) and Plummer (1983) that there is 'a fundamental affinity between the central tenets of symbolic interactionism and life history research'. Drawing from these arguments, they go on to state that there are three theoretical assumptions which are common to both traditions. The first assumption is that life is viewed as concrete experience. In other words, there is no point in studying abstractions of individuals or of social life. As Cooley (1956:

67) has put it, it is important to recognize that 'a separate individual is an abstraction unknown to experience, and so likewise is society when regarded as something apart from individuals'. Minichiello *et al.* (1990: 152) go on to argue that the central consequence of being concerned with life as concrete experience is that, as Plummer (1983: 54) has put it, 'in every case of study, we must acknowledge that experiencing individuals can never be isolated from their functioning bodies and their constraining social worlds'.

The second assumption highlighted by Minichiello *et al.* (1990) is that life is regarded as an ever-emerging relativistic perspective. In other words, human beings experience the world through their definitions of it. They quote Plummer (1983: 56) as follows: 'The reality shifts with a person's life and people act towards things on the basis of their understandings, irrespective of the "objective" nature of those things'. They conclude that if one accepts this theoretical assumption, then the most central and fundamental source of knowledge is the personal document, the life history which elicits 'the sense of reality' that human beings hold about their own worlds (Minichiello *et al.* 1990: 153).

The third assumption highlighted by Minichiello *et al.* (1990: 152) as being common to the symbolic interactionist and life history research traditions is that life is viewed as inherently marginal and ambiguous. This is tied to the two previous assumptions. They continue as follows:

> If we have taken one person's subjective reality seriously in a life history, and then considered it in relation to another person's, then there is always the possibility that ambiguity and incongruity will become evident in their definitions of the same situations.

They conclude that the message to the life history researcher is to move away from studying abstractions and get at the particular, the detailed and the experiential, thus allowing one to grasp the ambiguities and inevitability of different perspectives.

At this point it is instructive to outline Goodson's (1992: 6) crucial distinction between the life story and the life history. He elaborates on the distinction thus:

> The life story is the 'story we tell about our life'; the life history is a collaborative venture, reviewing a wider range of evidence. The life story teller and another (or others) collaborate in developing this wider account by interviews and discussions and by scrutiny of texts and contexts. The life history is the life story located within its historical context.

He concludes by reminding us that while a great deal of valuable work on teachers' stories or narratives was carried out in the 1980s by academics, much of it did not embrace contextual or intercontextual analysis.

With regard to the life history, as distinct from the life story, Allport (1942) and Denzin (1989) distinguished between the complete or comprehensive life history and the topical life history. The complete or comprehensive life history is concerned with all aspects of the individual's life from birth. It is usually a long and complex account which focuses on the overall flow of life of an individual. In contrast, the topical life history focuses on only one phase, aspect or issue of the individual's life. Also, the life history, whether a complete or comprehensive life history or a topical life history, may be edited with comments and analysis by the researcher, either interspersed with the narrative, or in a combination which includes introductory passages and analytical commentary after the narrative, or incorporated in a combined form. At the same time, as Denzin (1989: 217) points out, all three forms contain three central elements: the person's own story of his or her life; the social and cultural situation to which the subject and others see the subject responding; and the sequence of past experiences and situations in the subject's life.

The life histories to be developed in relation to the case studies proposed here will be edited topical life histories. The decision that they should be 'edited' was made in the light of Allport's (1942: 78) advice that while unique styles of expression, including argot and colloquial phrasing, should remain unedited, editing for the sake of clarity or to remove repetitious material would seem justified. The 'topic' is the interaction between current restructuring initiatives and the principals' innovations in curriculum, the teaching and learning taking place in their schools. The participants to be selected and forms of data collection and analysis to be utilized in the study in order to construct such edited topical life histories will now be considered.

The selection of the participants

An initial list of principals to be considered as possible participants in the study was drawn up on the basis of their reputations for attempting to promote adventurous change programmes to improve the quality of curriculum, teaching and learning in their schools. The present researchers became aware of these reputations over the period of a year through the consistency of reporting by district superintendents and central office administrators, and through evaluation reports by academics, informal contacts with consultants and hearsay from teachers and parents in the schools. Over a period of time corroborative evidence from these multiple sources emerged to facilitate the construction of a final list of principals. Following this, volunteers to participate were sought. In this regard, cognizance was taken of procedures outlined by Woods (1985a). He argued that in seeking volunteers for life history studies there is always an element of pressure, no matter how courteous and non-committal, in the direct approach. He then recommended that one set out a market-stall to groups of teachers and invite offers; 'there is an immediate sense of negotiation in the "offer", for, in the interests of motivation, they should be allowed to work their personal interests into the general framework of the research' (Woods 1985a: 14–15). The 'market-stall' would detail the broad aims of the research; the principles of the method; possible outcomes for education; possible outcomes for the teacher personally, 'such as greater understanding of self and career, and an aid to morale'. The latter, he says:

> ... may derive from knowledge of varieties of careers and career planning, and the general contextualising of one's own, which might touch on feelings of success and failure, and general job satisfaction. Above all, such a study promises to promote knowledge of self. As Stenhouse (1975, p. 144) argues, 'The outstanding characteristic of the extended professional is a capacity for autonomous professional self-development through systematic self-study'.
>
> (Woods 1985a: 15)

Finally, the 'market-stall' would also detail possible outcomes for the researcher and a statement of guarantees, such as anonymity at all times, respect and protection of privacy, and a teacher's right to correct or withhold transcripts.

From the principals who volunteered, six participants, three males and three females, have already been selected for this study. The selection was influenced by a desire to cast widely for a variety of perspectives, rather than to select a random sample, or choose a sample that would be representative of a total population. At the same time, a gender balance is reflected in the selection. Diversity is also to be found in the school catchment areas, whose socioeconomic status ranges from middle and higher income urban populations to lower income urban and rural communities.

Data collection and analysis

Data will be gathered and analysed concurrently in three stages.

Stage 1

In this stage, descriptive data will be gathered about each school, including its location, its history and the social background of its pupils. The purpose in generating such data is to assist in portraying the context within which each principal is working. Interviews will then be conducted with each principal separately. These interviews will be aimed at uncovering the principals' perspectives on what they have been doing to improve the quality of curriculum, teaching and learning in their schools, how they have been going about promoting such innovations, and why they feel they have been promoting them.

The semi-structured in-depth interview method (Taylor and Bogdan 1984: 76) will be utilized because it is concerned with creating the environment to encourage participants to discuss their lives and experiences in free-flowing, open-ended discussions. Also, it enables the researcher to interpret their views. In conducting the interviews, general principles as outlined by Spradley (1979) and Measor (1985: 63–73) will be followed. These include the following: having a clear purpose, which is made apparent to the participant; explaining why particular questions are being asked; using clear meaningful language; asking descriptive, structural and contrast questions; using open-ended questions to elicit rich qualitative responses; avoiding leading questions; framing the same questions in different time dimensions; using effective probing to obtain further elaboration, explanation and clarification; using cross-checks to investigate possible exaggerations and distortions; allowing the participant to do most of the talking; being non-judgemental and being sensitive to the participant's situation. Rogers' (1951) categories of intervention – evaluative, interpretative, reflective, supportive and probing – should also prove helpful in this regard.

The initial interview with each participant is likely to last approximately two hours. An *aide-memoire* (Burgess 1984), or semi-structured interview guide, will be developed around the following headings to enable the participants to frame their thoughts on the improvement of the quality of curriculum, teaching and learning in their schools as part of current restructuring: goals and objectives; enabling factors; constraining factors; dilemmas; stresses and stressors; actions taken; future directions; and feelings in retrospect about the whole process. However, neither the wording nor the ordering of the questions will be fixed. Furthermore, the participants will be given the *aide-memoire* prior to the interview in order to give them sufficient time to reflect on the headings. The adoption of such a procedure, it is felt, will facilitate the generation of both a quantity and quality of data which would be unlikely to emerge if reliance was to be placed on more immediate responses. Furthermore, because school restructuring matters are complex it is felt that the principals will need time to give due consideration to the questions they will be asked. In this way, the subtleties of events and meanings can be explored and captured.

Cognizant of Goetz and Le Compte's (1982: 41) argument that 'the optimum guard against threats to internal reliability' may be the presence of more than one researcher, the interviews with five of the six principals will be conducted jointly by two experienced interviewers so that later, during analysis, they can discuss the meaning of the participants' words until agreement is achieved. As themes arise, they will be pursued with the participants in 'a lengthy conversation piece' (Simons 1982: 37). In fact, the term 'conversation' is probably a much more appropriate term for the process than 'interview'. As Aspinwall (1992: 251) argues, the term 'interview' cannot convey the empathy and interest necessary to the process.

The conversations will be tape-recorded with the participants' consent. While tape-recording, the interviewers will also take notes. Woods (1985a: 20) has described the purpose of such note-taking as follows:

> These are rather like the rough notes made during ethnographic fieldwork, when one is being assailed by a torrent of data. The cryptic jottings made at the time are sufficient to stir the memory later, when one can record the full data or impression at length. Now the tape recorder may capture what is said. But it cannot capture fleeting thoughts and impressions, as something the teacher says prompts first this thought and then that – the second invariably displacing the first from memory. The briefest of notes can aid recall.

In reading over one's notes along with the transcribed interviews one should be able to identify points on which one wishes the participant to elaborate and points which one wishes the participant to clarify. This elaboration and clarification will take place with the participants for modification until they become accepted by them as representative of their position (Lincoln and Guba 1985: 314–16). Again, this process will be guided by a procedure outlined by Woods (1985a: 21):

> Initial conversations have to be followed up. In general, the points to look out for are of three kinds. (a) Corrective: These include inconsistencies, non sequiturs, omissions, lack of balance, implausibility, a too 'cut and dried' or 'black and white' account ... (b) Checking and in-filling: a copy of the transcript is returned to the teacher and he is asked to comment. Is he happy with it? Does it adequately represent his views? Does it say what he means to say? ... (c) Progressive: these are hints that are let fall of possible richness of data in areas according with the themes of the research.

In some cases, this will mean follow-up interviews after the initial one. Each of these interviews is likely to last approximately two hours.

Throughout all of the interviews in this and subsequent phases, cognizance will be taken of Langness and Frank's (1981: 34) contention that 'the key to successful anthropological fieldwork and also to successful life history taking is rapport'. At all times, the aim of the interviewers will be to be friendly and objective outsiders and to be cautious, diplomatic, persevering and patient. They will also seek to be good listeners, trying not to interrupt and using body language and short expressions to indicate that they are 'interestedly quiet' (Burgess 1982). The conversations will be conducted, where possible, in 'ordinary' teacher discourse. At the end of Stage 1 of the research, the total set of transcribed material will be analysed following the procedures outlined by Marton (1988: 15 5), with utterances in the transcripts being brought together into categories on the basis of their similarities and categories being differentiated from one another in terms of their variance.

Stage 2

The next stage in the research is to conduct semi-structured interviews with the participants on their life histories. The decision to engage in this aspect of the research following Stage 1, rather than the other way around, has been influenced by Langness and Frank's (1981: 39) argument that the taking of an adequate and reliable life history 'involves a degree of intimacy with the informant and a knowledge of the community as well, that comes only with exceptionally good rapport'. They go on to advise not to attempt a life history until one has known the person and been in the field for some time. The nature of the data gathering undertaken in Stage 1 will facilitate such a development.

Three weeks before the first life history interview the participants will each be given another *aide-memoire* so that they can have time to reflect on the themes, begin the process of recall and organize their recollections in a chronological sequence. The *aide-memoire* which will be developed for this occasion will be strongly influenced by Lancy's (1993: 204) suggestions. It will centre on the participants' family life, including their role as spouse and parent; personal school history, especially details of their professional training; their relationship with significant others, parents and favourite teachers; their higher education, including institutions attended, subjects taken, likes and dislikes, influential lecturers, and significant events at college; a sense of their daily routines and life-styles; the nature of the schools and the classroom environments in which they taught; the characteristics and backgrounds of the students they taught, especially regarding class and ethnicity; a sense of the climate of the schools within which they taught and the prevailing teaching ethos; classroom routines in which they engaged, including the use of prepared curricula, grouping arrangements, management strategies and the predominant instructional mode; professional development activities undertaken and recreational activities.

The adoption of a set of headings for the *aide-memoire* reflects the approach of Lemert (1951: 445–6) in his study of the life history of deviants. The contention is that those headings proposed by Lancy (1993: 204) are broad enough to be appropriate in investigating the lives of individual school principals. However, they will also be accompanied by a consideration of such factors as social class, religion and social and political climate. As Pollard (1980) argues, sensitively handled and portrayed, the influences of these can be seen in the acted-out life and the formulating self. The intention overall is to generate data sufficiently rich to construct the sort of portrait which, as Plummer (1983: 69) puts it, would enable us 'to perceive the intersection of the life history of human beings with the history of their society'. The headings of the *aide-memoire*, along with the broader headings of social class, religion, and social and political climate, can also be seen as constituting a set of uniform standards so that as each new case is developed comparisons can be made across them.

Woods (1985a: 19) makes the same point when he argues that the 'danger of reductionism and atomism should be guarded against from the beginning'. Quoting Dollard (1935), he states that this can be done in a number of ways, notably by situating personal and career developments within relevant frameworks, such as social class, ethnicity, gender or generation, and within the prevailing socioeconomic circumstances; and by focusing upon the culture of the primary groups within an individual's biography. In order to probe these issues it will be necessary for the researchers to familiarize themselves with the general history of WA over the last 40 years as well as with the history of education in the state over the same period.

Finally, when exploring each individual's life history, attention will be given to the point of Sikes *et al.* (1985: 20) that not all teachers necessarily experience smooth career progression; rather, 'a typical career is marked by critical incidents or phases'. Goodson and Walker (1991: 147) make the same point as follows:

> The new work on teachers' careers points to the fact that there are critical incidents in teachers' lives and specifically in their work which may crucially affect perception and practice. Certainly work on beginning teachers has pointed to the importance of certain incidents in moulding teachers' styles and practices.

Furthermore, cognizance will be taken of Sikes *et al.*'s (1985: 20) contention that while such incidents can give one's career and one's life 'a beneficial boost', they can also 'deal it a savage blow, or both at the same time'.

Stage 3

The final stage of the research involves further analysis of the life history data generated from the first interview with each participant. The aim is to explore those life history details that might explain both the manner in which and the reasons why he or she undertook adventurous programmes in the area of curriculum, teaching and learning. The decision to have this third stage of analysis was influenced particularly by Woods' (1992: 374) argument that because the participants' memories, thoughts and perceptions are of unknown scope and depth, even to themselves, accounts should be built up through successive discussions over a period of time. Accordingly, the previous conversations will be reviewed for accuracy and completeness.

Cognizance will also be taken of Mandelbaum's (1973) scheme for the analysis of life histories. Briefly, Mandelbaum has suggested that when analysing a life history we need to consider the dimensions of a person's life, the principal turnings and the person's characteristic means of adaptation. A dimension is 'made up of experiences that stem from a similar base and are linked in their effects on the person's subsequent actions' (Mandelbaum 1973: 180). They are biological, cultural, social and psychosocial. With regard to the first two, Mandelbaum states:

> The biological factors set the basic conditions for a life course; cultural factors mould the shape and content of a person's career. The cultural dimension lies in the mutual expectations, understandings and behavior patterns held by the people among whom a person grows up and in whose society he becomes a participant. Each culture provides a general scenario for the life course that indicates the main divisions, tells when transitions should be made, and imputes a social meaning to biological events from birth through death. Each scenario interprets and affects the biological dimension in its own way; each provides its own chart for the progress of a life.

The social dimension, in turn, consists of the social relations the person encounters during his or her life, the roles required of the person, the acts of personal choice characteristic of the group, and the commonly understood ways of working out recurrent conflicts. The psychosocial dimension refers to the individual's feelings, attitudes and subjective world in general. Mandelbaum recognizes that while each of these is individually experienced, each individual's experiences are also likely to be similar in important ways to others in the same culture.

Turnings are the major transitions that an individual makes during the course of a life. These are accomplished when 'the person takes on a new set of roles, enters into fresh relations with a new set of people and acquires a new self conception' (Mandelbaum 1973: 181). A turning can take place gradually, or it can be a single event. Also, it may be either improvised or in some way prescribed.

Finally, adaptations 'are changes that have a major effect on a person's life and on one's basic relations with others' (Mandelbaum 1973: 181). Mandelbaum goes on to argue that individuals change their ways: 'Each person changes his ways in order to maintain continuity whether of group participation or social expectation or self-image or simply survival'. He concludes that while some of these new conditions are imposed by the individual's own physical development, others arise from changing external conditions, whether of custom or climate, family or society.

Conclusion

To study the principalship by means of the edited topical life history research approach is to engage in a pioneering exercise. The motivation to adopt this approach arose out of an awareness of the limitations of the existing literature on the principalship, particularly within a context of unparalleled change and restructuring, and a recognition of the tendency to ignore the formative nature of past experiences on principals' present practices. However, the absence of a clear position on the study of the principalship from a life history perspective presents a major challenge. As a consequence, the underlying theoretical position and the guidelines for data gathering and analysis which have been presented in this proposal were developed from a wide variety of sources and woven into what we believe is a comprehensive and coherent plan.

Chapter 9

Retrospective interactionist longtitudinal studies

A point emphasised regularly throughout this book is that two main types of studies arise out of the central principles of the symbolic interactionist theoretical approach within the interpretivist paradigm. The second of these types, it will be recalled, consists of studies where the central concern is with how participants 'deal with' 'things'. In considering the latter type of studies emphasis was placed on the notion that they involve longitudinal research where the participants' perspectives, actions and interactions are studied over time. Sometimes, however, it is not possible to engage in such research, usually for such practical reasons as lack of access to research sites. At the same time, however, a sufficient number of participants and documentary evidence may exist to allow us to do the research retrospectively.

One difficulty with the retrospective approach is that the research may be dependent partly on participants' memories. Nevertheless, it is possible to go a long way towards addressing associated issues to do with trustworthiness if sufficient data are available to facilitate triangulation. Furthermore, the quantity and quality of documentary evidence available may be sufficient on its own to allow us to engage in a robust study.

My first engagement in studies of this type was with my former doctoral student and current colleague, Dr Simon Clarke. Our interest, which culminated in Dr Clarke's Doctor of Education thesis related to the phenomenon of enterprise bargaining within the education sector. The particular question which interested us was that of how the process of enterprise bargaining was dealt with at the school level in Western Australia (WA). To pose the question in this way, we realised, was to ask a typical symbolic interactionist question, but it quickly became apparent to us that our only hope of investigating it was through a retrospective study. This was primarily because the bargaining process for the particular enterprise agreement in which we were interested had been completed at the time of deciding to investigate the area and another round was not going to start for a number of years. The following proposal illustrates how we surmounted the problem by planning a retrospective study. The proposal also illustrates how the study was eventually conceptualised within a framework where the concept of micro-politics was linked to symbolic interactionism.

Project title

Pursuing an enterprise agreement: How the process was dealt with in one school.

Research aim

The stimulus to conceptualize the study being proposed here arose from observations on the process of enterprise bargaining in one Western Australian independent school. *The aim is to generate theory on how a school 'dealt' with the process of enterprise bargaining.* The study will focus on the period from the beginning of the bargaining process in 1993 to its conclusion in 1995. In the first part of 1995, non-government schools' enterprise agreements registered with the Western Australian Industrial Commission were of two types. The first type refers to the collective enterprise agreement framed by the Western Australian Catholic Schools' sector. The second type refers to the single enterprise agreement which all independent schools elected to pursue. All the enterprise agreements pertaining to the non-government schools' sector, which were registered with the Western Australian Industrial Commission in the first part of 1995, were applicable for one year, apart from one which applied for two years and two months. The particular school selected for this study is the one to which the latter agreement applies. Its selection was made by virtue of the uniqueness of its enterprise agreement.

The background

Since the late 1980s, the Australian system of industrial relations has been gradually changing from one based on a highly centralized model to one which places a focus on the workplace. The traditional approach emphasizing arbitrated decisions by central tribunals in order to achieve uniform wage increases without any consideration being given to productivity is being replaced by the practice of negotiation at the enterprise level. In pursuit of improving the efficiency and productivity of the workplace, legislative reforms have occurred at both Federal and State levels which present opportunities for individual enterprises to negotiate agreements defining terms and conditions which are considered to be most appropriate for their circumstances. In Western Australia, the single enterprise agreement is one such arrangement.

The potential of enterprise bargaining to present schools with the opportunity to reshape the nature of teachers' work and conditions, coupled with the paucity of knowledge that currently exists amongst the educational community about the process of enterprise bargaining in schools, invites the development of a research agenda which seeks to enhance an understanding of the phenomenon. This contention assumes greater import when it is considered that the efficacy of the response that is made throughout the education service as a whole to the new landscape of industrial relations could be largely contingent upon the ability of stakeholders to understand the process involved in workplace bargaining, thus engendering a confidence in procedures and requirements. A contribution to the proposed research agenda will be made by the study proposed here which addresses the question of how, in an attempt to reach an enterprise agreement for its teaching staff, the process of enterprise bargaining was dealt with in a Western Australian independent school.

Justification for the research in the light of the existing empirical research literature

Little is known about the nature of the interaction that has occurred within schools which have made a commitment to enterprise-based bargaining. Thus, the study proposed here, which is concerned with how a school dealt with the process of enterprise bargaining, is opportune. Although initial steps in work reorganization throughout the industrial sectors have been tentative, the stage has now been reached where enterprise-based bargaining can be assessed more fully. Many independent schools in Western Australia have already concluded enterprise agreements based on the 'Memorandum of Agreement' of 1994, a non-registered agreement co-signed by the employers' association, the Association of Independent Schools of Western Australia (AISWA), and the Union, the Independent Schools Salaried Officers' Association of Western Australia (the Union). Nevertheless, little is known about the nature of the interaction that occurred during the complex process of enterprise bargaining within the schools.

The study is also germane because of the paucity of knowledge about the understandings that are brought to bear on the process of enterprise bargaining by both employers and employees in a school situation. Indeed, the emphasis that research has placed on explicit procedures of bargaining and negotiation has meant that schools have received scant attention because they have not traditionally provided a context where this kind of activity has occurred openly (Hoyle 1986: 131). However, related research which has been applied to areas other than the education sector is also deficient in providing an adequate foundation for understanding the phenomenon. The research undertaken into negotiations, for example, has tended not to reveal what Fells (1995a: 268) has described as 'the cut and thrust of the 'real world' of negotiations'; a critique which complements Strauss's recommendation (1978: 11) that there is a need for research to consider the views of 'actors' as they enter and affect the negotiations.

The need for research to uncover the beliefs, values, perspectives and motivations of the participants in the bargaining process at the school level, is made more apparent when the particular circumstances which surround enterprise bargaining are considered. Firstly, the complete novelty of the phenomenon as it applies to schools prompts an investigation of participants' perspectives within a context of change and uncertainty. Indeed, as Fullan has postulated (1993), new ways of doing things in schools create an initial period of ambiguity which will inevitably affect the interpretations that are made of the phenomenon by the participants. A second circumstance is the notion of cooperation between employer and employee which underpins the process of enterprise bargaining in order to reach agreement. The desirability of this relationship is often evident in the rhetoric of the legislation which emphasizes the capacity of new workplace conditions to enable better cooperation and communication between the two parties. Notwithstanding such rhetoric, however, the cooperative dimension of the bargaining process will ultimately be defined by the interpretations of the individuals involved. Circumstances at the school level could be such that an impediment is placed in the path of achieving enhanced cooperation.

The education sector has, in fact, been slow to accept the new culture of industrial relations. As Angus has argued (1991: 78–9), teachers have found the notion of improving productivity within an 'industry' difficult to grasp as it applies to education. Indeed, many have regarded the economic objectives of workplace reform as an affront to their professionalism (Angus 1991). In this regard, teachers are particularly suspicious of the instrumental notions of schooling which have been embraced by the changes introduced into the industrial relations forum, as well as the requirement that education should become more productive (Angus 1991). Set against a background of scepticism, if not outright hostility, it may be the case that enterprise-based bargaining is not readily countenanced, which means that a school embarking on the process is likely to encounter difficulties from the outset. This factor in itself invites speculation as to how agreement can be reached according to a system of enterprise-based bargaining.

Another factor which could present an impediment to the cooperative basis of an agreement is a reluctance on the part of employers to reassess their position within an industrial relations environment predicated on a need for 'good faith' bargaining with employees. It seems likely that the efficacy of the bargaining process at the school will hinge, to some extent, on the willingness of management to accept more open and collaborative relationships with teachers than might have previously existed. If, however, an employing authority seeks to preserve its traditional 'management prerogative' to manage a school's affairs without interference, this attitude is likely to create a barrier to the kind of cooperation which is envisaged in the process of reaching an agreement. Similarly, a refusal to disclose crucial financial or other information may not further the cause of cooperation as espoused by the rhetoric (Gardner 1994).

A third dimension of enterprise bargaining in schools which may be strongly influenced by participants' interpretations is the rationale that is adopted for seeking an agreement. This observation relates to whether bargaining for an enterprise agreement within a school is motivated by a genuine desire to improve the quality of work life for teachers as a means of increasing the productivity of teaching and learning, or whether utilitarian and economic considerations take precedence. In this regard, the role of the union also needs to be taken into account. Kerchner and Caufman (1993: 19) use the term 'professional unionism' to describe a teaching association which 'balances teachers' legitimate self-interests with the larger interests of teaching as an occupation and education as an institution'. This model contrasts with 'industrial unionism' which is designed to 'protect teachers from the whims of managerial and political behaviour and to advance teachers' interests'. Professional unionism, Kerchner and Caufman (1993: 19) claim, provides a more promising basis for collaborative school reform.

It is evident, therefore, that the circumstances surrounding enterprise-based negotiations are likely to influence the perspectives that participants adopt regarding the phenomenon. If enterprise bargaining is to be regarded as a method of changing teachers' work for the benefit of the teachers as well as the school as a whole, it is imperative that an understanding is gained of bargaining as a social process. A variety of research approaches suggest themselves for this purpose. A research agenda using quantitative research methods could be developed with data being examined in terms of pre-formulated hypotheses about the phenomenon in question and either confirmed or rejected. To this end, data could be collected through surveys, structured interviews, and questionnaires, using a large sample. However, while such an approach may be appropriate for comprehending phenomena involving routinized behaviour (Hammersley 1989), it would be unlikely to provide insight into the complex and dynamic nature of the process of human interaction. If enterprise bargaining is to be understood as a process in the most holistic sense, research is required which, in Peshkin's words (1993: 28), 'gets to the bottom of things, dwells on complexity, and brings us very close to the phenomena we seek to illuminate'.

The study of the process of enterprise bargaining being proposed here is contiguous with Peshkin's objectives (1993: 28) by holding that a qualitative research orientation be adopted because of its underlying assumption that there are multiple realities emerging from personal interaction and perspectives. It is also proposed that the research should be undertaken from the theoretical perspective of symbolic interactionism because of its concern with the 'ways in which individual actors make sense of, analyze, or interpret any given situation' (Hitchcock and Hughes 1989: 33).

The theoretical location of the proposed research

Walton and McKersie (1965) were amongst the first group of researchers to investigate labour-management collective bargaining. By 1981 the field was sufficiently developed for Fisher and Ury (1981) to be able to offer a prescriptive framework for the consideration of bargaining concepts. Bargaining over positions, they contend, tends to lock negotiators into those positions and the exercise deteriorates into a contest of wills. Instead, they advocate an approach referred to as 'principled negotiation' which is based on four points: 'people', or separating the people from the problem; 'interests', meaning that the focus should be placed on interests and not positions; 'options', relating to the variety of possibilities that are required before making decisions; and finally, 'criteria', or the insistence that the result be predicated on some objective standard (Fisher *et al.* 1991: 11). These points, it is contended, present negotiators with the main mechanism for pursuing collaborative bargaining, a generic term for the 'win–win' approach which has been employed by an expanding number of districts and unions in the United States (Kerchner and Koppich 1993: 19).

The typology of bargaining defined by the research undertaken in the field of labour management collective bargaining, as well as the model for negotiation developed by Fisher and Ury, can help to illuminate and clarify practice. However, they are limited as a theoretical basis for research on the process of enterprise bargaining at the school level for three principal reasons. Firstly, they are deficient because of their exclusive focus on the formal, explicit manifestation of bargaining and their failure to recognize the more tacit dimensions of the interaction. Secondly, as a corollary of the emphasis put on explicit bargaining, there has been a neglect of the school context because it has not traditionally been the location of such activity (Hoyle 1986). Finally, there is no consideration of the political interaction associated with the bargaining process.

In an effort to fill the void in the conventional literature, the theoretical work of Bacharach and Lawler (1980) attempted to develop a closer connection between the fields of collective bargaining and organizations. According to Bacharach and Lawler (1980), the major deficiency of perspectives which have emerged from the structural analysis of organizations is their failure to acknowledge the power politics involved in coalitional bargaining. In particular, they regard Walton and McKersie's (1965) approach as inadequate on the grounds that there is very little mention of power. Furthermore, the approach focuses exclusively on labour management bargaining and is, consequently, too specific in its analysis. Bacharach and Lawler have therefore formulated a theory of bargaining relationships and bargaining tactics which is relevant to the power struggle and conflict which, they argue, form the basis of relations within any organization. More specifically, 'power, coalitions, and bargaining constitute the three basic themes of their theoretical treatise on organizational politics' (Bacharach and Lawler 1980: xi). They define bargaining as 'the give and take that occurs when two or more independent parties experience a conflict of interest' (Bacharach and Lawler 1980: 108). It is thereby considered to represent the action component of conflict.

By way of further explanation, a distinction arising out of the work of Walton and McKersie (1965) is also made by Bacharach and Lawler (1980) between direct or distributive bargaining and integrative bargaining. Bacharach and Lawler (1980) also identify what is described as the mode of bargaining, or the tacit-explicit dimension of the bargaining relationship. Explicit bargaining is specified as 'the conscious manifestation of bargaining' (Bacharach and Lawler 1980: 112) and is conceptualized by the exchange of offers and counter-offers which is designed to find a mutually acceptable solution to the conflict. An explicit bargaining context is characterized by relatively open lines of communication, a recognition that the relationship is a bargaining one, and consent to consider compromise. In contrast, tacit bargaining occurs when communication lines have been obstructed by the parties and the bargaining relationship may not even be recognized for what it is. Under these circumstances there are few explicit offers and counter-offers, but rather a more subtle employment of tactics aimed to outmanoeuvre and manipulate. Tacit bargaining, according to Bacharach and Lawler (1980), often precedes and is transformed into explicit bargaining. Furthermore, the essence of bargaining is regarded as tactical action and is depicted as an information manipulation game in which deception and bluff are critical ingredients.

The acknowledgement of the political dimension of an organization, and the related observation that issues may be handled in a less visible way, and according to explicit methods, constitutes a more fecund basis for a comprehensive analysis and understanding of what is involved in the bargaining process. The work of Mangham (1979) on organizational behaviour explores this contention more deeply and needs to be examined in order to establish its relevance for schools attempting to deal with the complexities of enterprise bargaining. However, an investigation of such a nature must also be located within a theoretical perspective. This prompts a consideration of the suitability of the micro-political approach and its connection with symbolic interactionism.

The micro-political perspective

At the heart of Mangham's (1979) perspective on organizational behaviour is the idea that social life is derived from the process of interaction which, in turn, is seen primarily as a political encounter. The emphasis on 'political encounter' is because when interaction takes place between individuals or groups there is usually some kind of benefit to be gained. Hence, it is asserted that the political realm of an organization is 'the struggle of reasonable men [sic] to have what they consider to be right and proper prevail' (Mangham 1979: xii). Political behaviour, according to this understanding, is not an insidious activity but a consequence of interaction predicated on a desire to achieve particular goals.

Underlying Mangham's (1979) depiction of organizational behaviour is the notion that people have the capacity to manipulate consciously their own behaviour as well as that of others, and that many fully utilize that capacity, for whatever purpose. This perspective entails an acceptance that people do cooperate and exhibit altruistic considerations in their dealings with others, but there is also recognition of the fact that people compete in order to achieve ends at the expense of another party. A realistic understanding of organizations, therefore, requires an acknowledgement that all dimensions of humanity are significant in determining the conduct of an enterprise. Organizations for Mangham (1979) may be viewed as micro-political arenas where assorted individuals, groups, coalitions and alliances, act in pursuit of their own sets of goals and objectives. According to this perspective, the activity of an organization is the product of interaction and is not defined by 'automatic machine-like interdependencies nor strongly influenced by principles of development nor homeostatic systems, but is the direct result of the power and skill of the proponents and opponents of the action in question' (Mangham 1979: 17). Mangham claims that this micro-political perspective can be used as a guide to action in a diversity of organizational settings (Mangham 1979: 18), but he makes no direct reference to schools.

The legitimacy of micro-politics in the more specific context of educational management and schools was formally acknowledged at a conference on 'The Politics of Educational Improvement' held at the University of Bristol in 1981 (Pratt 1982). At this conference the traditional model of organizational behaviour, with its stress on formal roles and channels of communication, was tempered by another view stipulating that as the political dimension of organizations was both inevitable and desirable, research should be seeking both to articulate the phenomenon more clearly and to build on it. In other words, the political process needed to be revealed and accepted as a vehicle for change and educational improvement (Pratt 1982).

This exhortation to promote a systematic study of the micro-politics of educational organizations was satisfied to some degree through the work of Ball (1987). In an attempt to rectify what he considered to be the inadequacy of functional theories in illuminating the way in which schools operate, Ball applied a micro-political perspective to the organization of schools. He asserted that schools are, in fact, sites of ideological struggle as demonstrated by their 'structural looseness'. Although acknowledging the possibility of consensus, Ball contended that schools are primarily, 'arenas of competition and contest over material advantage and vested interest. Careers, resources, status and influence are at stake in the conflicts between segments, coalitions and alliances' (Ball 1987: 279). It is, therefore, these processes which need to be explored so as to cultivate a more pragmatic and critical analysis of organizational activity than the abstract structural theories can offer.

Notwithstanding the considerable influence that Ball's political theory of school organization has had in the field, it has received some criticism on the grounds that the approach puts too much emphasis on the political processes of power, conflict, and domination at the expense of the cooperative activity that is also purported to occur in schools (Burlingame 1988; Townshend 1990). Nevertheless, this perceived weakness in Ball's work is addressed by Blase (1989; 1991), another prominent micro-political theorist. He views the micro-political perspective as a way of revealing the fundamentals of human behaviour and purpose. However, in contrast to Ball's position, Blase's definition of micro-politics also embraces the political processes that can be identified with cooperative relationships. Indeed, Blase (1991: 251) regrets the fact that, in his opinion, most studies of school level micro-politics neglect the positive and cooperative forms of political interaction. The recognition that the resolution of differences may be an outcome of political processes requires that his depiction of micro-politics is more circumspect in nature:

> Micro-politics is about power and how people use it to influence others and protect themselves. It is about conflict and how people compete with each other to get what they want. It is about cooperation and how people build support among themselves to achieve their ends. It is about what people in all social settings think about and have strong feelings about, but what is so often unspoken and not easily observed.
>
> (Blase 1991: 1)

This kind of activity, Mangham (1987) argues, is the product of interaction which is at the heart of micro-political behaviour and may be understood in terms of symbolic interactionism.

As revealed by the literature, there is only scant information about the enterprise bargaining process at the school level and hence an extremely limited knowledge base on which to build a research agenda. For these pragmatic reasons alone, it would be difficult to begin a study of enterprise bargaining with a preconceived theory and then attempt to verify it through an empirical study. More importantly, a research programme which is committed to symbolic interactionism should endeavour to be as open as possible to alternative constructions of reality and to many different explanations of observed phenomena, none of which can be eliminated prior to the study. It is therefore logical and epistemologically sound for the research enterprise to generate a theory which is grounded in the reality of the situation under question and 'fits' the data that have been generated.

The research plan

The research questions

Researchers adopting a symbolic interactionist perspective are fundamentally concerned with how individuals 'handle', 'manage', 'deal with', or 'cope with' particular phenomena within a given situation and over a given period of time. Accordingly, the major focus of the study is on discovering how, in an attempt to reach an enterprise agreement for its teaching staff, the process of enterprise bargaining undertaken has been dealt with in a Western Australian independent school.

As this research approach must accommodate multiple interpretations of the observed phenomenon, none of which can be eliminated prior to the study commencing, it is impossible from the outset to know what the sum total of sub-research questions will be as the study unfolds. However, a set of guiding questions is proposed initially which places the focus on revealing how the actors who participated directly in the exercise of enterprise bargaining at one school viewed their circumstances, how they interacted, and how these processes changed. These questions have been formulated as follows:

1 What were the individual perspectives attached to enterprise bargaining by the employer's and employees' representatives on the negotiating committee prior to the negotiation process taking place?
2 How did the initial perspectives attached to enterprise bargaining influence the early process of negotiation? What were the action/ interaction strategies engaged in by the participants?
3 What perspectives were held by the employer's and employees' representatives on the enterprise bargaining committee subsequent to the conduct of the negotiation process?

These guiding questions emerged from Blumer's (1969: 2) three basic premises of symbolic interactionism.

A clearer understanding of the term 'perspectives' may be gained by considering it as consisting of the notions of aims and intentions, significance, reasons and strategies (Blackledge and Hunt 1985: 234). On this basis, it seems pertinent to examine what an individual aims to do in the process of enterprise bargaining, what one considers to be significant about the process, the reasons given for pursuing the process, and the strategies employed as a part of it. However, it is not envisaged that the researcher should set out to answer these questions specifically; rather the questions are thought to provide the most productive means of generating data in order to generate a theory.

The unit of analysis

The study will be located in Western Australia. To focus on a particular state is justified since the enterprise bargaining that has occurred in schools has been encompassed by state jurisdiction. The constraints of time, finance and accessibility mean that the study must be further limited to the Perth metropolitan area. Moreover, it will be restricted to the non-government schools sector because, hitherto, most progress in enterprise bargaining has been achieved in the Western Australian education system by independent schools. An examination of the enterprise bargaining agreements which have been reached by schools within the Association of Independent Schools of Western Australia and registered with the Western Australian Industrial Relations Commission in 1995, reveals a great deal of uniformity. In terms of the respective agreements' structure and content, they have all been based on the framework which was originally recommended by the Memorandum of Agreement signed between the Association of Independent Schools of Western Australia (AISWA) and the Independent Schools Salaried Officers' Association of Western Australia (ISSOA) in May 1994.

The enterprise agreements that have been registered are of two types. The first type refers to the collective enterprise agreement concluded by the Western Australian Catholic Schools' sector. The second type refers to the single enterprise agreement which other AISWA schools have elected to pursue. All the single enterprise agreements adopted by the non-Catholic, AISWA schools and registered with the Western Australian Industrial Commission were operational for the duration of one year, except for one which was to apply for the longer term of two years and two months. The selection of the school which was the subject of this longer agreement as a case for the study has therefore been made on the basis of the difference that exists in the School's enterprise agreement which distinguishes it from those of other schools. This sampling strategy concurs with Goetz and LeCompte's (1984) notion of criterion-based sampling. According to this notion, the necessary criterion is first established for a unit to be included in the investigation and then a sample is found that matches the criterion. The school in question has, therefore, been selected because of its uniqueness, or in the words of Goetz and LeCompte (1984: 82), on the grounds of 'unique or rare attributes in a population'.

It could also be argued that the selection of the first school to have concluded an agreement applicable for longer than one year may add to the potential value of the research project. In other words, although the study will examine a specific instance, this should not detract from its capacity to extend generalizations to all those school contexts where longer agreements are being subsequently negotiated. This is particularly true when it is recognized that readers bring their own experience and understanding to reading a study of the kind that is reported here and that this can lead to generalizations as new data are added to old data (Stenhouse 1985: 287).

The decision to focus on a single school finds further justification in the potential of such a case to allow the researcher to get as close to the subjects of interest as possible and enable the uncovering of the subjective understandings of the phenomenon which are of most importance. In this regard, Burns (1994: 313) has described the case study as a 'rather portmanteau term'. Accordingly, it would be beneficial to define what is involved in this model of research more clearly. For the purposes of this exercise, Merriam's position (1988: 9) is especially enlightening. At the general level, a case study can be described as an 'examination of a specific phenomenon' and in this sense it constitutes a 'bounded system'. Merriam has also identified four essential properties of a qualitative case study. Firstly, a case study must be particularistic, meaning that a focus should be placed on a particular situation. This specificity of attention makes the case study an appropriate design for examining how people deal with a given problem. Secondly, a case study should be descriptive to the extent that the end product should be a 'thick' description of the phenomenon under study, which means a complete and literal description of the entity being investigated. Thirdly, a case study should be heuristic because it seeks to create the discovery of new meaning and a rethinking of the phenomenon presented. Finally, a case study should be inductive, meaning that generalizations, concepts or hypotheses should emerge from the data which are grounded in the context itself.

Data collection

Attention must now be given to the data-collection techniques to be utilized. In this connection, it is deemed appropriate that qualitative research methods of data collection be employed because of their concern for the empirical social world and their commitment to fieldwork. Participant observation is a major method of data gathering within the qualitative repertoire which enables the experiences of those inside the group to be penetrated. Assuming that entrée could be gained to a setting where sensitive information is being discussed, it would be appropriate for the researcher to observe enterprise bargaining meetings in order to record behaviour as it is occurring. A first-hand account of the negotiations would provide a useful supplement to other forms of data in the interpretation of what is happening. However, in view of the fact that the school which has been selected for the research has already concluded an enterprise agreement, the study has to be retrospective in nature. This feature of the research design automatically denies the appropriateness of participant observation in the collection of data and determines that there should be a reliance on the two other main qualitative techniques for obtaining data, namely, the interview and document study. Each of these data-gathering approaches is now described.

The interview process

As the research project seeks to contribute to the cultivation of insight and understanding of the enterprise bargaining process at the school level, the decision as to who should be interviewed has been made according to the potential of individuals to illuminate what happens on the basis of their direct involvement, as identified by previous observations. In other words, informants have been chosen because of their ability to provide rich descriptions of the experiences they encountered during enterprise bargaining at the school. It is possible to place the informants who have been selected into three categories based on the positions that they held during the negotiation process. Firstly, there is the employer, comprising three members of the School Council or the Governing Body. These particular members of Council have been assigned to assist with the study because of their prominence in the activities of the Governing Body related to the school's enterprise bargaining which resulted from occupying a key office. Secondly, there is the employer's bargaining committee, namely the headmaster, the deputy headmaster, and the bursar. Thirdly, there is the employees' bargaining committee which includes the Union representative on the staff of the school, an elected staff negotiator, and the Secretary of the Union who did not participate directly but was constantly aware of developments and provided advice to the employees.

Initial contact has already been made with each informant by telephone in order to obtain at least a provisional agreement to participate in the research project. This was confirmed shortly afterwards by a letter outlining the main purpose of the study and explaining the proposed format and function of the interview that will be undertaken. Consideration has also been given to the necessity for interviews to be held more than once, enabling particular topics to be pursued further. Enclosed with the letter was a code of conduct for the responsible practice of research which has been devised in collaboration with the headmaster of the school. According to this protocol, three main procedures were stipulated. It was made clear that the principles of anonymity and confidentiality will be observed at all times. Interview transcripts and research findings will be scrutinized by participants for accuracy, relevance and fairness. A declaration of the informant's support for the code of conduct will be signed before the interview commences.

Merriam (1988: 73) has identified three major variants of the interview: the highly structured, the semi-structured, and the unstructured. In its highly structured form, the interview questions as well as their order are predetermined, and it tends to be used when a large sample needs to be surveyed. At the opposite end of the interview 'continuum' is the unstructured format which is based on the assumption that informants can define the world in unique ways. It is therefore exploratory in its objectives and does not rely on a pre-prepared set of questions. A semi-structured approach, on the other hand, is also predicated on the epistemological assumption that there are multiple realities, but employs loosely defined questions for guidance during the conducting of the interview. Using this classification, it has been decided that the style of interview which is most appropriate for the study is a semi-structured one.

The primary function of the interview within the research agenda is to reveal the informants' perspectives on their own roles and those of others in the process of enterprise bargaining, their perspectives on the enterprise bargaining environment, and their perspectives on the experiences encountered. It is therefore necessary to provide the opportunity for a discourse between interviewer and interviewee which 'moves beyond surface talk to a rich discussion of thoughts and feelings' (Maykut and Morehouse 1994: 80). In order to elicit this depth of response from informants, two important elements of interview technique will be adopted. Firstly, each interview will be sufficiently long for rapport to be established between the two parties, probably between one-and-a-half to two hours. Secondly, because of the need for interviews to allow informants the freedom to recall and expound on events from their perspective, there will be no reliance on a standardized list of questions. Instead, initial questions will be more loosely based on the guiding questions already noted, and subsequent questions will be asked as they suggest themselves and as opportunities arise. The nature of the response will provide the direction that the interview should take next. In this way it could be claimed that questions will be used as an '*aide-memoire*' (Burgess 1984: 108) which serves three main purposes: the formulation of the *aide-memoire* will assist with the preparation of the interview (McHugh 1994: 59); the *aide-memoire* will also help to ensure that similar issues will be covered in all of the interviews; and, whilst providing guidance in the conducting of the interview, the *aide-memoire* will still permit the kind of flexibility required for the interviewer to respond to the emerging 'world view' of the informant as well as new ideas on the topic (Merrriam 1988: 74). Hence, the type of interview to be adopted in the study will conform to the notion that an interview may be construed as a 'conversation with a purpose' (Maykut and Morehouse 1994: 79).

Throughout all of the interviews, cognizance will be taken of Woods' (1992: 372) enumeration of the skills which are necessary to ensure that the interview is as productive as possible. These include active listening, which demonstrates that the interviewer is hearing, reacting, and occasionally constructing interpretations; focusing, or keeping the interview on the subject; explicating where material is incomplete or ambiguous; and checking for accuracy by pressing points, rephrasing and summarizing. In this way, the researcher will become a partner with the informant, with both of them working together to 'get the story straight' (Wilson and Hutchinson 1991: 270). The decision to employ semi-structured interviews has therefore been determined by the need to probe as deeply as possible into the individual's subjective experiences of the phenomenon in question. The use of semi-structured interviews also facilitates access to events which cannot be observed directly because of the retrospective nature of the study (Burns 1994: 280).

The interviews will be tape-recorded with the consent of the respondents and notes will be taken during the conversations in order to capture the things that the tape recorder is unable to record and which are necessary to further enhance the sense which the researcher will make of the interviewee's perspective (Maykut and Morehouse 1993: 99). The recorded interviews will then be transcribed verbatim by the researcher on the grounds that the verbatim transcription of interviews provides the best database for analysis (Merriam 1988: 82), and that involvement in the actual process of transcribing will bring the researcher closer to the data. Transcribing the interviews verbatim is also considered important to enable the use of quotations when writing up the descriptive and analytical sections of the research report for, as Ruddock (1993: 19) has indicated, 'some statements carry a remarkably rich density of meaning in a few words'. The use of quotes will also make it necessary to develop a system of codes in an attempt to maintain the anonymity of those people who will be interviewed. To this end, each interviewee will be assigned a code relating to whether the person is a negotiator for the employer, a member of the School Council, a staff negotiator, or a union official. A copy of the transcript will be sent to each respondent with an invitation to make any amendments considered necessary to enhance the representation of individuals' positions. At the end of this procedure the transcripts will be ready for analysis.

Document analysis

The second major technique which will be employed for data collection is document analysis. Goetz and LeCompte (1984: 153) have used the term 'artefact' to describe the assortment of written and symbolic records which have been kept by the participants in a social group. Such artefacts, as Merriam (1988: 109) has indicated, have both limitations and advantages. In view of the fact that they are generated independently of the research, artefacts can be fragmentary and may not fit the conceptual framework. However, their independence from the research agenda can also be considered an advantage because they are thereby non-reactive. As such, they are a product of a given context and are grounded in the 'real world'. This characteristic makes it likely that an analysis of a diversity of artefacts will help to develop insights relevant to the research problem.

The artefacts to be used in this study are exclusively printed material of various sorts. In this connection, Borg and Gall (1989: 813) have made a useful distinction between 'intentional documents' and 'unpremeditated documents'. According to this classification, intentional documents are those which serve primarily as a record of what happened, whereas unpremeditated documents are intended to serve an immediate purpose without any thought given to their future use in the recording of an event. For the function of investigating the process of enterprise bargaining at the school, it is possible to obtain in the first category of documents the agendas and minutes of enterprise bargaining meetings and whole staff meetings, draft enterprise agreements, and the headmaster's monthly reports to the School Council. Located in the second category are documents such as personal memos, the headmaster's letters and memoranda to staff, and communiqués from the headmaster to the employers' organization, AISWA. Collectively, the documents should not only provide a detailed account of the sequence of events that occurred during the process of enterprise bargaining at the school, but also indicate 'people's sensations, experiences, and knowledge which connote opinions, values and feelings' (LeCompte and Preissle 1993: 216).

Data analysis

The lack of research into the processes of enterprise bargaining (Fells 1995b), especially at the school level, means that there are many categories and properties of the phenomenon yet to be identified. Grounded theory methods of data analysis are particularly suited to this task. They offer a systematic approach to collecting, organizing, and analyzing data from the empirical world in question. They also constitute an approach to theory development based on the study of human conduct and the contexts and forces which impinge on human conduct (Chenitz and Swanson 1986: 14).

The constant comparative method of data analysis, which is fundamental to grounded theory modes of analysis, will be used in this study (Strauss 1987). Analysis will progress through the stages of open and axial coding (Strauss 1987; Strauss and Corbin 1990). Also in keeping with grounded theory modes of analysis, data collection and analysis will be undertaken simultaneously (Strauss and Corbin 1990). In this way, the study's substantive theory will be generated. The process will be further facilitated through 'theoretical sampling' (Strauss and Corbin 1990), building categories, writing memos, and drawing diagrams (Strauss and Corbin 1990).

The third type of coding used by grounded theorists, namely, selective coding, will not be utilized. This type of coding is necessary in a 'pure' grounded theory study, where the concern is with 'discovering' a core social-psychological problem and a corresponding social-psychological process. However, in the case of the study proposed here, the concern is with answering the central research question: how, in an attempt to reach an enterprise agreement for its teaching staff, the process of enterprise bargaining has been dealt with in a Western Australian independent school. The employment of open and axial coding will be sufficient for the development of propositions relating to this central question.

Chapter 10

Interactionist historical studies

The potential for engaging in particular types of historical studies using the symbolic interactionist theoretical approach within the interpretivist paradigm suggested itself to me a number of years ago. I had, as an educational historian, been struggling for a long period with how to go about research aimed at trying to understand how teachers in previous eras understood various aspects of their lives. I was particularly interested in this research agenda as it applied to lay people who taught alongside priests, brothers and nuns in Catholic schools in Australia. I got some early indications as to a way forward from the work of Silver (1980: 267) when he argued for 'the history of opinion'. This he defined as 'the history of how people, groups of people, people in action, have interpreted and reinterpreted their world'.

To pursue Silver's line of inquiry, it seemed to me, was to argue for the application of the 'hermeneutic' mode of historical research to the study of teachers' lives. It has been argued that such a mode is appropriate where there is an aspiration 'to explain events by referring to the motives, reasoning, meanings and intentions of the actors' (Fairburn 1999: 31). It is also a mode which relates very closely to the 'intentional explanation mode', where the investigator 'looks closely at the conscious desires, values, aims and purposes' of the members of the group being studied and relates these to their 'conscious beliefs about how the desired ends could be brought about' (Fairburn 1999: 26).

At the same time, I sought an approach that would be explicit in terms of clarifying and spelling out theoretical assumptions. In this I was influenced by contemporary trends in the writing of educational biography. A major breakthrough for me came on reading an outstanding Master of Education thesis by Dr Jenny Collins (2001) completed at Massey University in New Zealand. What Collins set out to do was to discover what the experience of religious life was like for a group of eight nuns who were members of a Catholic religious teaching order, the Dominican Sisters, and who chose teaching as a lifetime vocation in New Zealand in the first half of the twentieth century. In pursuit of this aim she very successfully utilized grounded theory methodology. It took only one more step in backward mapping to realise that this approach provided me with a methodology appropriate to my needs and that it could be positioned within the symbolic interactionist theoretical position within the interpretivist paradigm.

The following proposal indicates how I applied the latter outcome of my backward-mapping exercise to develop a history-of-education proposal on the experience of being a lay teacher in Western Australian Catholic schools during the period 1940–80. At the same time, however, I deemed it important to state that I recognised that this was not the only valid approach to engaging in research on the substantive area of interest under consideration here. Rather, the position taken was that it had a very significant part to play alongside other approaches. In particular, I held that it could lead to the development of the micro-perspectives necessary for those interested in investigating the area through research projects based on other frameworks, including structuralism, feminist theory and critical theory.

Project title

Changing Perspectives, Changing Performance: An Historical Analysis of Lay Teachers' Experiences in Western Australian Catholic Schools from 1940 to 1980.

Aims and background

The central aim of this project is to provide an historical analysis of the experience of being a lay teacher in Western Australian Catholic schools during the period 1940–1980. The project is based on three principal research questions:

1   What were the perspectives of lay teachers in Western Australian Catholic schools during the period 1940–1980 regarding what it meant to be a teacher?
2   How did the lay teachers carry out their work in light of those perspectives?
3   What was the relationship between the perspectives of the lay teachers and the wider socio-historical structure?

Both oral history and documentary sources will be drawn upon for this analysis.

The years 1940 to 1980 constitute a period of great change within the Catholic Church which impacted significantly on Catholic education in many countries, including Australia. The middle of the period, the 1960s, was characterized not only by enormous challenges to the 'traditional' Catholic 'mind-set' and religious practices arising from the activities of the Second Vatican Council (1962–5), but also by a major acceleration in the reduction in vocations to the religious life. The period also includes the year 1973, which ushered in 'the Whitlam era' in Australia, with promises of massive Federal Government aid to education, including Catholic schools, and this at a time when Catholic schools were being staffed more and more by lay teachers.

To focus on the period 1940–1980 is not to dismiss previous or subsequent periods as unworthy of attention. Rather, the argument is that these periods merit major projects in themselves. Also, to set out to generate oral history sources for the years prior to 1940 could be unproductive because of the likelihood of not having a reasonable number of participants available for interview. On the other hand, the likelihood of the numbers available increasing for the years after 1940 is great.

The general background is the situation whereby the Catholic community in Australia has been successful in maintaining and developing a substantial education sector independent of state education systems from the advent of legislation on education in all states in the latter half of the nineteenth century (O'Donoghue 2001: 19–21). Since the early decades of that century the teachers who worked in the Catholic education sector were categorized into the 'teaching religious' – members of religious teaching orders of priests, brothers and nuns – and the lay teachers who led what the Church viewed as the 'ordinary' unconsecrated life of being married or single (O'Donoghue 2001: 101–12). Relatively little is known about the perspectives and activities of these lay teachers. This project will make one contribution by concentrating on the experience of being a lay teacher in Catholic schools in Western Australia during the period 1940–1980.

The project is proposed at a time when the history of teachers' lives is beginning to receive much increased attention not only nationally, but also internationally. During the 1980s and early 1990s, educational historians in the United States (Altenbaugh 1992; Cuban 1984; Finkelstein 1989, 1998; Warren 1989) began to open up the field, particularly in relation to the lives of teachers in government schools. As the research output developed in both quality and extent, however, Silver (1994: 2616) argued that, apart from similar work in Canada – work which continues apace (Boutilier and Prentice 2000) – the remainder of the English-speaking world was not quite as active on the same front. Three years later, in 1997, attention was drawn to the situation whereby teachers in the UK constituted an occupational group whose lives historically were under-researched (Gardner and Cunningham 1997: 331). It is only very recently, with work like that of Goodman and Martin (2002), Robinson (2002) and Cunningham and Gardner (2004) that the situation has begun to be addressed for this context.

Historians in Australia have been more productive in the field. The early research of Spaull and colleagues on teaching and teacher unionisation (Spaull 1977, 1985; Spaull and Sullivan 1989) has provided essential historical views on the pressures under which teachers work today. Feminist historians (Kyle 1989; Mackinnon 1984; Theobald 1996) have also been major contributors and associated work on the gendered nature of women in teaching continues through works like that of Whitehead (2003). Research has also been undertaken on the role that teachers have played historically in the construction of masculinity (Crotty 2001) and femininity (Theobald 1994). Further insights into the history of Australian teachers are provided by a small body of research which has attempted to portray the economic, social and cultural contexts of their everyday working environments (Clarke 1985; Ford 1993; Selleck and Sullivan 1982), and also by significant biographical works on influential Australian educationalists (Cooper 1998). Some scholarly works have also begun to emerge on teachers and teaching in Catholic schools in Australia. Burley (1997, 2001) has opened up the complexity of the area by drawing attention to the various categories of Catholic teachers; female teachers in Catholic schools included, for example, 'choir nuns', 'lay nuns' and 'lay teachers'. The work of both 'types' of nuns, as teachers in Australian schools, has been examined by Kyle (1986), Lewis (1990) and Trimingham Jack (1998, 2003). Such contributions, while extremely valuable, also highlight the need for a much greater research project regarding the experience of what it meant to be a teacher in a Catholic school. To make this observation is not to overlook the extensive number of histories on Catholic educational institutions in various Australian states, including Western Australia (Carter 1997; Marchant 1996; McLay 1992; Plowman 2003). These are admirable as attempts to provide some record of the activities of the teaching religious. In general, however, they tend to be hagiographic. Also, they present the work of the religious orders as divinely inspired Catholic altruism and ignore the more secular perspective which would view their undertakings as the result of a complex interaction of political, social and economic forces. Furthermore, they tend to completely ignore the lay teachers who taught in Catholic schools. Thus, they perpetuate a practice of the Catholic Church in previous decades of viewing lay people in general as being of a lesser status than those who were priests, brothers and nuns (O'Donoghue and Potts 2004).

A major consequence of the dominance of the latter view in the past was that lay teachers tended to be employed in Catholic schools in Australia only when no teaching religious were available and they were excluded from school policy development. In this way, the teaching religious promoted the notion that lay teachers were of inferior rank. In particular, there was no consideration of the possibility that married life, or living as a single person outside of religious life, might enhance one's qualities as a teacher and a school manager. However, while these and related lenses through which the Catholic Hierarchy and the religious orders viewed the lay teachers are reasonably well understood (O'Donoghue 2004), there are hardly any studies on how the lay teachers viewed themselves. An investigation of this and associated issues would lead to a deeper knowledge of the history of the role and status of the lay teacher in Catholic education, and thus contribute to the growing knowledge-base on the history of the lives of teachers of all types both nationally and internationally.

Significance and innovation

The project will concentrate on the experience of being a lay teacher in Catholic schools in Western Australia during the period 1940–1980. It was during the middle of this period that major reforms took place within the Catholic Church (the Church) internationally (Hornsby-Smith 2000). These reforms, in turn, led to changes in the composition of the Catholic teaching force in many countries, including Australia. A major consequence is that nowadays young people being educated in Catholic schools in Australia, as in many other English-speaking countries, are usually taught by lay teachers, the principals in their schools are lay women and men, and lay people predominate on their school boards. Equally, the presence of members of religious orders of nuns, religious brothers and priests as teachers and administrators in the schools, is minimal (O'Donoghue 2004: 123–46). Yet, when many of the parents of those currently attending Catholic schools were themselves being educated, the Catholic teaching force was dominated by the teaching religious. The turning point was the mid 1960s and the opening up of the Church to the modern world as a result of the Second Vatican Council (1962–5). This opening up coincided with large numbers leaving the orders, a major drop off in new recruits and a consequent need to employ ever-greater numbers of lay teachers (Grace 2002).

The impact of the change on the lay teachers in Australian Catholic schools has not been the subject of much research. Certainly, there has been some work on the official perspective of the Church and of the teaching religious on the role and status of the lay teacher both before and after the Second Vatican Council (O'Donoghue 2004: 123–46). This work, however, has not been complemented by research projects aimed at investigating the lay teachers' own perspectives on their lives in the last years of the heyday of the teaching religious and the early years when the teaching religious were being rapidly replaced, how they carried out their work in light of those perspectives, and the relationship between their perspectives and the wider socio-historical structure. In seeking to address this deficit, the project proposed here on the experience of being a lay teacher in Catholic schools in Western Australia during the period 1940–80, is also influenced by the great lack of work on the social history of teaching in Australia more generally and by a belief that the most comprehensive way to begin to develop the field is to proceed on a state-by-state basis, concentrating on various categories of teachers in the different educational systems within each state through various historical periods.

Overall, the project will make a major contribution to understanding our region within the overlapping contexts of the Catholic and the educational world internationally. It will do so by developing a new and specialised account for the Australian context of schools as workplaces which constitute the arena of educational action, where curricula, pedagogies, and policies can be seen as dynamic processes shaped not only by teachers' professional concerns, but also by their personal lives. As well as filling a void in the literature on the social history of teaching in Catholic schools for the period in question, the account will open up the field for similar studies on other periods and on teachers in state educational sectors, as well as on teachers in schools of other religious denominations. In this way, the project can be seen as a response to Silver's comment in the early 1990s that the extensive corpus of research which had been built up on the history of education did not add up to 'a serious, widespread historical commitment to bringing the parochial school, the Catholic, the Christian, the religious experience into the canon of educational history' (Silver 1994: 2616); a comment which still holds true today, particularly with regard to studies on the experience of what it meant to be a lay teacher in Catholic schools.

The project is also a response to calls in recent years for a renewed scholarly interest in faith-based schooling as a result of recent international, regional and national developments motivated by religious ideology (Grace 2003). These developments have resulted in the growth of schools within the traditional non-government education systems, along with the expansion of 'fundamental' Christian schools, Islamic schools and schools of other non-Christian faiths. Catholic education, the largest non-government education sector, has also continued to grow and, in so doing, has continued to be dominated by lay people. Because of their level of influence, the lay teachers' ways of thinking need to be better understood. This oral history project will contribute to such an understanding by focusing on the period 1940–1980. It was during this period that the most fundamental changes took place in the 'traditional' Catholic mind-set. The project will illuminate how these changes in the Catholic Church internationally impacted on lay teachers in Australia and laid the foundations upon which much contemporary thinking on Catholic education in the nation takes place. In this way also, the project will contribute to our understanding of our region and the world.

The project will result in the development of:

a.   an outline of the Western Australian Catholic educational world during the period 1940–1980, including a profile of the number of teaching religious and lay teachers classified according to non-religious order and religious order-managed schools – with the latter sub-classified according to order-type – the location of the schools, the physical and social environments of the locations, the school curricula imparted and the pedagogical practices adopted;

b.   24 individual oral histories based on the 'life stories' (Kotre 1984) of lay teachers who taught in Western Australian Catholic schools during the period 1940–1980 regarding how they understood and negotiated their working lives;

c. an overall synthesis in the form of an historical analysis of the lives of lay teachers who taught in Western Australian Catholic schools during the period 1940–1980. The synthesis will be concerned with exploring if the perspectives of the lay teachers not only changed, but also if they were changed by the geographical, economic, social and cultural environments in which they worked.

Approach and methodology

Lancy (1993: 253) distinguishes between the 'narrative tradition' in historical research in which arguments about causation are implicit for the most part, and 'social science history' where theories, assumptions and methods of analyses are explicit. This project is conceptualised within the latter tradition. In particular, the principal research questions, in which the concept of 'perspective' is central, are derived from 'symbolic interactionism', a social theory which constitutes an appropriate theoretical framework for projects aimed at generating rich data of the type sought here (Woods 1992: 338). Symbolic interactionism is both a theory and an approach to the study of human behaviour; it examines the symbolic and the interactive together as they are experienced and organised in the worlds of everyday lives (Blumer 1969: 2). This long-established research tradition, which has been prominent at least during two periods in the last 100 years (Ritzer 1994), has over the last 10 years been reinstated once again as a central position within contemporary social theory (Prus 1996; Charon 2001). While its present-day variations have taken on various nuances, symbolic interactionism is still underpinned by three central principles made explicit by Blumer in 1969:

1 Human beings act toward 'things' on the basis of the meanings that the 'things' have for them.
2 This attribution of meaning to objects through symbols is a continuous process. The symbols are gestures, signs, language and anything else that may convey meanings.
3 The meanings are handled in, and modified through, an interpretative process used by the person in dealing with the things he or she encounters (Blumer 1969: 2).

It is on the basis of the operation of these principles that 'perspectives or 'frameworks through which people make sense of the world' (Woods 1992), are formed.

Blumer's principles of symbolic interactionism are fundamental to the three major research questions of this proposal. His concept of 'perspectives' is central to the first research question, namely, what were the 'perspectives' of lay teachers in Western Australian Catholic schools during the period 1940–1980 regarding what it meant to be a teacher? Also, his principle that human beings act toward 'things' on the basis of the meanings that the 'things' have for them, is central to the second research question, namely, how did the lay teachers carry out their work in light of those perspectives?; 'things' covers a range of phenomena, from the concrete – people, material objects and institutions – to the abstract, which includes the situations in which people find themselves and the principles that guide human life. The third research question, namely, what was the relationship between the perspectives of the lay teachers and the wider socio-historical structure?, is based on the notion that such conditions as 'time, space, culture, economic status, technological status, career history and individual biography' (Strauss and Corbin 1990: 103) can act to either facilitate or constrain the action/interactional strategies taken within a specific context by an individual or a group. Coupled with this is the assumption within symbolic interactionism that where these conditions do act to facilitate action/interactional strategies they have to be managed by the individual or group (Strauss and Corbin 1990: 103). Thus, while not totally in harmony with Giddens' (1984) notion of 'structuration', 'structure is not neglected in symbolic interactionism even though the emphasis is primarily on 'agency'.

The research will be undertaken in three stages.

Stage 1

The aim of this largely descriptive stage of the study is to portray the context within which Catholic teachers in Western Australia taught during the period under examination. This portrayal will be based mainly on a variety of documentary evidence, including annual reports on Catholic education in Western Australia, the 'rules and constitutions' and 'acts of chapter' of religious orders, school annuals and year books, and reports on education in *The Record*, the Western Australian Catholic newspaper. This evidence will be supplemented by descriptive data yielded through the individual oral histories of lay teachers to be conducted in Stage 2, even though the main focus in that stage is to elicit the 'life stories' of the teachers. In other words, the 'life story' interviews to be conducted in Stage 2 will also seek to unearth descriptive data on which the written evidence is silent, as well as extend and enrich that which is available. The result will be a profile of the social characteristics of lay teachers who taught in Western Australian Catholic schools during the period 1940–80, where they taught, the physical and social environments in which they taught, their pedagogical practices, and the curricula they imparted.

Stage 2

This stage of the study will result in 24 oral histories based on the 'life stories' (Goodson 1992: 6) of teachers who taught in Western Australian Catholic schools during the period 1940–1980 regarding how they understood and negotiated their working lives. The accounts will be elicited by means of semi-structured interviews.

The sample

Following on the position taken above, it is instructive to consider Cunningham and Gardner's (2004: 6) reiteration of the long-held position that one of the inherent and inevitable difficulties of any oral history project must be that it involves very small numbers of respondents in relation to the size of the original target group. Leaning heavily on both the position and experience of Foot (1998) and Thompson (2000), they conclude that, as a function of the natural mortality of potential respondents from that group, 'scientific sampling is simply not possible in this kind of work, even if it were seen as desirable'. Taking account of this position, the stance taken here is that participants can best be selected through a 'purposive sampling plan' (Punch 1998: 193). To this end, 24 individuals who were lay teachers during the period will be interviewed. Informal preliminary investigations indicate that such a goal can easily be met because of the existence of a wide pool of potential and willing participants.

The purposive sampling approach to be adopted seeks to enhance the possibility of gaining access to as wide a variety of perspectives as possible, while balancing the sample for gender. Thus, the selection will be as follows:

a. eight participants (four males and four females) who ceased teaching in Catholic schools prior to the meeting of the Second Vatican Council (1962–1965);
b. eight participants (four males and four females) who taught in Catholic schools both before, during and after the Second Vatican Council;
c. eight participants (four males and four females) who commenced employment in Catholic schools after the Second Vatican Council ceased to function.

Every effort will also be made to ensure that approximately two-thirds of the participants are individuals who taught in both urban and rural primary schools, the largest group of schools within the Catholic, as well as within the other Western Australian education sectors. The remaining participants will be secondary school teachers selected from across a range of teaching-subject areas and again with the aim of investigating experiences in both urban and rural settings.

While most participants are likely to be Catholics – at least in background – steps will also be taken to recruit a small number of non-Catholics around three to four. Also, every effort will be taken to sample across the various religious orders involved in Catholic education in the state. Western Australia is an excellent case to choose in terms of maximizing variety according to religious orders active in teaching at the time. For example, in 1960 the female teaching orders in the state included the Sisters of Mercy, 'Josephite Sisters', Presentation Sisters, Sisters of the Good Samaritan, Dominican Sisters, Sisters of St Brigid, Loreto Sisters and OLSH Sisters, while the male orders included the Jesuits, the Christian Brothers, the De La Salle Brothers and the Patrician Brothers. Selecting participants across this range will also ensure that 'voices' are heard from those who taught in the schools of those orders which catered for the relatively well-off proportion of the Catholic population as well as from those who taught the great majority. Finally, to interview 24 participants is to engage in a realistic exercise in a project extending over two years (Weiler 1992). Experience indicates that individual interviews in projects of this type, where the majority of the participants are retired teachers, usually take at least two hours each in the first round (Cunningham and Gardner 2004: 6). These are usually followed up by a second round also of two hours, where initial ideas prompted in the first round are pursued for clarification and further elaboration, and previously unexplored ideas are opened up. This represents 48 hours of interviewing a year and 96 hours of interviewing in total over two years.

The interviews

In the first year of the project 12 participants will be interviewed, while another 12 will be interviewed in the second year. Each participant will be interviewed twice for approximately two hours per interview as experience shows that this is around the length of time required to elicit extensive and in-depth accounts. The interviews will be semi-structured (Taylor and Bogdan 1984: 76). This method is concerned with creating the environment to encourage participants to discuss their lives and experiences in free-flowing, open-ended discussions and enables the researcher to interpret their views. In conducting the interviews, general principles as outlined by Measor (1985: 63–73) will be followed. The participants will be given an *aide-memoire* or semi-structured interview guide two weeks prior to the interviews to allow them to reflect on the headings. As themes arise they will be pursued with the participants in a 'lengthy conversation piece' (Simons 1982: 37). Each interview will be tape recorded providing that consent will be received from the participant. Where consent is not forthcoming, field notes will be made. Transcribed interviews will be 'checked back' with the participants until they become accepted as representative of their positions.

The researcher is alert to issues raised in oral history research regarding problems of memory and will safeguard for them along lines proposed in Lumis (1987) and Perks and Thomson (1998). It will also be necessary to keep in mind Thomson's (1998: 585) point that one of the most significant shifts in the last 25 years in oral history has been the recognition that 'the so-called unreliability of memory might be a resource, rather than a problem, for historical interpretation and reconstruction'. Primarily what is being referred to here is that memory can alert us to 'those aspects of one's past which become sedimented through regular repetition in life narratives' (Cunningham and Gardner's 2004: 5). Equally, one needs to be alert to the dangers of approaching research of the type proposed here with various historical questions arising out of other research agendas of interest to the researcher. It will be necessary to 'bracket' (Usher 1996: 21) or temporarily set aside such questions in order to identify the issues of importance to the participants at the time. In the same way, various 'outsider' constructs such as the industrial-relations' and 'teachers-work' models of teachers and teaching which are regularly used in the study of the history of teachers' unions and the sociology of 'teaching as an occupation', need to be eschewed so that what emerges are the 'insider' constructs of the participants themselves, as opposed to frameworks generated by filtering their 'voices' through pre-chosen constructs of the researcher.

Stage 3

This stage is concerned with the development of case studies of each of the three major groups of lay teachers already outlined: those who ceased teaching in Catholic schools prior to the meeting of the Second Vatican Council (1962–5), those who taught in Catholic schools both before and after the Council, and those who commenced employment in Catholic schools after the Council ceased to function. Such an approach is based on the notion that group perspectives may occur 'when people see themselves as being in the same boat and when they have the opportunity to interact with reference to their problems' (Becker *et al.* 1961: 36), but it also recognises that certain perspectives may not be shared by all and may be informed by individuals who see things differently.

Each of the transcripts from the individual case studies will be sorted into one of the three major groups of teachers noted above. Each group of transcripts will then be analysed using the 'inductive analysis' procedure outlined by Taylor and Bogdan (1984: 69). To this end also, grounded theory (Strauss and Corbin 1990: 96–115) modes of analysis, particularly the 'making of comparisons' and the 'asking of questions', will be used in the formulation of propositions.

The final product of each of the three stages in the research will go towards developing an overall synthesis in the form of an historical analysis of the experience of being a lay teacher in Western Australian Catholic schools during the period 1940–1980. In particular, it will be concerned with exploring the relationship between the lay teachers' perspectives regarding how they understood and negotiated their working lives, and the wider socio-historical structure. The details of the analytical approach are as outlined in Dimmock and O'Donoghue (1997, 1997a: 48–70).

National benefit

The project will contribute to understanding how changes in the Catholic Church internationally during the period 1940–80 impacted on lay teachers in Australia and laid the foundations upon which much contemporary thinking on Catholic education in the nation takes place. Such understanding is essential given that Catholic education is the largest non-government education sector in Australia and the recipient of very significant funding from the national coffers. It is also required at a time when there is renewed interest in, and often suspicion of, faith-based schooling as a result of recent international, regional and national developments motivated by religious ideology.

The project will also be of benefit in a more practical sense. Central to current policies aimed at improving both public and private education in Australia is an emphasis on having more flexible, responsive and student-oriented approaches to curriculum and pedagogy. However, while advice has been plentiful, relatively little of it has been based on empirical research. Over a decade ago Hargreaves (1993: 149) alerted us to a danger in this type of situation, arguing that one common reason for the failure of so many educational innovations is that they are based on 'so little knowledge about the nature of the everyday world of teachers, pupils and schools'. Projects on the social history of teaching, involving longitudinal perspectives not otherwise available to policy makers, have a significant role to play in responding to this observation by extending the empirical base. The project proposed here will contribute to the field for the Australian context by focusing on one group of key personnel, namely, lay teachers in Catholic schools in Western Australia.

The project will also lay the groundwork for related studies on the views of other major stakeholders in education, particularly parents and students. Furthermore, given the focus on a period of great change within the Catholic Church and Catholic education, it will be insightful for policy makers nationally by contributing to an understanding of how, over an extended period of time, teachers have responded to innovation and change. Such an understanding, based on four decades of collective practice, will constitute a major resource through which to reflect critically on the existing knowledge-base on teachers' careers (Day 1999), teachers' professional lives (Goodson 2000) and teachers' well-being (Holmes 2004). Also, it will yield a set of insights to complement those from other disciplines informing the current debate on the development of policies aimed at improving the quality of Australian education systems.

Chapter 11

The interpretivist paradigm and research based on 'problem-focused' ideas

The previous four chapters were concerned with research based upon 'concept-driven' ideas. The central concern in this chapter is with outlining a research proposal to illustrate how a symbolic interactionist theoretical position within the interpretivist paradigm can also be utilized to underpin research of the 'problem-focused' variety. Before examining the research proposal, however, it needs to be recognised that interpretivist research cannot accommodate research questions where one is searching for 'sure-fired' solutions to specific problems. The latter search tends to be the domain of those working within a positivist paradigm, particularly those who adopt an experimental methodology.

At the same time, it is arguable that the interpretivist paradigm has a crucial role to play in problem solving in a broader sense. Indeed, some would hold that the first task one needs to engage in when one sets out to consider how to approach what one perceives to be a problem, or set of related problems, is to develop a deeper understanding of the area. Broudy (1967) took up this point back in the 1960s in relation to problems which he characterised as belonging to the domain of education, although the position has applicability across the whole range of social issues and associated professions. His argument was that educationalists should know not only how to do their job, but should also be conditioned by reflection. Sutherland (1985) argued along similar lines when she stated that society demands, and has a legitimate interest in demanding, that individuals who are working in the field of education should have their practical action properly conditioned by reflection. This was consistent with Stanley's (1968) rejection of what he termed the 'craft mentality' in education when he contested the notion that educationalists are mere practitioners operating within a system and according to procedures dictated by others. It was also consistent with Broudy's case for what he termed the 'interpretive use of knowledge'; a use that enables one to conceptualise and understand a problem or issue. Another way of stating the latter point specifically with regard to the field of education is that one should engage in studies of educational problems with the aim of coming to understand them within a framework which 'utilizes the relationship of the school to the social order, and the aims, and the organization, and the curriculum of the school of a particular society' (Broudy 1967: iv).

Overall, what one can distil from the arguments of those in sympathy with the position of educationalists like Broudy is that there is a great need to engage in studies which allow one to gain a broad overview on educational problems. To hold this position is to be open to the possibility that what one considers in the initial stages to be a problem may strike one later as not a problem at all, while at this later stage also unforseen problems may present themselves unexpectedly as being the 'real' ones in need of solutions. This was the nature of the thinking brought to bear by Dr Michael Brennan when we embarked on preparing his Doctor of Education thesis proposal in the Graduate School of Education, The University of Western Australia, in the late 1990s. Dr Brennan was concerned that many of what were seen as specific problems within the Technical and Further Education (TAFE) sector in Western Australia were disconnected. Furthermore, he held that research projects which focused on this disconnected agenda were likely to come up with only temporary solutions to what were poorly understood problems in the first instance. Thus, he concluded, there was a need for a broader set of interpretive studies so that specific problems could be located contextually and, perhaps, even reconceptualized. This, in turn, led to the development of the following research proposal.

Project title

The involvement of 'TAFE WA' personnel with overseas students: Background, functions and concerns

Research aim

The phenomenon of overseas students studying in Australia is one that merits much serious research. The research project proposed here is one attempt to meet the challenge that exists. It focuses on a particular educational sector within Australia that is concerned with the education of overseas students, namely, the TAFE sector. Furthermore, it restricts its focus to TAFE in Western Australia (TAFE WA). This is partly to make the project manageable. However, it is also because of the proximity of Western Australia (WA) to South-East Asia and the likelihood that the state, through colleges in the TAFE sector, will become a main provider of technical and vocational education and training courses for South-East Asian students in the future.

The project has three particular aims:

1   The first aim is to develop an understanding of the background to overseas students studying at TAFE colleges in Western Australia.

2   The second aim is to develop an understanding of the present functions of TAFE WA in providing for overseas students who come to study at its colleges.

3   The third aim is to develop an understanding of the concerns of TAFE WA personnel who have had responsibilities relating to the provision of technical and vocational education and training for this student cohort.

The intention is that these research aims will be approached with 'practical' relevance in mind, in the sense that there is a desire that the findings will be insightful for improving practice related to the education and training of the student cohort in question. At the same time, the aims are broad enough to allow for a research orientation that goes beyond 'immediate relevance'. In this regard, the first aim is based on a recognition that the past can impact on the present and, consequently, needs to be always kept in mind in dealing with contemporary issues (Aldrich 1996). The second aim recognises that the functions that people in TAFE WA perform in providing for overseas students can extend well beyond those laid down in 'duty statements' and 'job description forms', while also realising that many expected functions might not be performed for various reasons. Finally, it is recognised that it is only with such a background in mind that issues raised in pursuit of the third aim could best be interpreted.

The context

Australia has a tradition of educating overseas students dating back at least to the beginning of the twentieth century. However, defined government policy in the area was not formalised until 1950 with the development of the Colombo Plan (O'Donoghue 1994: 2). This Plan, as a form of Australian government aid, provided overseas students with scholarships to study in Australian universities and colleges (Department of Employment, Education and Training 1992: 2). For the next 35 years increasing numbers of students from overseas came to Australia to study. These students were either directly supported by Australia's aid programme, or they received what was effectively a subsidy because their tuition fees did not cover the costs of the education provided. Since 1986, however, the Commonwealth Government has encouraged higher education institutions in the country to market Australia's educational services overseas (Industry Commission 1991). Much of the effort in this regard has centred on attracting full fee-paying students from Asia and its success is attested to by the fact that in 1997, overseas students contributed about $3.2 billion to the Australian economy (Downer 1998a: 2), of which around $1.121 billion came from fees paid by Asian students (Jolley 1997: 75). Also, the total number of overseas students in Australia in all sectors had increased from about 22,000 in 1986 (Department of

Employment, Education and Training 1992: 3) to more than 150,000 in 1997 (Sullivan 1998: 4).

By the second half of the 1990s, estimates suggested that there were approximately 1.35 million overseas students undertaking tertiary education outside their countries of origin, with Australia hosting more of these students on a per capita basis than the United States, the United Kingdom, or Canada (Downer 1997: 3). According to Shinn *et al.* (1999: 82), by 1995, Australia had joined the ranks of international players in the market for overseas students as one of the largest receiving countries. By and large, the industrialised countries tend to be net 'exporters' of tertiary education services, while the developing countries are net 'importers'. The United States, Western Europe, Australia and Canada are the countries most favoured by overseas students, while Japan, Italy and Finland are among the high-income industrialised countries that continue to send students overseas to study (Jolley 1997: 5). However, most of the overseas student population throughout the world comes from non-industrialised regions, namely, the Middle East, Latin America, Africa and Asia. The Philippines is an interesting case in that it receives students from North Korea and Pakistan, while at the same time it sends students to the United States.

For many years overseas students have studied in formal courses offered by Australian educational institutions. They have done so under a variety of arrangements, including the Colombo Plan scholarships, fellowships provided under aid programmes and projects, and the sponsored students' programme (Sullivan 1998: 4). Also, particularly since 1986, increasing numbers have come to Australia as full fee-paying students (Sullivan 1998: 4). Most of those students have come from the Asia-Pacific region (Downer 1998a: 2), which contains the countries that are Australia's closest neighbours, thus perpetuating the trend that has existed ever since overseas students first started coming to the country.

In 1985, the Federal Labor government in Australia generated a new policy for overseas students wishing to study in the country. One outcome of this policy was a categorisation of overseas students according to the origins of their financial backing. These student categories were entitled 'subsidised' – by the existing student-funded overseas student charge – 'sponsored' – by the Australian International Development Assistance Bureau – and 'full fee-paying students' (Industry Commission 1991: 21). O'Donoghue (1994: 4) argued that the designation of the latter category reflected the government's move towards economic rationalist policy making. He went on to note that earnings from education were expected to achieve $100 million by 1998. In fact, by the year 2000 export earnings far exceeded this figure, generating $3.5 billion per annum in fees, goods and services (Australian Broadcasting Corporation 2000).

Smart (1986) argued that tertiary institutions entered the arena of marketing educational services primarily through forms of government encouragement and coercion. Institutions were urged to look for new ways of showing 'educational entrepreneurship'. Part of the government's approach, according to Smart (1986), was to highlight the importance to Australia's national interest of improving the quality of Australia's education resources from the revenue gained from such fresh entrepreneurial initiatives. The provision of export development grants and the reduction of the existing Federal funding reinforced the notion that privatisation was the way forward (Smart 1986, 1987). In 1988, the argument was advanced further with the signalling that the introduction of fees for private overseas students was a way for universities to generate income and become less dependent on government funding.

Although all sectors of education, including schools, colleges and TAFE, were able to enter the private student market by 1987, the trend in overseas demand favoured university education over other education sectors. However, from 1991, a major expansion occurred in overseas demand in the vocational education and training sector. According to a government report into the export of education services at the time, a number of concerns had arisen in relation to the full fee-paying overseas student 'industry' (Industry Commission 1991: 185). Most of these concerns were raised in connection with overseas students studying in universities. This was because almost all overseas students in Australia at the time of the report were attending universities, with the TAFE sector enrolling only very small numbers, having taken longer than universities to pursue the government's policy in this regard. Nevertheless, the report also incorporated TAFE students through its deliberations and findings, maintaining that many of the concerns about universities were also relevant to the TAFE sector (Industry Commission 1991: 185). The report argued that:

> As numbers of students attending TAFE rise, and as funding pressures affecting places for domestic students build up, many of the same issues now being experienced by universities will come to the fore in the TAFE sector.
>
> (Industry Commission 1991: 185)

According to Alexander and Rizvi (1993: 19), a major problem with the move towards viewing education as a commodity to be sold was that higher education was now seen as a 'uniform product for consumption'. They held that because of this development, education ran the risk of becoming standardised and divorced from particular cultural concerns (Alexander and Rizvi 1993: 19). They also argued that Australian higher education institutions felt perfectly justified in providing the same range of subjects to all students and regarded teaching styles to be neutral with respect to particular cultural backgrounds. This was a particular issue in the case of students from many and varied South-East Asian countries, who were often mistakenly treated as if they were a homogeneous group. There was a concern that these students would be subject to the influence of a standardised Australian curriculum which would find its way into the work practices that the students would eventually follow in their different home countries. On this, Alexander and Rizvi (1993: 19) contended that when domestic practices in foreign countries acquired international characteristics, they inevitably undermined local traditions and practices.

Despite such warnings, however, there is still some truth in Jones' (1989) contention made more than a decade ago, that the literature on overseas students in Australia has neglected the educational and cultural aspects of overseas students in favour of financial, administrative and marketing concerns. Indeed, some would argue that Hodgkin's (1972: 16) observation of nearly 30 years ago still holds, namely, that there is a tendency for foreign students to be placed into 'exclusive categories such as "foreign" or "Asian"', which often leads to 'fallacious assumptions about adjustment problems, educational difficulties, and living patterns in the overseas situation'.

More recently, Volet and Kee (1993) claimed that most literature has given a stereotypical view of overseas students, thus neglecting their individual differences. This echoed Ballard's (1987) emphasis on the importance of developing an understanding of the cultures and the educational systems of the home countries of these students. In this connection, the guide for TAFE teachers of overseas students published in 1992 by the National TAFE Overseas Network (Mezger 1992), provided extremely valuable information for TAFE teachers. However, this manual did not contain accounts of first-hand experiences of being a TAFE staff member dealing with overseas students. It is arguable that an understanding of such experiences is essential for teachers, support staff and decision-makers. It is also arguable that it should deal with individual cultural groups.

Literature review

Three prominent themes emerge from the literature about students from developing countries who study overseas. In broad terms, these issues concern the welfare of the students, the teaching and learning they experience, and the curriculum they study. Each of these areas will now be briefly considered in turn.

The Australian academic literature on overseas students was developed in its earliest forms by personnel most closely connected with student welfare. These personnel included student counsellors and advisors (Ballard and Clanchy 1991, 1988, 1984; Ballard 1989, 1987, 1982; Bradley and Bradley 1984; Keats 1972; Rao 1976). The research that they produced was mainly concerned with the welfare issues associated with studying and living in a foreign country. Areas of concern centred on language difficulties, housing issues, cultural adjustments to Australian living and difficulties faced by students taking courses in a foreign language. These studies brought to the fore a recognition that overseas students were experiencing difficulties in adjusting to a culturally different way of life in Australia.

The appropriateness of the teaching styles adopted for the promotion of learning amongst overseas students constitutes another area of research. On this, Bilbow (1989: 85) drew attention to the possibility that the lecture-style of delivery might pose severe problems for those from non-English speaking backgrounds because of linguistic, discoursal and cultural sources. He went on to argue that this is an area that merits serious investigation.

The model of providing for the needs of overseas students that was prevalent for so long in Australia also suggested that social, cultural and intellectual adaptations were required of overseas students on entering higher education institutions in overseas countries. What was being argued was that overseas students needed to be assisted in 'adjusting' to the host country environment. Studies highlighting the importance of adjustment originate with works like those of Keats (1972), and were developed further by Gassin (1982), and Bock and Gassin (1982). No significant studies in this regard were developed in relation to TAFE. The works of Ballard (1982) and Ballard and Clanchy (1984), however, which offered instruction to Australian universities based on a 'deficit model', are likely to have been used extensively within the TAFE sector.

The third major area of research on overseas students focuses on the curriculum that they studied. By the 1990s disquiet was being expressed about the tendency to slot overseas students into courses designed for 'first world' situations without much consideration being given to the appropriateness of such courses for practice in their countries of origin. A related issue that emerged in Australia by the mid-1990s was dissatisfaction with the content of some of the courses being offered in that they did not fulfil the requirements that were necessary for registration in their profession in their home country (Smith 1994: 5).

The inefficacy of using curriculum material appropriate for one culture with other cultural groups has also been a subject of research. A number of the studies relate to expatriate international development consultants working with counterparts in developing countries (Leach 1993, 1994; O'Donoghue 1994; Scott-Stevens 1987; Ware 1994). The research undertaken by Ware (1994) in devising English-language programmes for Vietnamese and Cambodian students through Radio Australia is also instructive for those developing programmes for overseas students who come to study in Australia. To ensure accuracy and relevance of the programmes, Ware travelled to Cambodia and, as she put it:

> ... took every opportunity to engage local people in conversation, and observed a wide range of people at work, at home and at leisure, discussing

lifestyles and customs, government, the public service infrastructure, health, medicine and potential for business development.

(Ware 1994: 6)

Ware also engaged other Australian expatriates with regional experience to advise on particular needs of students beyond the capital city and she took many photographs concerning programme content (Ware 1994: 6). This material was then used by an illustrator in the development of the relevant text. The challenge to both the university and TAFE sectors in Australia is to learn from and build upon experiences such as this.

Much revenue has been generated in Australia as a result of the increasing number of overseas full fee-paying students. Nevertheless, in recent years a number of groups and individuals have raised serious ethical concerns about the process. In particular, they have objected to a notion of education as a commodity and as a service that can be viewed 'in terms of profitability or usefulness' (Kennedy 1991: 3). Burns (1991: 4), for example, argued that the drive for financial resources 'places lower value on other discourses such as the pedagogical, ethical and cultural'. Likewise, Jones (1989) questioned the priority given to financial, administrative and marketing matters to the detriment of educational and cultural concerns of overseas students on campus.

Concerns have also been voiced that, even from an economic perspective, the approach taken is not sensible in the long term. Crevola (1993), for example, has argued that the desire for profit in the short term gives the impression that Australian universities are regarding education as a business commodity and that this has not been well received, particularly in some countries in Asia. Similarly, Marginson (1993) declared that universities have taken a short-term approach aimed at raising additional revenue at the expense of building a good long-term educational relationship in the Asia-Pacific region. While Marginson argued that welfare and counselling services for overseas students have improved, he also contended that there has been less adjustment in curriculum design, particularly with respect to Asia-specific content and the cultural sensitivity of courses (Jolley 1997: 246).

It is also contended that the previous over-zealous marketing of Australian education has led to confusion about standards of education and has created a negative image of Australian education norms. In particular, there are concerns about possible discrepancies between what is marketed and what is delivered. There is also concern that the commercialisation required to boost numbers of full fee-paying students may have led to a decline in quality assurance. In an attempt to respond to the various concerns, the Australian Vice-Chancellors' Committee (AVCC) developed and disseminated a Code of Ethical Practice (CEP) that was endorsed by the Australian government. This Code was initiated to 'ensure that the potential benefits of full fee-paying overseas students who choose to study in Australia are fully realised for both the students and the host institutions' (Australian Vice-Chancellors' Committee 1987: 1). The Code went on to emphasise the importance of universities paying attention to a number of issues, including care, quality and 'the maintenance of academic standards' (Australian Vice-Chancellors' Committee 1987: 2). It also indicated to university staff that it was unethical to accept fees from overseas students without making appropriate adjustments to infrastructure support that facilitated training programmes and the establishment of support services that were responsive to the welfare and academic needs of overseas students. If one subscribes to such a position then it demands that, among other things, we develop an understanding of the experiences and concerns of those currently working in the field. It is the adoption of such a position that is taken as a justification for the particular study of the TAFE sector outlined in this proposal.

The research plan

Throughout the Western nations, issues associated with the increasing presence of overseas students on academic campuses are a result of the priority of the 'internationalisation' of education as a development strategy for the institutions. While most of the institutions in question have identified their potential for cultural, social and economic transformations, their initiatives have, in the main, been superficial. In particular, despite the plethora of policy initiatives, little research has been undertaken as to the effect of changing policy and practices on students, educators, administrators, or countries concerned. This deficit is serious, given the contention of authorities in the field of 'educational innovation and change' that a first step in any process aimed at improvement necessitates taking cognisance of the views of practitioners, along with an understanding of all the phenomena involved.

TAFE colleges nationally have had a relatively limited involvement in international education and training. Recently, however, the curricula of Australian TAFE have become progressively known and valued in countries in the Asia-Pacific region. Australian TAFE lecturers teaching overseas on secondment, and the growing number of overseas students studying in Australia, have given TAFE an increasing body of international market intelligence. Nevertheless, it seems that while the number of overseas students in TAFE has increased dramatically in recent years, the presence of these students in most colleges has preceded an understanding of the complexities of international programmes and strategic plans to meet these complexities (Australia TAFE International 1996: iv). One important step in improving the quality of TAFE programmes for overseas students would be to take into account the full range of relevant practitioners' understandings of the current situation. This is the assumption on which the study being proposed here is based.

The necessity of understanding people's contextual realities before introducing changes that hope to improve the quality of education in any context is well summarised by Fullan (1982: 2):

> In order to effect improvement, that is, to effect an introduced change that has the promise of increasing success and decreasing failure, the world of the people most closely involved must be understood.

It is this perspective that gave rise to the following research questions:

- What is the background to overseas students studying at TAFE colleges in Western Australia (TAFE WA)?
- What are the present functions of TAFE WA in providing for overseas students who come to study at its colleges?
- What are the concerns of TAFE WA personnel who have had responsibilities relating to the provision of technical and vocational education and training for this student cohort?

These questions are a specific application to the TAFE WA context of Fullan's (1982) claim as set out above. In particular, they are an application to the case of TAFE WA staff providing for overseas students. It is accepted that studies of this nature also need to be undertaken with other groups, particularly overseas students themselves, so that the 'full' picture can be developed.

Theoretical framework and the three research questions

The interpretivist paradigm has been chosen to underpin the research. The value of adopting an interpretivist approach to research is that it can uncover people's understandings of a phenomenon. This reflects a tradition in social science that fundamentally depends on observations taken in people's natural settings and interacting with them in their own language and on their terms (Kirk and Miller 1986: 9). A researcher adopting an interpretivist approach is concerned with revealing the meanings behind empirical observations. In such an approach, the researcher is the primary data-gathering instrument, using carefully constructed questions aimed at understanding a phenomenon through semi-structured or open-ended interviews with the people involved and in their own surroundings. Other important means of gathering data are through 'thick' description, review of documents and other records, and on-site observation. These methods rely on the interactional, adaptive, and judgemental abilities of the human inquirer. Keedy (1992: 162) considers that the adoption of qualitative research methods within an interpretive research approach enables the researcher to visualise how events or phenomena are perceived differently from multiple perspectives and from across similar events. Furthermore, the interpretivist approach can produce a vast amount of detailed information about a small number of people.

The first research question

The first research question is aimed at developing an understanding of the background to overseas students studying at TAFE colleges in Western Australia (TAFE WA). To this end the interpretivist paradigm will inform the work of the researcher in reviewing data contained in a wide range of public and private records and documents. This approach is consistent with Greene's (1994: 538) declaration that document review is one of the methods that offers the greatest consonance with the interpretivist perspective.

Various types of written data have already been collected from files compiled by government departments. The files contain mainly education and immigration details regarding overseas students studying in Australia, as well as miscellaneous organisational papers relating to the same matter. They are held in State and National archives. Included are the records of correspondence between the Head Offices of the separate Commonwealth Departments of Education and Immigration and their successors. Administrative documents, such as current working files, submissions and proposals, progress reports, agenda and minutes of meetings, official government announcements and other pronouncements intended for intra-government as well as external use are also central in the research process. Government inquiries into overseas students will also be drawn upon. Other printed sources to be consulted include conference papers and reports, as well as newspapers. Personal documents, such as certain individuals' files and memoranda, lecturers' teaching and learning resources, along with other pedagogic and curriculum material prepared for, or in regard to, overseas students, completes the array of documentary sources from which data will be gathered to address the first research question.

As the study is exploratory, it will not be possible from the outset to know the sum total of sub-research questions needed to guide the research with regard to this first research question. However, the following guiding questions have been deduced from it:

- *First research question*
  - What is the background to overseas students studying at TAFE colleges in Western Australia?

- *Guiding questions*
  - In what circumstances have overseas students studied at TAFE colleges in Western Australia?
  - Under what conditions have overseas students studied at TAFE colleges in Western Australia?

    – What policy changes have enabled overseas students to study at
      TAFE colleges in Western Australia?

Such guiding questions, of course, are not specific questions to be answered.
Rather, they are those that suggest themselves at this point as being the most
productive guides to generate data pertinent to the central area of interest.
From the guiding questions, an *aide-memoire* (Burgess 1984; Minichiello
et al. 1990) will be developed to initiate 'conversations'. As participants
raise unforeseen issues they will be allowed to pursue them. Further, as new
questions suggest themselves they will be pursued. Finally, where participants
are unable to respond meaningfully to questions, they will not be pressed on
them.

    The following illustrates how Guiding Question 1.1 outlined above can
be translated into a set of subordinate guiding questions in the initial *aide-
memoire*.

- *Guiding question*
  - In what circumstances have overseas students studied at TAFE
    colleges in Western Australia?

- *Examples of questions in the initial aide-memoire*
  - What is the record of overseas students enrolling at TAFE colleges
    in WA?
  - Who sponsored/paid for the students, both in regard to academic
    fees and living costs?
  - Why did overseas students attend TAFE colleges in WA, in preference
    to elsewhere in Australia?

Similar *aide-memoire* questions will be developed for the other guiding
questions. The total body of written data to be consulted will be analysed by
the researcher using 'grounded theory' methods.

The second research question

The second research question of the study aims to develop an understanding
of the present functions of TAFE WA in providing for overseas students who
come to study at its colleges. At this point it is necessary to explain what is
meant by the term 'function' within the present context. This refers simply
to activities that people working in TAFE WA carry out. Accordingly, it
incorporates not only those activities which are officially assigned to them, but
also actions they allocate to themselves. Also, for some people it encompasses
not fulfilling certain actions they are charged to perform.

    In addressing the second research question the interpretivist paradigm will
inform the work in two ways. One is the researcher's interpretation of a wide

range of contemporary, official records. These records consist principally of job description forms, job advertisements, organisation charts, and internal memoranda arising in or in connection with a number of TAFE institutions. The interpretivist paradigm will also guide a series of semi-structured interviews with TAFE administrators and lecturers.

The interviewing and record search regarding the second research question will be an iterative process. The initial source of data will come from interviews with TAFE WA personnel in colleges and administrative departments. In connection with these interviews, various documents are likely to be made available to the researcher by the interviewees. These should include formal administrative instructions emanating from the Western Australian Department of Training (WADOT) central office, TAFE International Western Australia (TIWA), and five TAFE colleges in the Perth metropolitan area, setting out policy and procedures to be followed in providing for overseas students. Also to be provided will be minutes of meetings of the TIWA Advisory Board, as well as reports of some general and specific-purpose meetings between college level personnel who provide for overseas students. Other workplace documents are likely to include examples of special teaching and learning worksheets prepared by lecturers explaining particular terms and definitions relevant to specific study areas that are unfamiliar to overseas students.

TAFE WA personnel to be interviewed have already been located at the central office and at five TAFE colleges in the metropolitan area. Full-time TAFE colleges are spread throughout both metropolitan and country areas and total nine in all. However, since overseas students began attending TAFE WA, they have studied almost exclusively at metropolitan institutions. This is the principal reason why metropolitan colleges have been chosen as the location of the study. In addition, constraints of time, finance and accessibility mean that the study will be further limited to the Perth metropolitan area. The decision as to who should be interviewed is based on the potential, as identified by the researcher's previous observations, of individuals to provide rich descriptions of their functions carried out during their work with, and in regard to, overseas students.

Sixty current TAFE WA staff members are likely to participate in the study. Accordingly, a very wide range of perspectives will be canvassed. To this end, participants will include personnel responsible for marketing of courses, recruiting of students, advising and counselling students, and administering immigration regulations in order for students to be granted right of entry to Australia and TAFE WA institutions. They will also include college-based TAFE WA personnel who are directly connected to teaching the students, including managing directors, assistant directors responsible for overseas students, directors of academic services/training in charge of different subject disciplines, heads of academic departments, heads of English Language Intensive Courses for Overseas Students (ELICOS) programmes, and lecturers in various study areas. Also included here will be learning resource centre (library) staff and laboratory and computer technicians. Another group of participants will be institution-based staff who are associated with what may be termed welfare and social issues. These are the student counsellors, overseas student coordinators, student services officers, travel and accommodation staff and canteen managers.

As with the first research question, this aspect of the study is also exploratory. Thus, it is not possible from the outset to know the sum total of sub-research questions needed to guide the research into this second research question. Again, however, some guiding questions can be deduced from this central question and can be laid out as follows:

- *Second research question*
  - What are the present functions of TAFE WA in providing for overseas students who come to study at its colleges?

- *Guiding questions*
  - What systems have been established by TAFE WA to deal with the sojourn of overseas students at its institutions in Western Australia?
  - What procedures have been established by TAFE WA to deal with the sojourn of overseas students at its institutions in Western Australia?
  - What have been the actual duties carried out by all TAFE WA staff who have had responsibilities relating to the provision of technical and vocational education and training for this student cohort?
  - What have been the actual tasks carried out by all TAFE WA staff who have had responsibilities relating to the provision of technical and vocational education and training for this student cohort?

Also, as previously pointed out in the case of the first research question, such guiding questions are not specific questions to be answered. Rather, they are those that suggest themselves at this point as being the most productive guides to generate data pertinent to the central area of interest. Accordingly, Guiding Question 2.1, for example, can be translated into a set of subordinate guiding questions in the initial *aide-memoire*, as shown below:

- *Guiding question*
  - What systems have been established by TAFE WA to deal with the sojourn of overseas students at its colleges?
- *Examples of questions in the initial aide-memoire*
  - What, if any, special arrangements were made in the college for overseas students?
  - What was done to plan and prepare for having overseas students in the institution?

Similar *aide-memoire* questions can be developed for the other guiding questions.

Using 'grounded theory' methods, the researcher will analyse the total body of the transcripts of interviews with TAFE WA personnel as well as written documents and records obtained in the course of the research. In doing this, the aim will be to interpret how those personnel interpret the functions they carry out in their involvement with overseas students. In particular, general ideas, themes or concepts will be sought as analytical tools for making generalisations.

The third research question

The third research question is aimed at developing an understanding of the concerns of TAFE WA personnel who have had responsibilities relating to the provision of technical and vocational education and training for the cohort of overseas students studying at TAFE colleges in Western Australia. In this context, 'concerns' are taken to be matters that affect or touch someone; they are subjects that occupy a person's interest, attention, or care.

In order to address the third research question, the researcher will rely on data that will come from the same body of interviews and documents as that referred to earlier in connection with the second research question. Again, as the study is exploratory, it is not possible from the outset to know the sum total of sub-research questions needed to guide the research with regard to this third research question. However, some guiding questions can be deduced from it and can be laid out as follows:

- *Third research question*
  - What are the concerns of TAFE WA personnel who have had responsibilities relating to the provision of technical and vocational education and training for this student cohort?

- *Guiding questions*
  - What issues and concerns have arisen in connection with the presence of overseas students at TAFE institutions in Western Australia?
  - What are the formal systems and procedures in place to deal with these issues and concerns?
  - How are issues and concerns dealt with in practice?

The following now illustrates how Guiding Question 3.1 can be translated into a set of subordinate guiding questions in the initial *aide-memoire*:

- *Guiding question*
  - What issues and concerns have arisen in connection with the presence of overseas students in TAFE institutions in Western Australia?

- *Examples of questions in the initial aide-memoire*
    - How has having overseas students in the institution caused concern to TAFE WA personnel in their work?
    - How have these concerns been dealt with in the institutions?

Similar *aide-memoire* questions will be developed for the other guiding questions.

The researcher will revisit and analyse again the transcripts of the interviews used and referred to earlier in connection with the second research aim, but this time the analysis will be guided by the third research question. Again, 'grounded theory' methods will be used in order to discover general ideas, themes or concepts as analytical tools for making generalisations about the data.

The quality of the data

For the positivist, 'unambiguous and precise, rigorous quantitative research reduces subjective influence and minimises the way in which information might be interpreted' (Kincheloe 1991: 129). Qualitative research of the type proposed here, however, has different techniques for ensuring 'trustworthiness'. In particular, it has procedures for enhancing the validity and reliability of studies in the sense in which these terms are understood by interpretivists.

The issue of the validity of the research may be considered under two headings, namely, internal validity and external validity. Internal validity deals with the question of how the findings of a study capture reality (Merriam 1988: 166). Reality, according to a general interpretivist researcher's understanding, is not an objective phenomenon but is, on the contrary, defined by individuals within any given situation. It is, therefore, incumbent upon the present researcher to demonstrate that what is presented in the final report is an honest portrayal of how the informants experienced and understood their functions and the concerns that arose for them in their involvement with overseas students in TAFE institutions in Western Australia.

Lincoln and Guba (1985) have provided a useful framework for describing procedures to promote validity. To begin with, there is more than one method of data collection. For this study, it has been deemed that the combination of 'thick description', semi-structured interviews and close analysis of relevant documents, is likely to result in a holistic understanding of the phenomenon. Such 'triangulation' is particularly appropriate for a study such as this that seeks to respond to the multiplicity of perspectives present in a highly complex social situation (Cohen and Manion 1989: 277).

Another practice that promotes the internal validity of a study is 'member checking'. This is the procedure of taking data and interpretations back to the people from whom they are derived and asking them if the results are plausible (Merriam 1988: 169). If a recognisable reality has been produced in the view of the research participants, the trustworthiness of the work is enhanced. To this end, key informants in the study will be consulted about the concepts as they emerge from the analysis of the data so that their validity can be corroborated.

The matter of external validity must also be considered. External validity has been defined as the degree to which a researcher's observations can be accurately compared to those of other groups (Kincheloe 1991: 135). Given that the aim of the study is to investigate the functions and concerns of personnel in TAFE colleges in Western Australia involved with overseas students, the production of knowledge that could be generalised is not a consideration. Indeed, it could be argued that interpretivist investigations such as this that aim to find the background, functions and concerns of certain groups of people are unique to their respective settings, making it impossible to transfer findings from one situation to another. Therefore, because circumstantial uniqueness is a major characteristic of an interpretivist study, the traditional notion of external validity is rendered meaningless.

Another way of viewing external validity relates to the proposition that the reader or user is able to 'generalise'. In other words, it relates to the extent to which the study's findings relate to the reader's own situation. In this sense, the researcher is attempting to facilitate the reader's own analysis rather than deliver 'generalizable' statements (Burns 1994). In order to enhance the possibility of this kind of 'generalizability', it is imperative that the study will provide rich, 'thick' description of the phenomenon in question. Readers' judgements about the appropriateness of transferability of findings to other contexts can, thereby, be based on sufficient information.

It is also important to consider the 'reliability' of the study. This often refers to the capacity for the study's findings to be replicated. In other words, if the study were to be repeated, would the same results be generated? Reliability is based on the assumption that there is a single objective reality that can be observed, known and measured. It is, however, a problematic concept when applied to a study founded on the premise that reality is a function of personal experiences and interpretations. Accordingly, for the present study, it has been deemed more appropriate to adopt Lincoln and Guba's (1985: 316) notion of 'dependability'.

To adopt the notion of 'dependability' demands that the reader should concur with the research findings, taking into consideration the data collected. The main technique to be used to enable the dependability of results is the 'audit trail'. This will allow the researcher to take the reader through the work from the beginning to the end so that the process by which conclusions have been drawn can be made apparent. People will thereby be able to judge the dependability or trustworthiness of the outcomes (Maykut and Morehouse 1994: 146). According to Lincoln and Guba (1985: 319), an audit trail 'cannot be conducted without a residue of records stemming from the inquiry'. Therefore, in keeping with audit requirements, the following information will be collected and stored: raw data, such as interview tapes, transcripts, documents provided by TAFE WA personnel, and written field notes; data reduction and analysis products, such as write-ups of field notes, unitised information on report cards, and theoretical memos; and data reconstruction and synthesis products, such as integrative diagrams connecting categories.

References

Abbs, P. (1974) *Autobiography in Education*, London: Heinemann Educational.

Abbs, P. (1976) *Root and Blossom*, London: Heinemann.

Adelman, C., Jenkins, D. and Kemmis, S. (1976) 'Rethinking case study', *Cambridge Journal of Education*, 6(3): 139–50.

Aldrich, R. (1996) *Education for the Nation*, London: Cassell.

Alexander, D. and Rizvi, F. (1993) 'Culturally constructed market relations – perceptions of quality of Australian higher education in Malaysia and Singapore', Paper presented at the 1993 IDP National Conference on International Education, 'Images of Quality: Perceptions and Best Practice in International Education', Canberra, 13–15 October.

Allport, G.W. (1944) *The Use of Personal Documents in Psychological Research*, New York, NY: Social Science Research Council.

Altenbaugh, R.J. (1992) *The Teacher's Voice*, London: Falmer Press.

Alvik, T. (1991) 'National curriculum in the primary school of Norway,' *Journal of Curriculum Studies*, 23(2): 181–4.

Anderson, L.W. (1990) *Time and School Learning*, Beckenham: Croom Helm.

Anderson, N. (1923) *The Hobo*, Chicago, IL: University of Chicago Press.

Angus, L.B. (1992) 'Quality schooling, conservative education policy and educational change in Australia', *Journal of Education Policy*, 7(4): 379–98.

Angus, M. (1991) 'Award restructuring: the new paradigm for school reform', *Unicorn*, 17(2): 78–84.

Aran, R. (1967) *Main Currents in Sociological Thought*, New York, NY: Basic Books.

Aspinwall, K. (1992) 'Biographical research: searching for meaning', *Management Education and Development*, 23(3): 248–57.

Assistant Masters and Mistresses Association (1991) *Assessment under the National Curriculum: Joint Union Advice on Workload*, London: College Hall Press.

Atkinson, P., Coffey, A. and Delamont, S. (2003) *Key Themes in Qualitative Research: Continuities and Change*, Walnut Creek, CA: Altamira Press.

Atkinson, P. and Housley, W. (2003) *Interactionism: An Essay in Sociological Amnesia*, London: Sage.

Australian Broadcasting Corporation (2000) 'Overseas students in Australia: background briefing', Broadcast, Sunday 5 March.

Australian Education Council Review Committee (1991) *Young People's Participation in Post-Compulsory Education and Training*, Canberra: Australian Government Publishing Service.

Australian TAFE International (1996) *National Guidelines on Best Practice for Program Delivery and Student Support Services for International Students in TAFE Systems and TAFE Institutes*, Brisbane: Australian National Training Authority.

Australian Vice-Chancellors' Committee (1987) *Code of Ethical Practice in the Provision of Full-fee Courses to Overseas Students by Australian Higher Education Institutions*, Canberra: AVCC.

Australian Vice-Chancellors' Committee (2003) *International Programs of Australian Universities*, Canberra: Australian Vice-Chancellors Committee.

Bacharach, S. and Lawler, L. (1980) *Power and Politics in Organisations*, San Francisco, CA: Jossey-Bass.

Ball, S. (1987) *The Micro-Politics of the School*, London: Methuen.

Ball, S. (1990) *Politics and Policy Making in Education*, London: Routledge.

Ball, S. (1993) 'Education policy, power relations and teachers' work', *British Journal of Educational Studies*, 41: 106–21.

Ball, S. (1994) *Educational Reform: A Critical and Post-structural Approach*, Buckingham: Open University Press.

Ballard, B. (1982) 'Language is not enough – responses to the academic difficulties of overseas students', in H. Bock, H. and J. Gassin (eds) Papers presented at the 'Communication at University: Purpose, Process and Produce' Conference, Melbourne: La Trobe University Press: 116–28.

Ballard, B. (1987) 'Academic adjustment: The other side of the export dollar', *Higher Education Research and Development*, 6(2): 109–19.

Ballard, B. (1989) 'Mutual misconceptions: the intellectual problems of overseas students in Australia', *Directions*, 11(1): 48–60.

Ballard, B. and Clanchy, J. (1984) *Study Abroad: A Manual for Asian Students*, Malaysia: Longman.

Ballard, B. and Clanchy, J. (1988) *Studying in Australia*, Melbourne: Longman Cheshire.

Ballard, B. and Clanchy, J. (1991) *Teaching Students from Overseas. A Guide for Lecturers and Teachers*, Melbourne: Longman Cheshire.

Beazley, K. (Chair) (1984) *Education in Western Australia: Report of the Committee of Inquiry into Education in Western Australia*, Perth: Education Department of Western Australia.

Becker, H., Geer, B., Hughes, E.C. and Strauss, A. (1961) *Boys in White: Student Culture in Medical School*, Chicago, IL: University of Chicago Press.

Becker, H.S., Geer, B., Riesman, D. and Weiss, D. (eds) (1968) *Institutions and the Person*, Chicago, IL: Aldine Publishing.

Beetham, D. (1987) *Bureaucracy*, Milton Keynes: Open University Press.

Beirne, J. (1994) *Homeschooling in Australia*, Paper presented at the Annual Homeschooling Conference, Sydney, 25 April 1994.

Bender, B., Valetutti, P. and Bender, R. (1976) *Teaching the Moderately and Severely Handicapped: Curriculum Objectives, Strategies and Activities*, Baltimore, MD: University Park Press.

Bilbow, G. (1989) 'Towards an understanding of overseas students' difficulties in lectures: a phenomenological approach', *Journal of Further and Higher Education*, 13(3): 85–9.

Blackledge, D. and Hunt, B. (1985) *Sociological Interpretations of Education*, London: Routledge.

Blackledge, D. and Hunt, B. (1991) *Sociological Interpretations of Education*, London: Routledge.

Blake, R.R. and Mouton, J.S. (1964) *The Managerial Grid*, Houston, TX: Gulf.

Blase, J. (1989) 'The micropolitics of the school: the everyday political orientation of teachers toward open school principals', *Educational Administration Quarterly*, 25(4): 377–407.

Blase, J. (1991) 'The micro political perspective', in J. Blase (ed.) *The Politics of Life in Schools: Power, Conflict, and Cooperation*, Newbury Park, CA: Sage: 1–18.

Blumer, H. (1969) *Symbolic Interactionism*, Englewood Cliffs, NJ: Prentice Hall.

Bogdan, R. (1974) *Being Different: The Autobiography of Jane Fry*, New York, NY: John Wiley.

Bogdan, R. and Biklen, S. (1982) *Qualitative Research for Education: An Introduction to Theory and Methods*, Boston, MA: Allyn and Bacon.

Bogdan, R. and Biklen, S. (1984) *Qualitative Research for Education: An Introduction to Theory and Methods*, Boston, MA: Allyn and Bacon.

Bogdan, R. and Biklen, S. (1992) *Qualitative Research for Education: An Introduction to Theory and Methods*, Boston, MA: Allyn and Bacon.

Borg, W.R. and Gall, M.D. (1983) *Educational Research: An Introduction* (4th edn), New York, NY: Longman.

Borg, W.R. and Gall, M.D. (1989) *Educational Research: An Introduction* (5th edn), New York, NY: Longman.

Bouma, G.D. (2000) *The Research Process*, Melbourne: Oxford University Press.

Boutilier, B. and Prentice, A. (eds) (2000) *Creating Historical Memory: English Canadian Women and the Work of History*, Toronto: University of Toronto Press.

Bradley, D. and Bradley, M. (1984) *Problems of Asian Students in Australia: Language, Culture and Education*, Canberra: Australian Government Publishing Service.

Broudy, H.S. (1967) *Philosophy of Education: An Organisation of Topics and Selected Sources*, Chicago, IL: University of Illinois Press.

Burgess, R.G. (1982) 'The unstructured interview as a conversation, in R.G. Burgess (ed.) *Field Research: A Sourcebook and Field Manual*, London: Allen and Unwin.

Burgess, R.G. (1984) *In the Field. An Introduction to Field Research*, London: Allen and Unwin.

Burley, S. (1997) 'Lost leaders from the convent and the classroom 1880–1925', in J. McMahon, H. Neidhart and J. Chapman (eds) *Leading the Catholic School*, Richmond, Victoria: Spectrum: 49–62.

Burley, S. (2001) 'Resurrecting the religious experiences of Catholic girls' schooling in South Australia in the 1920s', *Educational Research and Perspectives*, 28(1): 28–44.

Burlingame, M. (1988) 'Review of the micro-politics of the school: Towards a theory of school organization', *Journal of Curriculum Studies*, 20(3): 281–9.

Burns, R. (1991) 'Study and stress among first year students in an Australian university', *Higher Education Research and Development*, 10(1): 61–7.

Burns, R.B. (1994) *Introduction to Research Methods*, Melbourne: Longman.

Caldwell, B.J. and Spinks, J.M. (1988) *The Self-Managing School*, London: Falmer Press.

Campbell, R.J. and Neill, S. (1990) *1330 Days*, London: AMMA.

Candy, P. (1989) 'Alternative paradigms in educational research', *Australian Educational Researcher*, 16(3): 1–11.

Carmichael, L. (Chair) (1992) *The Australian Vocational Training Certificate System*, Canberra: Employment and Skills Formation Council.

Carspecken, P.F. (1996) *Critical Ethnography in Educational Research: A Theoretical and Practical Guide*, New York, NY: Routledge.

Carter, A. (1997) *Beyond All Telling: A History of Loreto in Western Australia 1897–1997*, Perth: The Institute of the Blessed Virgin.

Casey, K. (1994) *Teaching Children with Special Needs*, Wentworth Falls, New South Wales: Social Science Press.

Castells, M. (2000) *The Rise of the Network Society*, Oxford: Blackwell Publishers.

Catholic Education Commission of Western Australia (CECWA) (1983) *Pupil Enrolment Policy and Practice*, Perth: Catholic Education Commission of Western Australia.

Catholic Education Commission of Western Australia (CECWA) (1988) *Special Education Policy*, Perth: Catholic Education Commission of Western Australia.

Catholic Education Commission of Western Australia (CECWA) (1992) *Students with Special Needs – The Enrolment and Integration of Students with Disabilities*, Perth: Catholic Education Commission of Western Australia.

Chadbourne, R. and Clarke, R. (1994) *Devolution: The Next Phase, Western Australian Secondary Principals' Association: A Response*, Perth: Secondary Principals' Association.

Chalmers, R. (1994) 'The inclusion of children with severe or profound intellectual disability in regular classrooms: a synopsis of the literature', Paper presented at the 6th Joint National Conference of the National Council on Intellectual Disability and the Australian Society for the Study of Intellectual Disability. Fremantle, October 1994.

Chapman, A. and O'Donoghue, T.A. (2000) 'Home schooling: an emerging research agenda', *Educational Research and Perspectives*, 27(1): 19–36.

Chapman, J. (1987) 'Decentralization, devolution and the administration of schools', *Education Research and Perspectives*, 14(2): 62–75.

Charmaz, K. (2000) 'Qualitative interviewing and grounded theory analysis', in J.F. Gubrium and J.A. Holstein (eds) *Handbook of Interview Research: Context and Method*, Thousand Oaks, CA: Sage: 675–94.

Charmaz, K. (2002) 'Qualitative interviewing and grounded theory analysis', in J.F. Gubrium and J.A. Holstein (eds) *Handbook of Interview Research: Context and Method*, London: Sage.

Charon, J.M. (2001) *Symbolic Interactionism: An Introduction, An Interpretation, An Integration*, Upper Saddle River, NJ: Prentice Hall.

Chenitz, W. and Swanson, J. (1986) 'Qualitative Research Using Grounded Theory', in W. Chenitz and J. Swanson (eds) *From Practice to Grounded Theory*, Menlo Park, CA: Addison-Wesley: 3–15.

Cistone, P. (1989) 'School-based management/shared decision making: Perestroika in educational governance', *Education and Urban Society*, 21(2): 363–5.

Clark, C., Dyson, A., Millward, A. and Skidmore, D. (1997) *New Directions in Special Needs*, London: Cassell.

Clarke, E. (1985) *Female Teachers in Queensland State Schools: A History 1860–1983*, Brisbane: Department of Education Policy and Information Services Branch, June 1985.

Cocks, E., Fox, C., Brogan, M. and Lee, M. (eds) (1996) *Under Blue Skies: The Social Construction of Intellectual Disability in Western Australia*, Perth: Edith Cowan University.

Cohen, L. and Manion, L. (1989) *Research Methods in Education*, London: Routledge.

Collins, J. (2001) 'Hidden lives: the teaching and religious lives of eight Dominican sisters, 1931–1961', unpublished M.Ed thesis, Massey University, New Zealand.

Connole, H., Smith, B. and Wiseman, R. (1993) *Issues and Methods in Research: Study Guide*, Adelaide: University of South Australia.

Cooley, C.H. (1956) *Human Nature and the Social Order*, Glencoe, IL: The Free Press.

Cooper, A. (1998) 'A select bibliography', *The Australasian Catholic Record*, 25(2): 164–79.

Corbin, J. (1986) 'Coding, writing memos and diagramming', in W. Chenitz and J. Swanson (eds) *From Practice to Grounded Theory*, Menlo Park, CA: Addison-Wesley: 102–20.

Crabtree, B.F. and Miller, W.L. (eds) (1992) *Doing Qualitative Research*, Newbury Park, CA: Sage.

Creemers, B. (1993) 'New directions in the Netherlands', *Directions in Education*, 1(1): 3.

Cressey, P. (1932) *The Taxi Dance Hall*, Chicago, IL: University of Chicago Press.

Creswell, J.W. (2005) *Educational Research: Planning, Conducting, and Evaluating Quantitative and Qualitative Research*, Columbus, OH: Pearson.

Crevola, M. (1993) *Internationalising Education – Queensland University of Technology's Experience: A Research Report*, Brisbane: University of Queensland.

Crotty, M. (1998) *The Foundations of Social Research: Meaning and Perspective in the Research Process*, St Leonards: Allen and Unwin.

Crotty, M. (2001) *Making the Australian Male: Middle-Class Masculinity 1870–1920*, Melbourne: Melbourne University Press.

Crump, S. (1993) *School Centred Leadership*, Melbourne: Nelson.

Cuban, L. (1984) *How Teachers Taught: Constancy and Change in American Classrooms, 1890–1980*, New York, NY: Longman.

Cunningham, P. and Gardner, P. (2004) *Becoming Teachers: Texts and Testimonies 1907–1950*, London: Woburn Press.

Davis, D., Olsen, A. and Bohm, A. (eds) (2000) *Transnational Education Providers, Partners and Policy: Challenges for Australian Institutions Offshore*, Canberra: IDP Education Australia.

Day, C. (1999) *Developing Teachers: The Challenge of Lifelong Learning*, London: RoutledgeFalmer.

Denzin, N. and Lincoln, Y. (1994) 'Introduction: entering the field of qualitative research', in N. Denzin and Y. Lincoln (eds) *Handbook of Qualitative Research*, Thousand Oaks, CA: Sage Publications: 1–19.

Denzin, N.K. (1989) *Interpretitive Interactionism*, Thousand Oaks, CA: Sage Publications.

Department of Employment, Education and Training (1992) *International Students Policy Handbook*, Canberra: Australian Government Publishing Service.

Derouet, J.L. (1991) 'Lower secondary education in France: From uniformity to institutional autonomy', *European Journal of Education*, 26(2): 119–32.

Diesing, P. (1972) *Pattterns of Discovery in the Social Sciences*, London: Routledge and Kegan Paul.

Dimmock, C. and O'Donoghue, T.A. (1997) *Innovative School Principals and Restructuring: Life History Portraits of Successful Managers of Change*, London: Routledge.

Dimmock, C. and O'Donoghue, T.A. (1997a) 'The edited topical life history approach', *Leading and Managing*, 3(1): 48–70.

Dinham, S. (1994) 'The use of the telephone interview in educational research: one case study', *Education Research and Perspectives*, 21(2): 17–27.

Doenau, S. (1984) *Edging to Integration – The Australian Experience*, Sydney: Advance Publications.

Dollard, J. (1935) *Criteria for the Life History*, New York, NY: Libraries Press.

Dove, L.A. (1986) *Teachers and Teacher Education in Developing Countries*, London: Croom Helm.

Downer, A. (1997) 'Our Global Future: Harnessing Education's Power', Occasional Address by the Hon. Alexander Downer, MP, Australian Minister for Foreign Affairs, Canberra: Department of Foreign Affairs and Trade. Available online at www.dfat.gov.au/pub/speeches/fa-sp/faspeech-menu.html.

Downer, A. (1998) 'Australia, Indonesia and the Region – Increasing Understanding', Speech to the launch of the Institute of International Education, Flinders University, Adelaide, Canberra: Department of Foreign Affairs and Trade. Available online at www.dfat.gov.au/pub/speeches/fa-sp/faspeech-menu.html.

Downer, A. (1998a) *Australia, Indonesia and the Region – Increasing Understanding*, Canberra: Department of Foreign Affairs and Trade.

Dye, T. (1976) *Policy Analysis*, Tuscaloosa, AL: University of Alabama Press.

Eisner, E. (1983) 'The art and craft of teaching', *Educational Leadership*, January: 5–13.

Eisner, E. (1985) *The Art of Educational Evaluation*, London: Falmer Press.

Emery, M. (1986) 'Introduction', in M. Emery (ed.) *Qualitative Research*, Canberra: Australian Association for Adult Education.

Employment and Skills Formation Council (1992) *The Australian Vocational Certificate Training System*, Canberra: National Board for Employment, Education and Training.

Entwistle, H. (1971) 'The relationship between theory and practice', in J.S. Tibble (ed.) *An Introduction to the Study of Education*, London: Routledge and Kegan Paul: 95–113.

Erwin, J.E. and Soodak, L.C. (1995) 'I never knew I could stand up to the system: families' perspectives on pursuing inclusive education', *Journal of the Association of Persons with Severe Handicaps*, 17(4): 205–12.

Evetts, J. (1989) 'Married women and career: career history accounts of primary headteachers', *Qualitative Studies in Education*, 2(2): 89–105.

Fairburn, M. (1999) *Social History: Problems, Strategies and Methods*, London: Macmillan Press.

Feiman-Nemser S. and Floden, R.E. (1986) 'The cultures of teaching', in M.C. Wittrock (ed.) *Handbook of Research on Teaching*, New York, NY: Macmillan Publishing: 505–26.

Fells, R. (1995a) 'Negotiating workplace change: an overview of research into negotiation behaviour', in D. Mortimer and P. Leece (eds) *Workplace Reform and Enterprise Bargaining: Issues, Cases, and Trends*, Centre of Employment Relations, Nepean: University of Western Sydney: 267–84.

Fells, R. (1995b) 'Enterprise bargaining and the process of negotiation: a case study', *Journal of Industrial Relations*, 37(3): 219–35.

Finch, J. (1986) *Research and Policy*, London: Falmer Press.

Finkelstein, B. (1989) *Governing the Young: Teacher Behaviour in Popular Primary Schools in Nineteenth Century United States*, London: Falmer Press.

Finkelstein, B. (1998) 'Classroom management in the United States', in N.K. Shimahara (ed.) *Politics of Classroom Life: Classroom Life in International Perspective*, New York, NY: Garland Publishing: 11–48.

Fisher, R. and Ury, W. (1981) *Getting to Yes: Negotiating Agreement Without Giving In*, New York, NY: Penguin.

Fisher, R., Ury, W. and Patton, B. (1991) *Getting to Yes*, London: Random Century.

Floden, R.M. and Huberman, M. (1989) 'Teachers' professional lives: The state of the art', *International Journal of Educational Research*, 13: 455–66.

Foot, J.M. (1998) 'Words, songs and books. Oral history in Italy: a review and discussion', *Journal of Modern Italian Studies*, 3(2): 164–74.

Ford, O. (1993) 'Voices from below: family, school and community in the Braybrook Plains 1854–1892', M.Ed. thesis, University of Melbourne.

Foster, L. and Harman, K. (1992) *Australian Education: A Sociological Perspective*, Sydney: Prentice Hall.

Fulcher, G. (1989) *Disabling Policies? A Comparative Approach to Education Policy and Disability*, London: Falmer Press.

Fullan, M. (1982) *The Meaning of Educational Change*, New York, NY: Teachers College, Columbia University.

Fullan, M. (1993) *Change Forces. Probing the Depths of Educational Reform*, London: Falmer Press.

Gardner, P. (1994) 'Teaching an old dog new tricks', *The Australian Nursing Journal*, 2(4): 16–17.

Gardner, P. and Cunningham, P. (1997) 'Oral history and teachers' professional practice', *Cambridge Journal of Education*, 27(3): 331–42.

Gassin, J. (1982) 'The learning difficulties of the foreign student', *Herdsa News*, 4(3): 13–16.

Geertz, C. (1973) 'Thick description: towards an interpretive theory of culture', in C. Geertz (ed.) *The Interpretation of Cultures*, New York, NY: Basic Books.

Giddens, A. (1984) *The Constitution of Society: Outline of the Theory of Structuration*, Cambridge: Polity Press.

Glaser, B. (1978) *Theoretical Sensitivity*, Mills Valley, CA: Sociology Press.

Glaser, B. (1992) *Basics of Grounded Theory Analysis: Emergence vs Forcing*, Mills Valley, CA: Sage.

Glaser, B. and Strauss, A. (1965) *Awareness of Dying*, Chicago, IL: Aldine Publishing.

Glaser, B. and Strauss, A. (1967) *The Discovery of Grounded Theory: Strategies for Qualitative Research*, Chicago, IL: Aldine Publishing.

Glaser, B. and Strauss, A. (1968) *Time for Dying*, Chicago, IL: Aldine Publishing.

Goddard, D. (1992) 'Ideology and the management of change in education: developments in Western Australian State Education 1983–1989', Unpublished D.Phil. thesis, The University of Western Australia.

Goetz, J. and Le Compte, M. (1984) *Ethnography and Qualitative Design in Education Research*, Orlando, FL: Academic Press.

Goetz, M.D. and le Compte, J.P. (1982) 'Problems of reliability and validity in ethnographic research', *Review of Educational Research*, 52(1): 31–60.

Goodman, J. and Martin, J. (2002) (eds) *Gender, Colonialism and Education: The Politics of Experience*, London: Woburn Press.

Goodson, I. (1977) 'Evaluation and evolution', in N. Norris (ed.) *Theory in Practice*, Centre for Applied Research in Education, Norwich: University of East Anglia.

Goodson, I. (1991) 'Teachers' lives and educational research', in I.F. Goodson and R. Walker (eds) *Biography, Identity and Schooling: Episodes in Educational Research*, London: Falmer Press.

Goodson, I. (1992) (ed.) *Studying Teachers' Lives*, London: Routledge.

Goodson, I. (2002) 'Professional knowledge and the teacher's life and work', in C. Day, A. Fernandez, T.E. Hauge and J. Moller (eds) *The Life and Work of Teachers: International Perspectives in Changing Times*, London: RoutledgeFalmer: 13–25.

Goodson, I. and Sikes, P. (2001) *Life History Research in Educational Settings: Learning from Lives*, Buckingham: Open University Press.

Gordon, L. (1992) 'The state, devolution and educational reform in New Zealand', *Journal of Education Folio*, 7(2): 187–203.

Gow, L. (Chair) (1989) *Review of Integration in Australia: Summary Report*, Canberra: Commonwealth Schools Commission.

Grace, G. (2002) *Catholic Schools: Mission, Markets and Morality*, London: RoutledgeFalmer.

Grace, G. (2003) 'Educational studies and faith-based schooling: moving from prejudice to evidence-based argument', *British Journal of Educational Studies*, 51(2): 149–67.

Greene, J. (1994) 'Qualitative program evaluation: practice and promise', in N. Denzin and Y. Lincoln (eds) (1994) *Handbook of Qualitative Research*, Thousand Oaks, CA: Sage Publications: 530–44.

Groves, R.M and Kahn, R.L. (1979) *Surveys by Telephone*, New York, NY: Academic Press.

Guba, E. (1981) 'Criteria for assessing the trustworthiness of naturalistic inquiry,' *Educational Communication and Technology Journal*, 29: 79–92.

Guba, E. and Lincoln, Y. (1994) 'Competing paradigms in qualitative research', in N. Denzin and Y. Lincoln. (eds) *Handbook of Qualitative Research*, Thousand Oaks, CA: Sage: 105–17.

Habermas, J. (1972) *Knowledge and Human Interests*, London: Heinemann.

Hage, J. and Powers, C. (1992) *Post-industrial Lives: Roles and Relationships in the 21st Century*, New York, NY: Sage.

Haigh, G. (1995) 'Home truths', *Times Educational Supplement*, 5 May.

Hall, J. (1997) *Social Devaluation and Special Education*, London: Jessica Kingsley Publishers.

Hallinger, P., Leithwood, K. and Murphy, J. (eds) (1993) *Cognitive Perspectives on Educational Leadership*, New York, NY: Teachers' College Press.

Ham, C. and Hill, M. (1993) *The Policy Process in the Modern Capitalist State*, Hemel Hempstead: Harvester Wheatsheaf.

Hammersley, M. (1989) *The Dilemma of Qualitative Method. Herbert Blumer and the Chicago Tradition*, London: Routledge.

Hammersley, M. and Atkinson, P. (1983) *Ethnography – Principles in Practice*, London: Tavistock.

Hargreaves, D. (1993) 'Whatever happened to symbolic interactionism', in M. Hammersley (ed.) *Controversies in Classroom Research*, Buckingham: Open University Press: 135–52.

Haring, T.G. (1996) 'The role of research in the continuing development of the field of severe disabilities', *Journal of the Association for Persons with Severe Handicaps*, 21(1): 6–8.

Hess, G.A. (1991) *Chicago and Britain: Experiments in Empowering Parents*, Paper presented at 'The annual meeting of the American Educational Research Association, Chicago', April.

Hewett, F. and Forness, S. (1984) *Education of Exceptional Learners*, Boston, MA: Allyn and Bacon.

Hill, M. (1997) *The Policy Process in the Modern State*, Hemel Hempstead: Harvester Wheatsheaf.

Hitchcock, G. and Hughes, D. (1989) *Research and the Teacher*, London: Routledge.

Hodgkin, M. (1972) 'The Cultural Background of South-East Asian Students in Australia', in S. Bochner and P. Wicks (eds) *Overseas Students in Australia*, Sydney: University of New South Wales Press: 25–30.

Hogwood, B. and Gunn, L. (1981) *The Policy Orientation*, University of Strathclyde: Centre for the Study of Public Policy.

Holmes, E. (2004) *Teacher Well-being*, London: RoutledgeFalmer.

Hopkins, D. (1993) *A Teacher's Guide to Classroom Research*, Buckingham: Open University Press.

Hornsby-Smith, M.P. (2000) 'Catholic schooling in England and Wales', in M. Eaton, J. Longmore and A. Naylor (eds) *Commitment to Diversity: Catholics and Education in a Changing World*, London: Cassell: 184–219.

Hoyle, E. (1986) *The Politics of School Management*, London: Hodder and Stoughton.

Hoyle, E. (1988) 'Micropolitics of educational organisations', in A. Westoby (ed.) *Culture and Power in Educational Organisations*, Milton Keynes: Open University: 255–69.

Hughes, M.G. (1976) 'The professional as administrator: The case of the secondary school head', in R.S. Peters (ed.) *The Role of the Head*, London: Routledge and Kegan Paul.

Hunter, R. (1990) 'Home schooling', *Unicorn*, 16(3): 194–6.

Hunter, R. (1994) 'The home school phenomenon', *Unicorn*, 20(3): 28–37.

Husén, T. (1988) 'Research paradigms in education', in J. Keeves (ed.) *Educational Research, Methodology, and Measurement: An International Handbook*, Oxford: Pergamon Press: 17–20.

Industry Commission (1991) *Exports of Education Services (Report No. 12)*, Canberra: Commonwealth of Australia.

International Development Program of Australian Universities and Colleges (IDP) (2002) *International Students Enrolled in Australian Universities, 1994–2002*, Canberra: IDP Education Australia.

Jackson, P.W. (1968) *Life in Classrooms*, New York, NY: Holt, Rinehart and Winston.

James, W. (1958 edn) *Talks to Teachers on Psychology: And to Students on Some of Life's Ideals*, New York, NY: W.W. Norton.

Jolley, A. (1997) *Exporting Education to Asia*, Melbourne: Victoria University Press for the Centre for Strategic Economic Studies.

Jones, C. (1991) 'Qualitative interviewing', in G. Allen and C. Skinner (eds) *Handbook for Research Students in the Social Sciences*, London: Falmer Press: 203–14.

Jones, P. (1989) 'Overseas students in Australia: a profile', in B. Williams (ed.) *Overseas Students in Australia: Policy and Practice*, Canberra: International Development Program of Australian Universities and Colleges: 25–42.

Keats, D. (1972) 'New study patterns', in Bochner, S. and Wicks, P. (eds) *Overseas Students in Australia*, Sydney: University of New South Wales Press: 105–18.

Keedy, J. (1992) 'The interaction of theory with practice in a study of successful principals: an interpretive research in process', *Theory into Practice*, 31(2): 157–64.

Kennedy, K. (1991) 'Towards a national curriculum in Australia: policy developments as a prescription for action', unpublished paper: 1–7.

Kennedy, M.M. (1979) 'Generalizing from single case studies', *Evaluation Quarterly*, 3(4): 661–79.

Keogh, B.K. (1990) 'Narrowing the gap between policy and practice', *Exceptional Children*, 57(2): 186–90.

Kerchner, C.T. and Caufman, K.D. (1993) 'Building the airplane while it's rolling down the runway', in C.T. Kerchner, and J.E. Koppich (eds) *A Union of Professionals. Labor Relations and Educational Reform*, New York, NY: Teachers College Press: 1–24.

Kerchner, C.T. and Koppich, J.E. (1993) 'Organising the other half of teaching', Paper prepared for the National Commission on Teaching and America's Future.

Kerlinger, F. (1970) *Foundations of Behavioural Research*, New York, NY: Holt, Rinehart and Winston.

Kincheloe, J. (1991) *Teachers as Researchers: Qualitative Inquiry as a Path to Empowerment*, London: Falmer.

Kirk, J. and Miller, M. (1986) *Reliability, Validity and Qualitative Research*, Beverly Hills, CA: Sage.

Knight, J. (1990) 'Current reforms in education: Implications for teachers', *Unicorn*, 16(3): 139–41.

Kotre, J. (1994) *Outliving the Self: Generativity and the Interpretation of Lives*, Baltimore, MD: Johns Hopkins University Press.

Kuhn, T. (1970) *The Structure of Scientific Revolutions*, Chicago, IL: University of Chicago Press.

Kyle, N.K. (1986) *Her Natural Destiny*, New South Wales: NSW University Press.

Kyle, N.K. (ed.) (1989) *Women as Educators in 19th and 20th Century Australia*, Wollongong: University of Wollongong, School of Learning Studies.

Lancy, D. (1993) *Qualitative Research in Education. An Introduction to the Major Trends*, New York, NY: Longman.

Langness, L.L. and Frank, G. (1981) *Lives: An Anthropological Approach to Biography*, Novato, CA: Chandler and Sharp Publishers.

Lawton, D. (1992) *Education and Politics in the 1990's: Conflict or Consensus*, London: Falmer Press.

Layder. D. (1995) *Understanding Social Theory*, Thousand Oaks, CA: Sage.

Leach, F. (1993) 'Counterpart personnel: a review of the literature with implications for education and development', *International Journal of Educational Development*, 13(4): 315–30

Leach, F. (1994) 'Expatriates as agents of cross-cultural transmission', *Compare*, 24(3): 217–31.

LeCompte, M.D. and Preissle, J. (1993) *Ethnography and Qualitative Design in Educational Research*, New York, NY: Academic Press.

Leithwood, K.A., Begley, P.T. and Cousins, B. (1994) *Developing Expert Leadership for Future Schools*, London: Falmer Press.

Lemert, E.A. (1955) *Social Pathology*, New York, NY: McGraw-Hill.

Lewins, F. (1992) *Social Science Methodology: A Brief but Critical Introduction*, Melbourne: Macmillan.

Lewis, C.N. (1990) *Provision for the Education of Catholic Women in Australia since 1840*, Ph.D. thesis, University of Melbourne.

Lincoln, Y. and Guba, E. (1985) *Naturalistic Inquiry*, Beverly Hills, CA: Sage Publications.

Lindblad, S. (1984) 'The practice of school-centred innovation: a Swedish case,' *Journal of Curriculum Studies*, 16(2): 165–72.

Lingard, B. (1991) 'Policy-making for Australian schooling: the new corporate federalism', *Journal of Education Policy*, 6(1): 85–90.

Lipsky, M. (1908) *Street-Level Bureaucracy: Dilemmas of the Individual in Public Services*, New York, NY: Russell Sage Foundation.

Lofland, J (1971) *Analyzing Social Settings: A Guide to Qualitative Observation and Analysis*, Belmont, CA: Wadsworth.

Lumis, T. (1987) *Listening to History: The Authenticity of Oral Evidence*, London: Hutchinson.

Mackinnon, A. (1984) 'A new point of departure', *History of Education Review*, 13(2): 1–4.

Majchrzak, A. (1984) *Methods for Policy Research*, Newbury Park, CA: Sage.

Mandelbaum, D.G. (1973) 'The study of life history: Ghandi', *Current Anthropology*, 14(3): 177–206.

Mangham, I.L. (1979) *The Politics of Organisational Change*, London: Associated Business Press.

Mangham, I.L. (1987) 'A matter of context', in I.L. Mangham (ed.) *Organization Analysis and Development. A Social Construction of Organizational Behaviour*, Chichester: John Wiley: 1–22.

Mann, C. and Stewart, F. (2000) 'Internet interviewing', in J.F. Gubrium and J.A. Holstein (eds) *Handbook of Interview Research: Context and Method*, Thousand Oaks, CA: Sage: 603–27.

Marchant J.R. (1996) *Cork to Capricorn: A History of the Presentation Sisters in Western Australia 1891–1991*, Perth: The Congregation of the Presentation Sisters of Western Australia.

Marginson, S. (1993) *Education and Public Policy in Australia*, Cambridge: Cambridge University Press.

Marsh, C. and Stafford, K. (1988) *Curriculum: Practices and Issues*, Sydney: McGraw-Hill.

Marton, F. (1985) 'Phenomenography: A research approach to investigating different understandings of reality', in R.G. Burgess (ed.) *Qualitative Research in Education: Focus and Methods*, London: Falmer Press: 141–61.

Marton, F. (1988) 'Phenomenography: a research approach to investigating different understandings of reality' in R.R. Sherman and R.W. Webb (eds) *Qualitative Research in Education: Focus and Methods*, London: Falmer Press: 141–61.

Matza, D. (1969) *Becoming Deviant*, Englewood Cliffs, NJ: Prentice-Hall.

Mayberry, M. (1989) 'Home-based education in the United States: demographics, motivations and educational implications', *Educational Review*, 47(3): 275–87.

Mayer Committee (1992) *Employment Related Competencies: A Proposal for Consultation*, Melbourne: Mayer Committee.

Maykut, P. and Morehouse, R. (1994) *Beginning Qualitative Research. A Philosophic and Practical Guide*, London: Falmer Press.

McCulloch, G. (2004) *Documentary Research in Education, History and the Social Sciences*, London: RoutledgeFalmer.

McHugh, J.D. (1994) 'The Lords' will be done: interviewing the powerful in education', in G. Walford (ed.) *Researching the Powerful in Education*, London: University College London Press: 55–66.

McLay, A. (1992) *Women out of their Sphere: A History of the Sisters of Mercy in Western Australia*, Perth: Vanguard Press.

Mead, G.H. (1934) *Mind, Self and Society*, Chicago, IL: University of Chicago Press.

Measor, L. (1985) 'Interviewing: A strategy in qualitative research', in G.R. Burgess (ed.) *Strategies of Educational Research*, London: Falmer Press: 63–73.

Meighan, R. (1995) 'Home-based education effectiveness research and some of its implications', *Educational Review*, 47(3): 275–87.

Meltzer, B.B., Petras, J.W. and Reynolds, L.T. (1975) *Symbolic Interaction: Genesis, Varieties and Criticism*, London: Routledge and Kegan Paul.

Merriam, S.B. (1988) *Case Study Research in Education*, San Francisco, CA: Jossey Bass.

Merton, R.K (1968) 'On sociological theories of the middle range', in R.K. Merton (ed.) *Social Theory and Social Structure*, New York, NY: Free Press: 39–72.

Mezger, J. (1992) *Bridging the Intercultural Communication Gap*, A Guide for TAFE Teachers of International Students, Tasmania: National TAFE Overseas Network.

Minichiello, V., Aroni, R., Timewell, E. and Alexander, L. (1990) *In-depth Interviewing: Researching People*, Melbourne: Longman Cheshire.

Ministry of Education (Western Australia) (1987) *Better Schools in Western Australia: A Programme for Improvement*, Perth: Ministry of Education.

Myers, S.S. (1990) 'The management of curriculum time as it relates to student engaged time', *Educational Review*, 42(1): 13–23.

National Project on the Quality of Teaching and Learning (1993) *National Schools Project: Report of the National External Review Panel*, Canberra: Australian Government Publishing Service.

O'Donoghue, T.A. (1994) 'Overseas Students in Australia: A Literature Review, unpublished report, Perth: Graduate School of Education, The University of Western Australia.

O'Donoghue, T.A. (2001) *Upholding the Faith: The Process of Education in Catholic Schools in Australia, 1922–65*, New York, NY: Peter Lang.

O'Donoghue, T.A. (2004) *Come Follow Me and Forsake Temptation: Catholic Schooling and the Recruitment and Retention of Teachers for Religious Teaching Orders, 1922–1965*, Bern: Peter Lang.

O'Donoghue, T.A. and Chalmers, R. (2000) 'How teachers manage their work in inclusive classrooms', *The Journal of Teaching and Teacher Education*, 16(7): 889–904.

O'Donoghue, T.A. and Potts, A. (2004) 'Researching the lives of Catholic teachers who were members of religious orders: historiographical considerations', *History of Education*, 33(4): 469–82.

Open University (1972) *School and Society (Course E282)*, Milton Keynes: Open University Press.

Ouchi, W.G. (1981) *Theory Z: How American Business Can Meet the Japanese Challenge*, Reading: Addison-Wesley.

Ozga, J. (2000) *Policy Research in Educational Settings: Contested Terrain*, Buckingham: Open University Press.

Pearman, E.L., Huang, A.H. and Mellbom, C.I. (1997) 'The inclusion of all students: Concerns and initiatives of educators', *Education and Training in Mental Retardation Disabilities*, March: 11–20.

Perks, R. and Thomson, A. (1998) (eds) *The Oral History Reader*, London: Routledge.

Peshkin, A. (1993) 'The goodness of qualitative research', *Educational Researcher*, 22(2): 24–30.

Peters, T.J. and Waterman, R.H. (1982) *In Search of Excellence: Lessons from America's Best-Run Companies*, New York, NY: Harper and Row.

Piper, K. (1992) 'National curriculum: An historical perspective', *Unicorn*, 18(3): 20–4.

Plowman, D.H. (2003) *Enduring Struggle: St. Mary's Tardun Farm School*, Perth: Scholastic Press.

Plummer, K. (1983) *Documents of Life*, Sydney: Allen and Unwin.

Polit, D.F., Beck, C.T. and Hungler, B.P. (2001) *Essentials of Nursing Research: Methods, Appraisal and Utilization*, New York, NY: Lippincott.

Pollard, A. (1980) 'Teacher interests and changing situations of survival threat in primary school classrooms', in P. Woods (ed.) *Teacher Strategies*, London: Croom Helm: 34–60.

Popkewitz, T. (1984) *Paradigm and Ideology in Educational Research: The Social Functions of Intellectuals*, London: Falmer Press.

Porter, P. (1990) 'The crisis in the teaching profession: the importance of excellence and equity', *Unicorn*, 16(3): 149–55.

Potts, A. (1997) *College Academics*, Charlestown, New South Wales: William Michael Press.

Pratt, D. (1980) *Curriculum Design and Development*, San Diego, CA: Harcourt Brace Jovanovich.

Pratt, S. (1982) 'Editorial: Enter micropolitics', *Educational Management and Administration*, 10(2): 77–85.

Prickett, R.L., Flanigan, J.L., Richardson, T.M.D. and Petrie G.E. (1991) 'Who knows what?: Site-based management', Paper presented at the meeting of the University Council for Educational Administration, Pittsburgh, PA, October 1990.

Prunty, J. (1984) *A Critical Reformulation of Educational Policy Analysis*, Geelong: Deakin University.

Prus, R. (1996) *Symbolic Interaction and Ethnographic Research*, Albany, NY: State University of New York Press.

Punch, H. and Wildy, H. (1995) 'Grounded theory in educational administration: leadership and change', Paper presented at the 'International Conference of the Australian Council for Educational Administration', Sydney, July.

Punch, K. (1988) *Introduction to Social Research: Quantitative and Qualitative Approaches*, London: Sage.

Punch, K. (1998) *Introduction to Social Research: Quantitative and Qualitative Methods*, London: Sage.

Punch, K. (2000) *Developing Effective Research Proposals*, London: Sage Publications.

Punch, K. (2005) *Introduction to Social Research: Quantitative and Qualitative Approaches* (2nd edn), London: Sage.

Purkey, S.C. and Smith, M.S. (1985) 'School reform: the district policy implications of the effective schools literature', *The Elementary School Journal*, 85: 353–89.

Quality of Education Review Committee (1985) *Quality of Education in Australia*, Canberra: Australian Government Publishing Service.

Ranson, S. (1996) 'Educational policy', in Peter Gordon (ed.) *A Guide to Educational Research*, London: Woburn Press: 247–76.

Rao, G. (1976) *Overseas Students in Australia: Some Major Findings from a Nation-wide Survey*, Canberra: ANU Education Research Unit.

Ribbins, P. and Sherratt, B. (1992) 'Managing the secondary school in the 1990s: a new view of headship', *Educational Management and Administration*, 20(3): 151–60.

Ritzer, G. (1983) *Sociological Theory*, New York, NY: Alfred A. Knopf.

Ritzer, G. (1994) *Sociological Beginnings: on the Origins of Key Ideas in Sociology*, New York, NY: McGraw-Hill.

Robertson, S.L. and Soucek, V.V. (1991) 'Changing social realities in Australian schools: a study of teacher perceptions and experiences of current reforms', Paper presented at 'The Comparative and International Education Society Conference', University of Pittsburgh, PA, March.

Robinson, W. (2002) *Pupil Teachers and their Professional Training in Pupil-teacher Centres in England and Wales, 1870–1914*, Lewiston, NY: Edwin Mellen Press.

Rogers, C.R. (1951) *Client Centred Therapy*, Boston, MA: Houghton Mifflin.

Rose, A.M. (ed.) (1962) *Human Behaviour and Social Processes*, London: Routledge and Kegan Paul: 3–19.

Ruddock, J. (1993) 'The theatre of daylight: qualitative research and school profile studies', in M. Schratz. (ed.) *Qualitative Voices in Educational Research*, London: Falmer Press: 8–23.

Sachs, J. and Logan, L. (1990) 'Control or development? A study of inservice education', *Journal of Curriculum Studies*, 22(5): 473–81.

Schatzman, L. and Strauss, A. (1973) *Field Research: Strategies for a Natural Sociology*, Englewood Cliffs, NJ: Prentice Hall.

Schwandt, T. (1994) 'Constructivist, interpretivist approaches to human inquiry', in N. Denzin and Y. Lincoln (eds) *Handbook of Qualitative Research*, Thousand Oaks, CA: Sage Publications: 118–37.

Schwartz, H. and Jacobs, J. (1979) *Qualitative Sociology: A Method to the Madness*, New York, NY: The Free Press.

Scott-Stevens, S. (1987) *Foreign Consultants and Counterparts: Problems in Technology Transfer*, Boulder, CO: Westview Press.

Selleck, R.J.W and Sullivan, M.G. (1982) (eds) *Not so Eminent Victorians*, Melbourne: Melbourne University Press.

Shaw, C. (1931) *The Natural History of a Delinquent Career*, Chicago, IL: University of Chicago Press.

Shaw, C. (1966) *The Jack Roller*, Chicago, IL: University of Chicago Press.

Shean, R. (Chair) (1993) *The Education of Children with Disabilities and Specific Learning Difficulties – Recognising Special Needs in Education*, Perth: Ministry of Education.

Shils, E. and Finch, H. (eds) (1949) *Max Weber on the Methodology of the Social Sciences*, New York, NY: The Free Press.

Shinn, C., Welch, A. and Bagnall, N. (1999) 'Culture of competition? Comparing international student policy in the United States and Australia', *Journal of Further and Higher Education*, 23(1): 81–100.

Shulman, L. (1985) 'Knowledge and teaching: foundations of the new reform', *Harvard Educational Review*, 57(1): 1–22.

Sikes, P.J., Measor, L. and Woods, P. (1985) *Teacher Careers: Crises and Continuities*, London: Falmer Press.

Silver, H. (1980) 'Nothing but the present, or nothing but the past', in Gordon, P. (ed.) *The Study of Education: A Collection of Inaugural Lectures*, London: Woburn Press: 265–84.

Silver, H. (1994) 'Historiography of education', in T. Husen and T.N. Postlethwaite (eds) *The International Encyclopaedia of Education*, London: Pergamon: 2607–18.

Silverman, D. (2005) *Doing Qualitative Research*, London: Sage.

Simons, H. (1982) *Conversation Piece*, London: Grant McIntyre.

Sindell, P.S. (1974) 'Some discontinuities in the enculturation of Mistassini children', in G.D. Spindler (ed.) *Education and Cultural Process: Towards an Anthropology of Education*, New York, NY: Holt, Rinehart and Winston: 333–41.

Skilbeck, M. (1990) 'National curriculum within the OECD', *Unicorn*, 16(3): 9–13.

Smart, D. (1986) 'The financial crises in Australian higher education and the inexorable push towards privatisation', *Australian Universities Review*, 30: 16–21.

Smart, D. (1987) 'Diversifying the higher education financial base: escaping over-reliance on Canberra's dwindling funds', *Unicorn*, 13(1): 32–8.

Smith, D. and Lovatt, T. (1991) *Curriculum: Action on Reflection*, Wentworth Falls, New South Wales: Social Science Press.

Smith, S. (1994) 'Foreign students call on universities to improve service', *Campus Review*, September/October: 5.

Spaull, A. (1977) (ed.) *Australian Teachers from Schoolmasters to Militant Professionals*, South Melbourne: Macmillan.

Spaull, A. (1985) *A History of Federal Teachers' Unions in Australia, 1921–85*, Canberra: Australian Teachers' Federation.

Spaull, A. and Sullivan, M. (1989) *A History of the Queensland Teachers' Union*, Sydney: Allen and Unwin.

Spradley, J.P. (1979) *The Ethnographic Interview*, New York, NY: Holt, Rinehart and Winston.

Stainback, W. and Stainback, S. (1984) 'A rationale for the merger of special and regular education', *Exceptional Children*, 51: 102–11.

Stake, R.E. (1978) 'The case study method in social inquiry', *Educational Researcher*, 7: 5–8.

Stanley, W.O. (1968) 'The social foundations subjects in the professional education of teachers', *Educational Theory*, 18(3): 224–36.

Stenhouse, L. (1975) *An Introduction to Curriculum Research and Development*, London: Heinemann.

Stenhouse, L. (1985) 'A note on case study and educational practice', in R. G. Burgess, (ed.) *Field Methods in the Study of Education*, Lewes: Falmer Press: 263–71.

Strauss, A. (1978) *Negotiations. Varieties, Contexts, Processes, and Social Order*, San Francisco, CA: Jossey-Bass.

Strauss, A. (1987) *Qualitative Analysis for Social Scientists*, Cambridge: Cambridge University Press.

Strauss, A. and Corbin, J. (1990) *Basics of Qualitative Research. Grounded Theory Procedures and Techniques*, Newbury Park, CA: Sage.

Strauss, A. and Corbin, J. (1994) 'Grounded theory methodology: an overview', in N. Denzin and Y. Lincoln (eds) *Handbook of Qualitative Research*, Thousand Oaks, CA: Sage Publications: 273–85.

Sullivan, K. (1998) 'Getting our education partnerships right', Speech delivered on 23 April 1998 by The Hon. Kathy Sullivan, the Minister assisting the Minister for Foreign Affairs and Trade, Canberra: Australian Agency for International Development. Available online at www.ausaid.gov.au/publications/speeches/sullspch23apr.html.

Sultana, R. (1991) 'Social movements and the transformation of teachers' work: case studies from New Zealand', *Research papers in Education*, 6(2): 113–52.

Sutherland, E. (1937) *The Professional Thief*, Chicago, IL: University of Chicago Press.

Sutherland, M.B. (1985) 'The place of theory of education in teacher education', *British Journal of Educational Studies*, 33(1): 222–34.

Sverker L. (1984) 'The practice of school-centred innovation: a Swedish case', *Journal of Curriculum Studies*, 23(2): 165–72.

Taylor, S.J. and Bogdan, R. (1984) *Introduction to Qualitative Research Methods: The Search for Meanings*, New York, NY: John Wiley and Sons Inc.

Taylor, S.J. and Bogdan, R. (1998) *Introduction to Qualitative Research Methods*, New York: John Wiley and Sons.

Theobald, M. (1994) 'History of women's education in Australia', in Husen, T. and Postlethwaite, T.N. (eds) *The International Encyclopaedia of Education*, London: Pergamon: 6731–5.

Theobald, M. (1996) *Knowing Women: Origins of Women's Education in 19th Century Australia*, Cambridge: Cambridge University Press.

Thomas, G. (1997) 'Inclusive schools for an inclusive society', *British Journal of Special Education*, 24(3): 103–7.

Thomas, G. (1997a) 'What's the use of theory', *Harvard Educational Review*, 67(1): 75–104.

Thomas, W.I. and Thomas, D.S. (1928) *The Child in America: Behavior Problems and Programs*, New York, NY: Knopf.

Thomas, W.I. and Znaniecki, F. (1918–20) *The Polish Peasant in Europe and America*, New York, NY: Dover Publications.

Thompson, P. (2000) *The Voice of the Past: Oral History*, Oxford: Oxford University Press.

Thomson, A. (1998) 'Fifty years on: an international perspective on oral history', *Journal of American History*, 85(2): 581–95.

Thrasher, F. (1927) *The Gang*, Chicago, IL: University of Chicago Press.

Townshend, R.G (1990) 'Toward a broader micropolitics of the school', *Curriculum Inquiry*, 20(2): 216–24.

Trimingham Jack, C. (1998) 'The lay sister in educational history and memory', Paper presented at the Annual Conference of the Australian and New Zealand History of Education Society, Auckland, New Zealand, June.

Trimingham Jack, C. (2003) *Growing Good Catholic Girls: Education and Convent Life in Australia*, Melbourne: Melbourne University Press.

Trond A. (1991) 'National curriculum in the primary school of Norway', *Journal of Curriculum Studies*, 23(2): 181–4.

Uhrmacher, P.B. (1993) 'Coming to know the world through Waldorf education', *Journal of Curriculum and Supervision*, 9(1): 87–104.

United Nations (1971) *Declaration on the Rights of Mentally Retarded Persons*, New York, NY: UNESCO.

United Nations (1975) *Declaration on the Rights of Disabled Persons*, New York, NY: UNESCO.

Usher, R. (1996) 'A critique of the neglected epistemological assumptions of educational research', in D. Scott and R. Usher (eds) *Understanding Educational Research*, London: Routledge: 9–32.

Volet, S. and Kee, J. (1993) *Studying in Singapore – Studying in Australia: A Student Perspective*, Murdoch: Murdoch University.

Volet, S. and Pears, H. (1994) *International Students. Murdoch University and TAFE International Western Australia research study on international students at TAFE Colleges in Western Australia*, Murdoch: Murdoch University.

Walton, R.E. and McKersie, R.B. (1965) *A Behavioral Theory of Labor Negotiations*, New York, NY: McGraw-Hill.

Ware, Y. (1994) *International Education: Do We Account for the Real Cultural and Contextual Needs?*, Paper presented at the conference 'Teaching for development; An international review of Australian formal and non-formal education for Asia and the Pacific,' held in Canberra in September, 1994, organised by the Australian Development Studies Network.

Waring, M. (1979) *Social Pressure and Curriculum Innovations: A Study of the Nuffield Foundation Science Teaching Project*, London: Methuen.

Warnock, H.M. (Chair) (1979) *Special Educational Needs: Report of the Committee of Inquiry into the Education of Handicapped Children and Young People*, London: H.M. Stationery Office.

Warren, D. (1989) 'Messages from the inside', *International Journal of Educational Research*, 13: 379–90.

Weiler, H.N. (1989) 'Decentralization in educational governance: an exercise in contradiction?', Paper presented at an International Conference on the project 'National Evaluation and the Quality of Education', Oslo, Norway, May.

Weiler, K. (1992) 'Remembering and representing life histories: A critical perspective on teachers' oral history narratives', *Qualitative Studies in Education*, 5(1): 39–50.

Whitehead, K. (2003) *The New Women Teachers Come Along*, Sydney: Australian and New Zealand History of Education Society Monograph Series.

Wildavsky, A. (1979) *Speaking Truth to Power: The Art and Craft of Policy Analysis*, Boston, MA: Little, Brown and Company.

Wilson, H. and Hutchinson, S. (1991) 'Pearls, pith, and provocation. Triangulation of qualitative methods: Heideggerian hermeneutics and grounded theory', *Qualitative Health Research*, 1(2): 263–75.

Wirth, L. (1928) *The Ghetto*, Chicago, IL: University of Chicago Press.

Wise, A. (1979) *Legislated Learning – The Bureaucratization of the American Classroom*, Berkeley, CA: University of California Press.

Wolcott, H.F. (1973) *The Man in the Principal's Office; An Ethnography*, New York, NY: Holt, Rinehart and Winston.

Wolcott, H.F. (1992) 'Posturing in qualitative research', in M. LeCompte, W. Milroy and J. Preissle (eds) *Handbook of Qualitative Research in Education*, San Diego, CA: Academic Press: 3–52.

Woods, P. (1983) *Sociology and the School*, London: Routledge and Kegan Paul.

Woods, P. (1985) 'Conversations with teachers: a potential source of their professional growth', *Curriculum Inquiry*, 12(3): 239–55.

Woods, P. (1985a) 'Conversations with teachers: Some aspects of life history method', *British Educational Research Journal*, 11(1): 13–26.

Woods, P. (1986) *Inside Schools: Ethnography in Educational Research*, London: Routledge and Kegan Paul.

Woods, P. (1992) 'Symbolic interactionism: theory and method', in M. LeCompte, W. Milroy and J. Preissle (eds) *Handbook of Qualitative Research in Education*, San Diego, CA: Academic Press: 337–404.

Woods, P. (2006) *Successful Writing for Qualitative Researchers*, London: Routledge.

Young, M.F.D. (ed.) (1971) *Knowledge and Control: New Directions for the Sociology of Education*, London: Collier-Macmillan.

Zorbaugh, H. (1929) *The Gold Coast and the Slum*, Chicago, IL: University of Chicago Press.

Index